CISM®

Certified Information Security Manager® Practice Exams

Second Edition

Peter H. Gregory

New York   Chicago   San Francisco
Athens   London   Madrid   Mexico City
Milan   New Delhi   Singapore   Sydney   Toronto

McGraw Hill books are available at special quantity discounts to use as premiums and sales promotions, or for use in corporate training programs. To contact a representative, please visit the Contact Us pages at www.mhprofessional.com.

CISM® Certified Information Security Manager® Practice Exams, Second Edition

1 2 3 4 5 6 7 8 9   LCR   27 26 25 24 23

ISBN   978-1-264-69374-0
MHID   1-264-69374-5

Sponsoring Editor Wendy Rinaldi	**Technical Editor** Jay Burke	**Composition** KnowledgeWorks Global Ltd.
Editorial Supervisor Patty Mon	**Copy Editor** William McManus	**Illustration** KnowledgeWorks Global Ltd.
Project Manager Radhika Jolly, KnowledgeWorks Global Ltd.	**Proofreader** Lisa McCoy	**Art Director, Cover** Jeff Weeks
Acquisitions Coordinator Caitlin Cromley-Linn	**Production Supervisor** Thomas Somers	

To Rebekah, the love of my life.

ACKNOWLEDGMENTS

I am particularly grateful to Wendy Rinaldi for affirming the need to have this book published on a tight timeline. My readers, including current and future security managers, deserve nothing less.

Deepest thanks to Wendy Rinaldi and Caitlin Cromley-Linn for expertly managing and coordinating this project, facilitating rapid turnaround, and equipping us with the information and guidance we needed to produce the manuscript.

I would like to thank my former consulting colleague, Jay Burke, who took on the task of tech reviewing the manuscript. Jay carefully and thoughtfully scrutinized the entire draft manuscript and made scores of valuable suggestions that have improved the book's quality and value for readers. Without Jay's help, this book would be less than it is.

Many thanks to Patty Mon and Radhika Jolly for managing the editorial and production ends of the project and to Bill McManus for copy editing the book and further improving readability. Much appreciation to KnowledgeWorks Global Ltd. for laying out the pages.

Many thanks to my literary agent, Carole Jelen, for her diligent assistance during this and other projects. Sincere thanks to Rebecca Steele, my business manager and publicist, for her long-term vision and for help in keeping me on track and my life in balance.

Despite having written more than 50 books, I have difficulty putting into words my gratitude for my wife, Rebekah, for tolerating my frequent absences (in the home office and away on business travel) while I developed the manuscript. This project could not have been completed without her loyal and unfailing support.

ABOUT THE AUTHOR

Peter H. Gregory, CISM, CISA, CRISC, CDPSE, CISSP, CIPM, DRCE, CCSK, is a 30-year career technologist and a security leader in a regional telecommunications company. He has been developing and managing information security management programs since 2002 and has been leading the development and testing of secure IT environments since 1990. Peter has also spent many years as a software engineer and architect, systems engineer, network engineer, and security engineer. Throughout his career, he has written many articles, white papers, user manuals, processes, and procedures and has conducted numerous lectures, training classes, seminars, and university courses.

Peter is the author of more than 50 books about information security and technology, including *Solaris Security* (Prentice Hall, 1999), *CISSP Guide to Security Essentials* (Cengage Learning, 2014), *CISM Certified Information Security Manager All-In-One Exam Guide* (McGraw Hill, 2018), *CISA Certified Information Systems Auditor All-In-One Exam Guide* (McGraw Hill, 2016), and *The Art of Writing Technical Books* (Waterside, 2022). He has spoken at numerous industry conferences, including RSA, Interop, (ISC)² Security Congress, ISACA CACS, SecureWorld Expo, West Coast Security Forum, IP3, Society for Information Management, the Washington Technology Industry Association, and InfraGard. Interviews of Peter appear in *SC Magazine, U.S. News & World Report, CNet News, SearchSecurity, Information Security Magazine, CIO, The Seattle Times,* and *Forbes*.

Peter serves on advisory boards for cybersecurity continuing education programs at the University of Washington and the University of South Florida. For nine years, he was the lead instructor, and still serves as an advisory board member, for the University of Washington certificate program in cybersecurity. He is a former board member of the Washington State chapter of InfraGard and a founding member of the Pacific CISO Forum. He is a 2008 graduate of the FBI Citizens' Academy and a member of the FBI Citizens' Academy Alumni Association. Peter is an executive member of the CyberEdBoard and the Forbes Technology Council.

Peter resides with his family in Washington State and can be found online at www.peterhgregory.com.

About the Technical Editor

Jay Burke, CISSP, CISM, RBLP-T, is a highly accomplished information security professional with more than 20 years of operational and executive experience across a variety of industries.

Jay has worked with customers of different sizes and types to build, enhance, and manage best-in-class cybersecurity programs. As an executive-level security professional, he has led detailed maturity assessments and facilitated executive workshops to assist CISOs in maturing their cybersecurity programs. His practical experience includes engagements addressing strategic consulting, project management, regulatory compliance (Sarbanes–Oxley, PCI, NERC CIP, HIPAA, SOC 1, and SOC 2), and cybersecurity program development leveraging ISO 27001/2, NIST 800-53, Cloud Security Alliance CCM, Shared Assessments SIG, and Unified Compliance Framework.

Jay currently serves as the strategic service manager for Tenable, helping customers gain visibility of cyber risk by leveraging the Tenable Cyber Exposure platform while also providing the executive suite and board of directors with insight to focus on the issues that matter most and make better strategic decisions. Additionally, Jay is a partner at Sage Advisory, LLC, which helps young professionals find their voice in the workplace and supports the SMB market in the cybersecurity space.

CONTENTS

INTRODUCTION

Welcome to the practice exams book for the CISM Certified Information Security Manager certification.

Since you are reading this book, you're probably well-versed in the four CISM job practice areas and you're refining your study by practicing taking exam questions. But if you are earlier in your journey and still accumulating knowledge and skill, I suggest you pick up a copy of the companion book, *CISM Certified Information Security Manager All-In-One Exam Guide, Second Edition* (McGraw Hill, 2023). That book is filled with discussions, details, and real-life examples throughout the CISM domains.

Let's get one thing out of the way: the CISM certification exam is difficult. The folks at ISACA do an outstanding job of developing certification exam questions for CISM—with questions that rely on professional judgment and experience, not just questions that rely on your ability to memorize an impressive number of facts. The CISM certification does not rely on your ability to memorize a lot of facts and other matters instead, it's a reflection of years of security and risk management experience. No book can claim to be a substitute for that experience. I've taken the CISM exam myself, and like many who take exams for advanced certifications, I was not sure whether I had passed it or not. Back to ISACA for a moment: I've participated in their certification exam "item writing workshops" for the CRISC certification, so I can attest to the rigor and the attention to quality for every certification exam question. Long story short, if you are expecting that this book will make it "easy" for you to pass the CISM exam, let me influence you just a little bit: reading this can make it *easier,* because it enables you to practice answering difficult questions that are not unlike those you'll encounter in the actual exam.

Let me explode another myth, if I may. Earning advanced certifications does not mean you will soon land that dream CISO or other security management job. Organizations are—for the most part—smart enough to know that someone with a single certification, or an impressive list of them, is not necessarily the right person for a specific job. But I can tell you this: earning and keeping advanced certifications such as CISM will open doors for you, provided you also work just as hard on your soft skills such as oral and written communications.

Okay, if you're still with me, then you are one of the more serious CISM candidates focusing on an important milestone in your career. If you already have at least some security management experience, or have worked on a team and have been observing a security manager for a while, this book can help you from the perspective of experiencing a long series of difficult security brain-twisting questions.

Best of luck on your exam! And I hope that this proves to be one of those milestones that propels your career further along.

Purpose of This Book

Practice makes perfect. This adage applies to many things in life, including those brutal security certification exams. For many of you, preparing for the big day means practicing answering exam questions. I've provided 450 practice questions throughout all of the CISM domains to help you feel more confident that you will pass the actual exam.

Rather than just tell you whether you're "correct" or "wrong," this book explains why the correct answers are correct and why the incorrect answers are incorrect. This feedback loop helps you add to your knowledge, even when you answer a practice exam incorrectly. The web-based practice exams don't provide this feedback, because they are designed to more closely resemble the actual certification exam (which does not tell you whether each question is correct or incorrect, or the reason).

How This Book Is Organized

Aside from this front matter section that introduces the CISM certification, this book is organized into chapters corresponding to the four principal domains in the CISM job practice: Information Security Governance, Information Security Risk Management, Information Security Program, and Incident Management. The number of study questions for each domain is in proportion to the weight of each domain on the certification exam.

In addition to the 300 exam questions in this book, you can access another 150 exam questions online. You'll find instructions for accessing these web-based exam questions in the book's appendix.

About This Second Edition

ISACA has historically recalibrated the contents of its certifications every five years or so. I learned that ISACA would update the CISM job practice (the basis for the exam and the requirements to earn the certification) in early 2022, effective in mid-2022. To ensure that this information is up to date, Wendy Rinaldi and I developed a plan for the second edition of this book and the *CISM All-In-One Exam Guide* as quickly as possible; both books are the result of that effort.

The new CISM job practice information was made available in March 2022. We began work at that time to update both of these books. This has been updated to reflect all of the changes in the CISM job practice and changes in information security and information technology since the first edition was published.

Changes to the CISM Job Practice

For the 2022 CISM job practice, ISACA reformatted how the practice areas are described. Previously, each job practice had a set of Knowledge Statements and Task Statements. In the 2022 model, each job practice consists of two major categories with three to six subtopic areas each. This is followed by 37 Supporting Tasks for CISM that are not specifically associated with the four domains. Table 1 illustrates each previous and current CISM job practice and its corresponding chapters in this book, along with the structure of the new job practice and coverage in this book.

As is typical for each new job practice and revision of *CISM All-In-One Exam Guide* and this *CISM Practice Exams,* I performed a gap analysis to understand what subject matter was added to the new job practice and what was eliminated. My conclusion: ISACA made no significant additions or changes to the 2022 CISM job practice, besides numerous structural changes and changes in the weighting between domains.

By the time we completed this book, even more new developments, technologies, techniques, and breaches provided additional insight and the promise of still more changes. Like the surface

2016 CISM Job Practice		2022 CISM Job Practice		All-in-One and Practice Exam Coverage
1. Information Security Governance	24%	1. Information Security Governance	17%	
		A. Enterprise Governance		Chapter 1
		B. Information Security Strategy		Chapter 2
2. Information Risk Management	30%	2. Information Security Risk Management	20%	
		A. Information Security Risk Assessment		Chapter 3
		B. Information Security Risk Response		Chapter 4
3. Information Security Program Development and Management	27%	3. Information Security Program	33%	
		A. Information Security Program Development		Chapter 5
		B. Information Security Program Management		Chapter 6
4. Information Security Incident Management	19%	4. Incident Management	30%	
		A. Incident Management Readiness		Chapter 7
		B. Incident Management Operations		Chapter 8

Table 1 Previous and Current CISM Job Practices and Corresponding Chapters

of Jupiter's moon, Io, our profession is ever-changing. The technology boneyard is filled with vendors, products, protocols, techniques, and methodologies that once held great promise, later replaced with better things. This underscores the need for security leaders (and IT, audit, and risk professionals) to stay current by reading up on current events, new technologies, and techniques. Some last-minute changes that may not be fully reflected in the manuscript include the following:

- ISO/IEC 27001:2013 was replaced by ISO/IEC 27001:2022 in late 2022.
- ISO/IEC 27002:2013 was replaced by ISO/IEC 27002:2022 in early 2022.
- A new U.S. national law on privacy may have been voted upon and perhaps enacted.
- Additional U.S. presidential executive orders on the topic of cybersecurity may have been issued.

Becoming a CISM Professional

To become a CISM professional, you must pay the exam fee, pass the exam, prove that you have the necessary education and experience, and agree to uphold ethics and standards. To keep your CISM certification, you must take at least 20 continuing education hours each year (120 hours in three years) and pay annual maintenance fees. This life cycle is depicted in Figure 1.

The following list outlines the primary requirements for becoming certified:

- **Experience** A CISM candidate must submit verifiable evidence of at least five years of professional work experience in information security management. Experience must be verified and gained within the ten years preceding the application date for certification or within five years from passing the exam. Experience waivers are available for as many as two years.

- **Ethics** Candidates must commit to adhering to ISACA's Code of Professional Ethics, which guides the personal and professional conduct of those certified.

- **Exam** Candidates must receive a passing score on the CISM exam. A passing score is valid for up to five years, after which the passing score is void. A CISM candidate who passes the exam has a maximum of five years to apply for CISM certification; candidates who pass the exam but fail to act after five years must retake the exam if they want to become CISM certified.

- **Education** Those who are certified must adhere to the CISM Continuing Professional Education Policy, which requires a minimum of 20 continuing professional education (CPE) hours each year, with a total requirement of 120 CPEs over each three-year certification period.

- **Application** After successfully passing the exam, meeting the experience requirements, and reading through the Code of Professional Ethics and Standards, a candidate is ready to apply for certification. An application must be received within five years of passing the exam.

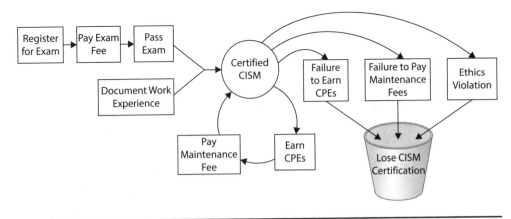

Figure 1   The CISM certification life cycle (Source: Peter Gregory)

Experience Requirements

To qualify for CISM certification, you must have completed the equivalent of five years of total work experience in information security management. Additional details on the minimum certification requirements, substitution options, and various examples are discussed next.

 NOTE Although it is not recommended, a CISM candidate can take the exam before completing any work experience directly related to information security management. As long as the candidate passes the exam and the work experience requirements are filled within five years of the exam date and ten years from the application for certification, the candidate is eligible for certification.

Direct Work Experience You must have a minimum of five years of work experience in the field of information security management. This is equivalent to roughly 10,000 actual work hours, which must be related to three or more of the CISM job practice areas, as follows:

- **Information security governance** Establish and/or maintain an information security governance framework and supporting processes to ensure that the information security strategy is aligned with organizational goals and objectives.

- **Information security risk management** Manage information risk to an acceptable level based on risk appetite to meet organizational goals and objectives.

- **Information security program** Develop and maintain an information security program that identifies, manages, and protects the organization's assets while aligning to information security strategy and business goals, thereby supporting an effective security posture.

- **Incident management** Plan, establish, and manage the capability to detect, investigate, respond to, and recover from information security and disaster incidents to minimize business impact.

All work experience must be completed within the ten-year period before completing the certification application or within five years from the date of initially passing the CISM exam. You will need to complete a separate Verification of Work Experience form for each segment of experience.

Substitution of Experience Up to two years of direct work experience can be substituted with the following to meet the five-year experience requirement. Only one waiver is permitted.

Two Years

- Certified Information Systems Auditor (CISA) in good standing

- Certified Information Systems Security Professional (CISSP) in good standing

- MBA or master's degree in information security or a related field; transcripts or a letter confirming degree status must be sent from the university attended to obtain the experience waiver

One Year

- Bachelor's degree in information security or a related field
- Skill-based or general security certification
- One full year of information systems management experience

Here is an example of a CISM candidate whose experience and education are considered for CISM certification: A candidate graduated in 2002 with a bachelor's degree in computer science. They spent five years working for a software company managing IT, and in January 2015, they began managing information security. In January 2017, they took some time off work for personal reasons. In 2019, they earned their CompTIA Security+ certification and rejoined the workforce in December 2019, working as a risk manager for a public company in its enterprise risk management department. The candidate passed the CISM exam in June 2022 and applied for CISM certification in September 2022. Do they have all of the experience required? What evidence will they need to submit?

- **Skills-based certification**   The candidate obtained their CompTIA Security+ certification, which equates to a one-year experience substitution.
- **Two years of direct experience**   They can count their two full years of information security management experience in 2015 and 2016.
- **One-year substitution**   They cannot take into account one year of IT management experience completed between January 2002 to January 2007, because it was not completed within ten years of their application.
- **One-year direct experience**   The candidate would want to utilize their new risk manager experience for work experience.

The candidate would need to send the following with their application to prove the experience requirements are met:

- Verification of Work Experience forms filled out and signed by their supervisors (or any superior) at the software company and the public company, verifying both the security management and non–security management work conducted
- Transcripts or letters confirming degree status sent from the university

---

 TIP   Read the CISM certification qualifications on the ISACA website. ISACA changes the qualification rules from time to time, and I want you to have the most up-to-date information available.

ISACA Code of Professional Ethics

Becoming a CISM professional means adhering to the ISACA Code of Professional Ethics, a formal document outlining what you will do to ensure the utmost integrity in a way that best supports and represents the profession. Specifically, the ISACA Code of Professional Ethics requires ISACA members and certification holders to do the following:

- Support the implementation of, and encourage compliance with, appropriate standards and procedures for the effective governance and management of enterprise information systems and technology, including audit, control, security, and risk management.

- Perform their duties with objectivity, due diligence, and professional care, in accordance with professional standards.

- Serve in the interest of stakeholders in a lawful manner, while maintaining high standards of conduct and character and not discrediting their profession or the association.

- Maintain the privacy and confidentiality of information obtained in the course of their activities unless disclosure is required by legal authority. Such information shall not be used for personal benefit or released to inappropriate parties.

- Maintain competency in their respective fields and agree to undertake only those activities they can reasonably expect to complete with the necessary skills, knowledge, and competence.

- Inform appropriate parties of the results of work performed, including the disclosure of all significant facts known to them that, if not disclosed, may distort the reporting of the results.

- Support the professional education of stakeholders in enhancing their understanding of the governance and management of enterprise information systems and technology, including audit, control, security, and risk management.

Failure to comply with this Code of Professional Ethics can result in an investigation into a member's or certification holder's conduct and, ultimately, disciplinary measures, including the forfeiture of hard-won certification(s).

You can find the full text and terms of enforcement of the ISACA Code of Ethics at www.isaca.org/ethics.

The Certification Exam

The certification is offered throughout the year. You have several ways to register; however, I highly recommend planning and registering early, regardless of your chosen method.

In 2022 the schedule of exam fees in U.S. dollars is

- CISM application fee: $50

- Regular registration: $575 member/$760 nonmember

As I write this, we're emerging from the global COVID-19 pandemic. During the pandemic, ISACA and other certification bodies adapted and developed remotely proctored exams that permitted test-takers to sit for a certification exam from their residence. I have observed that ISACA has returned to tests administered at testing centers while continuing to offer remotely proctored exams for those who prefer remote testing. I'll discuss both options in this section.

NOTE Pay close attention to information on ISACA's website regarding testing logistics and locations.

Once your registration is complete, you will immediately receive an e-mail acknowledging this. Next, you will need to schedule your certification exam. The ISACA website will direct you to the certification registration page, where you will select a date, time, and (optionally) location to take your exam. When you confirm the date, time, and location for your exam, you will receive a confirmation via e-mail. You will need the confirmation letter to enter the test location—make sure to keep it unmarked and in a safe place until test time.

Onsite Testing Center

When you arrive at the test site, you will be required to sign in, and you may be required to sign an agreement. Also, you will be asked to turn in your smartphone, wallet or purse, and other personal items for safekeeping. The exam proctor will read aloud the rules you must follow while taking the exam. These rules will address matters such as breaks, drinking water, and snacks. While you take the exam, you will be supervised by the proctor, who may monitor you and your fellow test-takers by video surveillance in the test center to ensure that no one can cheat.

Remote Proctored Testing

If you have registered for a remote proctored exam, you must meet all of the technical requirements. ISACA has published the "Remote Proctoring Guide" that includes all of the necessary technical requirements and describes the step-by-step procedures for taking the exam.

A remote proctored exam means you'll be taking the exam on your computer in your residence or other location. You'll be in live contact with an exam proctor, and your webcam will be turned on throughout the exam so that the proctor can observe while you take the exam to ensure you are not cheating through the use of reference materials (books or online). You will also be required to use your webcam to show the entire room to your proctor, to demonstrate that you are alone and do not have reference materials or information anywhere in view.

To be eligible for a remote proctored exam, you must have a supported version of Windows or macOS, a current Google Chrome or other Chromium (such as Brave, SRware Iron) browser, a webcam with at least 640×480 resolution, a microphone, and a stable broadband Internet connection. You must be able to install the PSI Secure Browser and modify firewalls and other administrative tasks on the day of the exam (this requires administrative privileges on the computer you are using, which might be a problem if you are using a company-issued computer).

You'll be required to log in to your My ISACA account when your exam is scheduled. Next, you'll navigate to your certifications, find the exam you have scheduled, and launch the exam. You'll be directed to perform several tasks, including installing the secure browser and closing several other programs on your computer, such as other web browsers and programs such as Adobe Reader, Word, Excel, and any others that could include reference material.

You are not permitted to speak or perform gestures during the exam. In short, you cannot be seen to perform any action that may be an indication of aid by an accomplice.

You'll be required to verify your ID by holding it near your webcam so that the proctor can see it to confirm that you, not someone else, are taking the exam. You will also be required to use your webcam to show the entire room to your proctor.

After completing all steps, the proctor will release the exam, and you may begin.

Exam Questions

Each registrant has four hours to take the exam, with 150 multiple-choice questions representing the four CISM job practice areas. Each question has four answer choices; you must select only one best answer. You can skip questions and return to them later, and you can also flag questions you want to review later if time permits. While you are taking your exam, the time remaining will appear on the screen.

When you have completed the exam, you'll be directed to close the exam. At that time, the exam will display your pass or fail status, reminding you that your score and passing status are subject to review. You will be scored for each job practice area and then provided one final score. All scores are scaled. Scores range from 200 to 800; a final score of 450 is required to pass.

Exam questions are derived from a job practice analysis study conducted by ISACA. The selected areas represent tasks performed in a CISM's day-to-day activities and the background knowledge required to develop and manage an information security program. You can find more detailed descriptions of the task and knowledge statements at www.isaca.org/credentialing/cism/cism-exam-content-outline.

Exam Coverage

The CISM exam is quite broad in its scope. It covers four job practice areas, as shown in Table 2.

Independent committees have been developed to determine the best questions, review exam results, and statistically analyze the results for continuous improvement. Should you come across a horrifically difficult or strange question, do not panic. This question may have been written for another purpose. A few questions on the exam are included for research and analysis purposes and will not be counted against your score. The exam contains no indications in this regard, so do your best to answer every question.

Preparing for the Exam

The CISM certification requires that CISM candidates possess much knowledge and experience. You need to map out a long-term study strategy to pass the exam. The following sections offer some tips to help guide you to, through, and beyond exam day.

Domain	CISM Job Practice Area	Percentage of Exam
1	Information security governance	17%
2	Information security risk management	20%
3	Information security program	33%
4	Incident management	30%

Table 2 CISM Exam Job Practice Areas

Before the Exam

Consider the following list of tips on tasks and resources for exam preparation. They are listed in sequential order.

- **Read the Certification Exam Candidate Guide**   For information on the certification exam and requirements for the current year, go to www.isaca.org/credentialing/exam-candidate-guides and select the guide in your language of choice.

- **Register**   If you can, register early for any cost savings and solidify your commitment to moving forward with this professional achievement.

- **Schedule your exam**   Find a location, date, and time, and then commit.

- **Become familiar with the CISM job practice areas**   The job practice areas serve as the basis for the exam and requirements. As previously noted, beginning with the 2022 exam, the job practice areas have changed. Ensure that your study materials align with the current list at www.isaca.org/credentialing/cism.

- **Download and study the ISACA Glossary**   It's important for you to be familiar with ISACA's vocabulary, which you can download from www.isaca.org/resources/glossary.

- **Know your best learning methods**   Everyone has preferred learning styles, whether self-study, a study group, an instructor-led course, or a boot camp. Try to set up a study program that leverages your strengths.

- **Self-assess**   Run through practice exam questions in this book, as well as those available online (see the appendix for more information). ISACA may also offer a free online CISM self-assessment.

- **Iterative study**   Depending on your work experience in information security management, I suggest you plan your study program to take at least two months but as long as six months. During this time, periodically take practice exams and note your areas of strength and weakness. Once you have identified your weak areas, focus on those areas weekly by rereading the related sections in this book, retaking practice exams, and noting your progress.

- **Avoid cramming**   We've all seen the books on the shelves with titles that involve last-minute cramming. The Internet reveals various websites that teach individuals how to cram for exams. Research sites claim that exam cramming can lead to susceptibility to colds and flu, sleep disruptions, overeating, and digestive problems. One thing is certain: many people find that good, steady study habits result in less stress and greater clarity and focus during the exam. Because of the complexity of this exam, I highly recommend the long-term, steady-study option. Study the CISM job practice areas thoroughly. There are many study options. If time permits, investigate the many resources available to you.

- **Find a study group**   Many ISACA chapters and other organizations have formed specific study groups or offer less expensive exam review courses. Contact your local chapter to see whether these options are available to you. In addition, be sure to keep your eye on the ISACA website. And use your local network to find out whether there are other local study groups and helpful resources.

- **Confirmation letter**   Recheck your confirmation letter. Do not write on it or lose it. Put it in a safe place and note on your calendar when you will need to arrive at the site. Confirm that the location is the one you selected and is nearby.

- **Logistics check**   Check the Certification Exam Candidate Guide and your confirmation letter for the exact time you are required to report to the test site (or log in from home if you registered for a remote proctored exam). A few days before the exam, check the site—become familiar with the location and tricks to getting there. If you are taking public transportation, be sure to look at the schedule for the day of the exam: if your CISM exam is on a Saturday, public transportation schedules may differ from weekday schedules. If you are driving, know the route and where to park your vehicle.

- **Pack**   The night before, place your confirmation letter and a photo ID in a safe place, ready to go. Your ID must be a current, government-issued photo ID that matches the name on the confirmation letter and must not be handwritten. Examples of acceptable forms of ID are passports, driver's licenses, state IDs, green cards, and national IDs. Leave behind food, drinks, laptops, cell phones, and other electronic devices, because they are not permitted at the test site. For information on what can and cannot be brought to the exam site, see the Certification Exam Candidate Guide at www.isaca.org/credentialing/exam-candidate-guides.

- **Notification decision**   Decide whether you want your test results e-mailed to you. You will have the opportunity to consent to e-mail notification of the exam results. If you are fully paid (zero balance on exam fee) and have agreed to the e-mail notification, you should receive a one-time e-mail approximately eight weeks from the exam date with the results.

- **Sleep**   Make sure you get a good night's sleep before the exam. Research suggests that you should avoid caffeine at least four hours before bedtime. Keep a notepad and pen next to the bed to capture late-night thoughts that might keep you awake, eliminate as much noise and light as possible, and keep your room at a suitable temperature for sleeping. In the morning, rise early so as not to rush and subject yourself to additional stress.

Day of the Exam

On the day of the exam, follow these tips:

- **Arrive early**   Check the Bulletin of Information and your confirmation letter for the exact time you are required to report to the test site. The confirmation letter and the Certification Exam Candidate Guide explain that you must be at the test site *no later* than approximately 30 minutes *before* testing time. The examiner will begin reading the exam instructions at this time, and any latecomers will be disqualified from taking the test and will *not* receive a refund of fees.

- **Observe test center rules**   There may be rules about taking breaks. This will be discussed by the examiner, along with exam instructions. If you need something during the exam and are unsure about the rules, be sure to ask first. For information on conduct during the exam, see the ISACA Certification Exam Candidate Guide at www.isaca.org/credentialing/exam-candidate-guides.

- **Answer all exam questions**   Read questions carefully, but do not try to overanalyze. Remember to select the *best* solution based upon the CISM job practice and ISACA's vocabulary. There may be several reasonable answers, but one is *better* than the others. If you aren't sure about an answer, mark the question, so that after working through all the questions, you can return to any marked questions (and others) to read them and consider them more carefully. Above all, don't try to overanalyze questions, and do trust your instincts. Do not try to rush through the exam; there is plenty of time to take as many as a few minutes for each question. But at the same time, do watch the clock so that you don't find yourself going so slowly that you won't be able to answer every question thoughtfully.

- **Note your exam result**   When you have completed the exam, you should see your pass/ fail result. Your results may not be in large, blinking text; you may need to read the fine print to get your preliminary results. If you passed, congratulations! If you did not pass, observe any remarks about your status; you will be able to retake the exam—you'll find information about this on the ISACA website.

If You Do Not Pass

Don't lose heart if you do not pass your exam on the first attempt. Instead, remember that failure is a stepping stone to success. Thoughtfully take stock and determine your improvement areas. Be honest about areas where you need to learn more. Then reread the chapters or sections and return to this book's practice exams. If you participated in a study group or training, contact your study group coach or class instructor if you believe you may get advice about how to study the topics you need to master. Take at least several weeks to study those topics, refresh yourself on other topics, and then give it another go. Success is granted to those who are persistent and determined.

After the Exam

A few weeks from the exam date, you will receive your exam results by e-mail or postal mail. Each job practice area score will be noted in addition to the final score. All scores are scaled. Should you receive a passing score, you will also receive the application for certification.

Those unsuccessful in passing will also be notified. These individuals will want to closely look at the job practice area scores to determine areas for further study. They may retake the exam as often as needed on future exam dates, as long as they have registered and paid the applicable fees. Regardless of pass or fail, exam results will not be disclosed via telephone, fax, or e-mail (except for the consented e-mail notification).

 NOTE   You are not permitted to display the CISM moniker until you have completed certification. Passing the exam is *not* sufficient to use the CISM moniker anywhere, including e-mail, resumés, correspondence, or social media.

Applying for CISM Certification

You must submit evidence of a passing score and related work experience to apply for certification. Remember that you have five years to apply for CISM certification after you receive a passing exam score. After this time, you will need to retake the exam before you can apply. In addition, all work experience submitted must have occurred within ten years of your new certification application.

To complete the application process, you need to submit the following information:

- **CISM application** Note the exam ID number in your exam results letter, list the information security management experience and any experience substitutions, and identify which CISM job practice area (or areas) your experience pertains to.
- **Verification of Work Experience forms** These must be filled out and signed by your immediate supervisor or a person of higher rank in the organization to verify your work experience noted on the application. You must fill out a complete set of Verification of Work Experience forms for each separate employer.

After you've submitted the application, you will wait approximately eight weeks for processing. Then, if your application is approved, you will receive an e-mail notification, followed by a package in the postal mail containing your letter of certification, certificate, and a copy of the Continuing Professional Education Policy. You can then proudly display your certificate and use the "CISM" designation on your résumé, e-mail, social media profiles, and business cards.

 NOTE You are permitted to use the CISM moniker *only* after receiving your certification letter from ISACA.

Retaining Your CISM Certification

There is more to becoming a CISM professional than passing an exam, submitting an application, and receiving a paper certificate. Becoming a CISM professional is an ongoing and continuous lifestyle. Those with CISM certification agree to abide by the ISACA Code of Ethics, meet ongoing education requirements, and pay annual certification maintenance fees. Let's take a closer look at the education requirements and explain the costs of retaining certification.

Continuing Education

The goal of professional continuing education requirements is to ensure that individuals maintain CISM-related knowledge to help them successfully develop and manage security management programs. To maintain CISM certification, individuals must obtain 120 continuing education hours within three years, with a minimum requirement of 20 hours per year. Each CPE hour accounts for 50 minutes of active participation in educational activities.

What Counts as a Valid CPE Credit? For training and activities to be utilized for CPEs, they must involve technical or managerial training directly applicable to information

security and information security management. The following activities have been approved by the CISM certification committee and can count toward your CPE requirements:

- ISACA professional education activities and meetings
- ISACA members can take *ISACA Journal* CPE quizzes online or participate in monthly webcasts, earning CPEs after passing a quiz
- Non-ISACA professional education activities and meetings
- Self-study courses
- Vendor sales or marketing presentations (10-hour annual limit)
- Teaching, lecturing, or presenting on subjects related to job practice areas
- Publication of articles and books related to the profession
- Exam question development and review for any ISACA certification
- Passing related professional examinations
- Participation in ISACA boards or committees (20-hour annual limit per ISACA certification)
- Contributions to the information security management profession (10-hour annual limit)
- Mentoring (10-hour annual limit)

For more information on acceptable CPE credit, see the Continuing Professional Education Policy at www.isaca.org/credentialing/how-to-earn-cpe/#cpe-policy.

Tracking and Submitting CPEs   Not only are you required to submit a CPE tracking form for the annual renewal process, but you also should keep detailed records for each activity. Records associated with each activity should include the following:

- Name of attendee
- Name of sponsoring organization
- Activity title
- Activity description
- Activity date
- Number of CPE hours awarded

It is best to track all CPE information in a single file or worksheet. ISACA has developed a tracking form for your use in the Continuing Professional Education Policy. To make it easy on yourself, consider keeping all related records, such as receipts, brochures, and certificates, in the same place. Documentation should be retained throughout the three-year certification period and for at least one additional year afterward. Evidence retention is essential, as you may someday be audited. If this happens, you will be required to submit all paperwork. So why not be prepared?

For new CISMs, the annual and three-year certification period begins on January 1 of the year following certification. You are not required to report CPE hours for the first partial year after your certification; however, the hours earned from the time of certification to December 31 can be utilized in the first certification reporting period the following year. Therefore, should you get certified in January, you will have until the following January to accumulate CPEs. You will not have to report them until you report the totals for the following year, in October or November.

This is known as the *renewal period*. You will receive an e-mail directing you to the website to enter CPEs earned over the year. Alternatively, the renewal will be mailed to you, and then CPEs can be recorded on the hard-copy invoice and sent with your maintenance fee payment. CPEs and maintenance fees must be received by January 15 to retain certification.

Notification of compliance from the certification department is sent after all the information has been received and processed. You will be contacted directly if ISACA has questions about your submitted information.

Sample CPE Records   Table 3 contains an example of CPE records.

Name John Jacob

Certification Number 67895787

Certification Period 1/1/2023 to 12/31/2023

Activity Title/Sponsor	Activity Description	Date	CPE Hours	Support Docs Included?
ISACA presentation/lunch	PCI compliance	2/12/2023	1	Yes (receipt)
ISACA presentation/lunch	Security in SDLC	3/12/2023	1	Yes (receipt)
Regional Conference, RIMS	Compliance, risk	1/15–17/2023	6	Yes (CPE receipt)
BrightFly webinar	Governance, risk, and compliance	2/16/2023	3	Yes (confirmation e-mail)
ISACA board meeting	Chapter board meeting	4/9/2023	2	Yes (meeting minutes)
Presented at ISSA meeting	Risk management presentation	6/21/2023	1	Yes (meeting notice)
Published an article in XYZ	Journal article on SOX ITGCs	4/12/2023	4	Yes (article)
Vendor presentation	Learned about GRC tool capability	5/12/2023	2	Yes
Employer-offered training	Change management course	3/26/2023	7	Yes (certificate of course completion)

Table 3   Sample CPE Records

CPE Maintenance Fees

To remain CISM certified, you must pay CPE maintenance fees each year. These annual fees are (as of late 2022) $45 for members and $85 for nonmembers. The fees do not include ISACA membership and local chapter dues (though neither is required to maintain your CISM certification). More information is available from www.isaca.org/credentialing/cism/maintain-cism-certification.

Revocation of Certification

A CISM-certified individual may have their certification revoked for the following reasons:

- Failure to complete the minimum number of CPEs during the period
- Failure to document and provide evidence of CPEs in an audit
- Failure to submit payment for maintenance fees
- Failure to comply with the Code of Professional Ethics, which can result in investigation and ultimately lead to revocation of certification

If you have received a revocation notice, contact the ISACA Certification Department at https://support.isaca.org/ for more information.

Living the CISM Lifestyle

Being a CISM-certified individual involves much more than passing the exam, participating in continuous learning, and paying the annual maintenance fees. There are numerous opportunities to get involved in local, national, and global activities and events to help you grow professionally and meet other cyber risk management professionals.

Find a Local Chapter

ISACA has more than 200 chapters in about 100 countries around the world. Chances are there is a chapter near you. I attended many ISACA chapter meetings and other events in Seattle when I lived there, where engaging speakers spoke on new topics, and I met many like-minded security and audit professionals over the years.

Local chapters rely entirely on volunteers, and there is room for you to help in some way. Some chapters have various programs, events, study groups, and other activities that enrich participants professionally. Most of my ISACA experiences happen in my local chapter.

Attend ISACA Events

ISACA puts on fantastic in-person conferences with world-class keynote speakers, expert presentations, vendor demonstrations and exhibits, a bookstore, and opportunities to meet other security, risk, and audit professionals. I find ISACA conferences enriching to the point of being overwhelming. With so many learning and networking opportunities, I have found myself nearly exhausted at the end of an ISACA conference.

Join the Online Community

ISACA has an online community known as Engage, in which participants can discuss any topic related to security, risk, audit, privacy, and IT management. You can read and participate in online discussions, ask questions, help others with their questions, and make new professional connections. You can join Engage at https://engage.isaca.org/.

Pay It Forward Through Mentorship

If you are at the point in your career where you qualify for and have a reasonable prospect of passing the CISM exam, chances are you have had a mentor or two earlier, and maybe you have one now. As you grow in your professional stature, others will look to you as a potential mentor. Perhaps someone will ask if you would consider mentoring them. The world needs more, and better, information security professionals and leaders. Mentoring is a great way to "pay it forward" by helping others get into the profession and grow professionally. Mentoring will enrich your life as well.

Volunteer

As a nonprofit organization, ISACA relies upon volunteers to enrich its programs and events. There are many ways to help, and one or more of these volunteer opportunities may suit you:

- **Speak at an ISACA event**   Whether you make a keynote address or host a session on a specific topic, speaking at an ISACA event is a mountaintop experience. You can share your knowledge and expertise on a particular topic with attendees, but you'll learn some things too.

- **Serve as a chapter board member**   Local chapters don't run by themselves; they rely on volunteers—working professionals who want to improve the lot of other professionals in the local community. Board members can serve in various ways, from financial management to membership to events.

- **Start or help a CISM study group**   Whether part of a local chapter or a chapter at large, consider starting or helping a group of professionals who want to learn the details of the CISM job practice. I am a proponent of study groups because study group participants make the best students: they take the initiative to take on a big challenge to advance their careers.

- **Write an article**   ISACA has online and paper-based publications that feature articles on various subjects, including current developments in security, privacy, risk, and IT management from many perspectives. If you have specialized knowledge on some topic, other ISACA members can benefit from this knowledge if you write about it.

- **Participate in a credential working group**   ISACA works hard to ensure that its many certifications remain relevant and up to date. Experts worldwide in many industries give of their time to ensure that ISACA certifications remain the best in the world. ISACA conducts online and in-person working groups to update certification job practices, write certification exam questions, and publish updated study guides and practice exams. I contributed to the first CRISC certification working group in 2013 when ISACA initially developed the CRISC certification exam; I met many like-minded professionals, some of whom I am still in regular and meaningful contact with.

- **Participate in ISACA CommunITy Day**   ISACA organizes a global effort of local volunteering to make the world a better, safer place for everyone. Learn about the next CommunITy day at https://engage.isaca.org/communityday/.
- **Write certification exam questions**   ISACA needs experienced subject matter experts willing to write new certification exam questions. ISACA has a rigorous, high-quality process for exam questions that includes training. You could even be invited to an in-person exam item writing workshop. You can find out more about how this works at www.isaca.org/credentialing/write-an-exam-question.

Please take a minute to reflect upon the quality and richness of the ISACA organization and its many world-class certifications, publications, and events. These are all fueled by volunteers who made ISACA into what it is today. Only through your contribution of time and expertise will ISACA continue in its excellence for future security, risk, privacy, and IT professionals. And one last thing you can only experience on your own: volunteering helps others and enriches you. Will you consider leaving your mark and making ISACA better than you found it? For more information about these and many other volunteer opportunities, visit www.isaca.org/why-isaca/participate-and-volunteer.

Continue to Grow Professionally

Continual improvement is a mindset and lifestyle built into IT service management and information security, and it's even a formal requirement in ISO/IEC 27001! I suggest you periodically take stock of your career status and aspirations, be honest with yourself, and determine what mountain you will climb next. If needed, find a mentor who can guide you and give you solid advice.

While this may not immediately make sense to you, know this: helping others, whether through any of the volunteer opportunities listed here, or in other ways, will enrich you personally and professionally. I'm not talking about feathers in your cap or juicy items in your résumé, but rather the growth in character and wisdom that results from helping and serving others, particularly when you initiated the helping and serving.

Professional growth means different things to different people. Whether it's a better job title, more money, a better (or bigger, or smaller) employer, a different team, more responsibility, or more certifications, embarking on long-term career planning will pay dividends. Take control of your career and your career path. This is yours to own and shape as you will.

Summary

Becoming and being a CISM professional is a lifestyle, not just a one-time event. It takes motivation, skill, good judgment, persistence, and proficiency to be a strong and effective leader in information security management. The CISM certification was designed to help you navigate the security management world more easily and confidently.

The following chapters contain 300 CISM certification exam practice questions across all of the CISM job practice areas. Detailed explanations help you understand why answers are correct or incorrect. You can also take online exam practice questions—see the appendix for more information.

PART I

Information Security Governance

Enterprise Governance

This domain includes questions from the following topics:
- Organizational culture
- Types of legal and regulatory requirements
- Organization structure, roles, and responsibilities
- Ethics and codes of conduct

This chapter covers Certified Information Security Manager (CISM) job practice 1, "Information Security Governance," part A, "Enterprise Governance." The entire Information Security Governance domain represents 17 percent of the CISM examination.

Supporting Tasks in the CISM job practice that align with the Information Security Governance / Enterprise Governance domain include

4. Integrate information security governance into corporate governance.
8. Define, communicate, and monitor information security responsibilities throughout the organization and lines of authority.
21. Identify legal, regulatory, organizational, and other applicable compliance requirements.

When properly implemented, security governance is the foundation that supports security-related strategic decisions and all other security activities. *Governance* is a process whereby senior management exerts strategic control over business functions through policies, objectives, delegation of authority, and monitoring. Governance is management's oversight of all other business processes to ensure that business processes effectively meet the organization's business vision and objectives.

Organizations usually establish governance through steering committees responsible for setting long-term business strategy and making changes to ensure that business processes continue to support business strategy and the organization's overall needs. This is accomplished through the development and enforcement of documented policies, standards, procedures, and requirements. Various reporting metrics provide feedback to business leaders on organizational performance and the results of their decisions.

1. Which of the following best describes information security governance?
    A. Information security policies
    B. Information security policies along with audits of those policies
    C. Management's control of information security processes
    D. Benchmarks of metrics as compared to similar organizations

2. In a risk management process, who is the best person(s) to make a risk treatment decision?
    A. Chief risk officer (CRO)
    B. Chief information officer (CIO)
    C. Process owner who is associated with the risk
    D. Chief information security officer (CISO)

3. The ultimate responsibility for an organization's cybersecurity program lies with whom?
    A. The board of directors
    B. The chief executive officer (CEO)
    C. The chief information officer (CIO)
    D. The chief information security officer (CISO)

4. In a U.S. public company, a CISO will generally report the state of the organization's cybersecurity program to:
    A. The Treadway Commission
    B. Independent auditors
    C. The U.S. Securities and Exchange Commission
    D. The audit committee of the board of directors

5. A new CISO in an organization is building its cybersecurity program from the ground up. To ensure collaboration among business leaders and department heads in the organization, the CISO should form and manage which of the following?
    A. A risk committee of the board of directors
    B. A cybersecurity steering committee
    C. An audit committee of the board of directors
    D. Business-aligned security policy

6. Who is the best person or group to make cyber-risk treatment decisions?
    A. The chief information security officer (CISO)
    B. The audit committee of the board of directors
    C. The cybersecurity steering committee
    D. The chief risk officer (CRO)

7. Which is the best party to conduct access reviews?

   A. Users' managers

   B. Information security manager

   C. IT service desk

   D. Department head

8. Which is the best party to make decisions about the purpose and function of business applications?

   A. Business department head

   B. IT business analyst

   C. Application developer

   D. End user

9. Which of the following is the best definition of custodial responsibility?

   A. A custodian protects assets based on the customer's defined interests.

   B. A custodian protects assets based on the custodian's own defined interests.

   C. A custodian makes decisions based on the custodian's own defined interests.

   D. A custodian makes decisions based on the customer's defined interests.

10. What is the primary risk of IT acting as custodian for a business owner?

   A. IT may not have enough interest to provide quality care for business applications.

   B. IT may not have sufficient staffing to care for business applications properly.

   C. IT may have insufficient knowledge of business operations to make good decisions.

   D. Business departments might not give IT sufficient access to manage applications properly.

11. An organization needs to hire an executive who will build a management program that will consider threats and vulnerabilities and determine controls needed to protect systems and work centers. What is the best job title for this position?

   A. CSO

   B. CRO

   C. CISO

   D. CIRO

12. An organization needs to hire an executive who will be responsible for ensuring that the organization's policies, business processes, and information systems are compliant with laws and regulations concerning the proper collection, use, and protection of personally identifiable information. What is the best job title for the organization to use for this position?

   A. CSO

   B. CIRO

   C. CISO

   D. CPO

13. The Big Data Company is adjusting several position titles in its IT department to reflect industry standards. Included in consideration are two individuals: The first is responsible for the overall relationships and data flows among its internal and external information systems. The second is responsible for the overall health and management of systems containing information. Which two job titles are most appropriate for these two roles?

   A. Systems architect and database administrator

   B. Data architect and data scientist

   C. Data scientist and database administrator

   D. Data architect and database administrator

14. What is the primary distinction between a network engineer and a telecom engineer?

   A. A network engineer is primarily involved with networks and internal network media, while a telecom engineer is primarily involved with networks and external (carrier) network media.

   B. A network engineer is primarily involved with networks and external (carrier) network media, while a telecom engineer is primarily involved with networks and internal network media.

   C. A network engineer is primarily involved with layer 3 protocols and above, while a telecom engineer is primarily involved with layer 1 and layer 2 protocols.

   D. There is no distinction, as both are involved in all aspects of an organization's networks.

15. An organization that is a U.S. public company is redesigning its access management and access review controls. What is the best role for internal audit in this redesign effort?

   A. Develop procedures

   B. Design controls

   C. Provide feedback on control design

   D. Develop controls and procedures

16. A security operations manager is proposing that engineers who design and manage information systems play a role in monitoring those systems. Are design and management compatible with monitoring? Why or why not?

   A. Personnel who design and manage systems should not perform a monitoring role because this is a conflict of interest.

   B. Personnel who design and manage systems will be more familiar with the reasons and steps to take when alerts are generated.

   C. Personnel who design and manage systems will not be familiar with response procedures when alerts are generated.

   D. Personnel who design and manage systems are not permitted access to production environments and should not perform monitoring.

17. The statement "Complete migration of flagship system to latest version of vendor-supplied software" is an example of what?

    A. Mission statement

    B. Vision statement

    C. Purpose statement

    D. Objective statement

18. Ernie, a CISO who manages a large security group, wants to create a mission statement for the CISO group. What is the best approach for creating this mission statement?

    A. Start with the organization's mission statement.

    B. Start with Ernie's most recent performance review.

    C. Start with the results of the most recent risk assessment.

    D. Start with the body of open items in the risk register.

19. Samuel is the CISO in an organization that is a U.S. public company. Samuel has noted that the organization's internal audit function concentrates its auditing efforts on "financially relevant" applications and underlying IT systems and infrastructure. As an experienced CISO, what conclusion can Samuel draw from this?

    A. The audits performed by internal audit on underlying IT systems and infrastructure are value-added activities.

    B. Internal audit's scope is too narrow and must include all applications and IT systems.

    C. The scope of internal audit is of no consequence or value to the CISO.

    D. The scope of internal audit's auditing activities is as expected for a U.S. public company.

20. What is the purpose of metrics in an information security program?

    A. To measure the performance and effectiveness of security controls

    B. To measure the likelihood of an attack on the organization

    C. To predict the likelihood of an attack on an organization

    D. To predict the method of an attack on an organization

21. Of what value is a third-party risk management (TPRM) process for a CISO who is developing a long-term security strategy for an organization?

    A. TPRM provides valuable insight into the security capabilities of critical service providers.

    B. TPRM provides valuable insight into the organization's procurement process.

    C. TPRM provides a list of all service providers used by the organization.

    D. TPRM does not provide value to the CISO because it is concerned only with business processes.

22. Joseph, a new security leader in an online retail organization, is developing a long-term security strategy. Joseph has developed a detailed description of the future state of the security organization. What must Joseph do before developing a strategy to realize the future state?

   A. Perform an audit of existing security controls to understand their effectiveness.

   B. Understand the current state and perform a gap analysis to identify the differences.

   C. Perform a risk assessment to identify potential pitfalls in the strategy.

   D. Commission a penetration test to identify unknown vulnerabilities in critical systems.

23. Joseph, a new security leader in an online retail organization, is developing a long-term security strategy. In his research, Joseph is seeking documents describing the current security program. Which of the following documents would *not* provide the best value in this analysis?

   A. Security program charter

   B. Security team job descriptions

   C. Information security policy

   D. Meeting minutes for the cybersecurity steering committee

24. Quincy is a security leader who wants to formalize information security in his organization. What is the best first step to formalizing the program?

   A. Start an information security intranet site.

   B. Start an information security newsletter.

   C. Develop an information security policy.

   D. Develop an information security program charter.

25. Ravila, a security leader, has assessed the maturity of the information security capabilities in the organization using the CMMI model. The average maturity of business processes in the organization is 3.2. What should Ravila do next?

   A. Compare the current maturity levels to desired maturity levels and develop a strategy to achieve desired levels.

   B. Determine the steps necessary to raise process maturity to 5.

   C. Identify the processes with the lowest maturity and develop a strategy to raise them to the level of other processes.

   D. Perform a root cause analysis (RCA) to determine why business process maturity has fallen to this level.

1. C		**14.** A	
2. C		**15.** C	
3. A		**16.** B	
4. D		**17.** D	
5. B		**18.** A	
6. C		**19.** D	
7. D		**20.** A	
8. A		**21.** A	
9. D		**22.** B	
10. C		**23.** B	
11. B		**24.** D	
12. D		**25.** A	
13. D			

1. Which of the following best describes information security governance?

   A. Information security policies

   B. Information security policies along with audits of those policies

   C. Management's control of information security processes

   D. Benchmarks of metrics as compared to similar organizations

   ☑ C. ISACA defines governance as a set of processes that "[e]nsures that stakeholder needs, conditions and options are evaluated to determine balanced, agreed-on enterprise objectives to be achieved; setting direction through prioritization and decision making; and monitoring performance and compliance against agreed-on direction and objectives."

   ☒ A, B, and D are incorrect. A is incorrect because, although information security policies are an essential part of information security governance, there are several other components to governance as well. B is incorrect because security policies and activities (such as audits) to measure their effectiveness are only one component of information security governance. D is incorrect because the comparison of metrics to other organizations is not a significant part of a governance program. Indeed, many organizations forego benchmarking entirely.

2. In a risk management process, who is the best person(s) to make a risk treatment decision?

   A. Chief risk officer (CRO)

   B. Chief information officer (CIO)

   C. Process owner who is associated with the risk

   D. Chief information security officer (CISO)

   ☑ C. The department head (or division head or business owner, as appropriate) associated with the business activity regarding the risk treatment decision should be the person making the risk treatment decision. This is because a risk treatment decision is a business decision that should be made by the person who is responsible for the business function.

   ☒ A, B, and D are incorrect. A is incorrect because the chief risk officer (CRO) should not be making business function risk decisions on behalf of department heads or business owners. At best, the CRO should be facilitating discussions leading to risk treatment decisions. B is incorrect because the CIO should not be making business function risk decisions on behalf of department heads or business owners. D is incorrect because the CISO should not be making risk treatment decisions. Instead, the CISO should, at best, be facilitating discussions that lead to risk treatment decisions made by department heads or business owners.

3. The ultimate responsibility for an organization's cybersecurity program lies with whom?

    A. The board of directors

    B. The chief executive officer (CEO)

    C. The chief information officer (CIO)

    D. The chief information security officer (CISO)

    ☑ **A.** The ultimate responsibility for everything in an organization, including its cybersecurity program, lies with its board of directors. Various laws and regulations define board member responsibilities, particularly in publicly traded organizations in the United States and in other countries.

    ☒ **B, C,** and **D** are incorrect. **B** is incorrect, except in unusual cases when an organization does not have a board of directors. **C** is incorrect because this is about *ultimate responsibility,* which lies with the board of directors. **D** is incorrect because the CISO's role should be one of a facilitator, wherein other members of executive management, as well as board members, make business decisions (including cybersecurity-related decisions) on behalf of the organization.

4. In a U.S. public company, a CISO will generally report the state of the organization's cybersecurity program to:

    A. The Treadway Commission

    B. Independent auditors

    C. The U.S. Securities and Exchange Commission

    D. The audit committee of the board of directors

    ☑ **D.** In most U.S. publicly traded companies, the CISO will report the state of the organization's cybersecurity program to members of the audit committee of the board of directors. Although this is the best answer, in some organizations, the CIO or CEO may instead report on the cybersecurity program.

    ☒ **A, B,** and **C** are incorrect. **A** is incorrect because an organization would not report anything to the Treadway Commission. **B** is incorrect because the CISO would typically not report the state of the cybersecurity program to independent auditors. In public companies, however, the CISO and independent auditors will periodically meet to discuss the cybersecurity program. **C** is incorrect because the CISO would not be reporting to the U.S. Securities and Exchange Commission (SEC). An organization's internal auditor or CFO will, however, submit reports about the organization's financial results to the SEC, although these filings will rarely include information about cybersecurity, unless there has been a security incident that had material impact on the organization.

5. A new CISO in an organization is building its cybersecurity program from the ground up. To ensure collaboration among business leaders and department heads in the organization, the CISO should form and manage which of the following?

   A. A risk committee of the board of directors

   B. A cybersecurity steering committee

   C. An audit committee of the board of directors

   D. Business-aligned security policy

   ☑ **B.** A cybersecurity steering committee, consisting of senior executives, business unit leaders, and department heads, when properly facilitated by the CISO, can discuss organization-wide issues related to cybersecurity and make strategic decisions about cyber risk.

   ☒ **A, C,** and **D** are incorrect. **A** is incorrect because the CISO will not be involved in the formation and management of a board of directors risk committee. **C** is incorrect because a CISO would not be involved in the formation or management of a board of directors audit committee. **D** is incorrect because a business-aligned security policy, while important, would not significantly foster collaboration among business leaders.

6. Who is the best person or group to make cyber-risk treatment decisions?

   A. The chief information security officer (CISO)

   B. The audit committee of the board of directors

   C. The cybersecurity steering committee

   D. The chief risk officer (CRO)

   ☑ **C.** The cybersecurity steering committee, which should consist of senior executives, business unit leaders, and department heads, should openly discuss, collaborate, and decide on most risk treatment issues in an organization. If decisions are made by individuals such as the CISO or CRO, then business leaders may be less likely to support those decisions, as they may not have had a part in decision-making.

   ☒ **A, B,** and **D** are incorrect. **A** is incorrect because the CISO unilaterally making risk treatment decisions for the organization is less likely to get buy-in from other business leaders, who may feel they did not have a voice in making these decisions. **B** is incorrect because audit committee members rarely get involved in risk treatment decision-making. **D** is incorrect because the CRO unilaterally making risk treatment decisions will result in less buy-in and support from business leaders than if they participated in these decisions.

7. Which is the best party to conduct access reviews?

   A. Users' managers

   B. Information security manager

   C. IT service desk

   D. Department head

☑ **D.** The persons who are responsible for business activities should be the ones who review users' access to applications that support their business activities. All too often, however, access reviews are performed by persons less qualified to make decisions about which persons should have access (and at what levels or capabilities) to systems and applications critical to their business processes. Commonly, IT personnel perform these reviews as a proxy for business owners, but often IT personnel do not have as much knowledge about business operations and are, therefore, less qualified to make quality decisions about user access. IT personnel can perform a user access review only if they have a sound understanding of user roles; but even then, business owners should be informed of user access reviews and their outcomes.

☒ **A, B,** and **C** are incorrect. **A** is incorrect because the managers of users with access to systems and applications are not the best parties to review access. **B** is incorrect because information security managers have insufficient knowledge about business operations and the persons using them. **C** is incorrect because IT service desk personnel have insufficient knowledge about business operations and the persons using them. More often, IT service personnel are the ones who carry out access changes. Since they are the ones carrying out changes (in most cases), they should not also be the party reviewing who has access, because they would be reviewing their own work.

8. Which is the best party to make decisions about the purpose and function of business applications?

   A. Business department head

   B. IT business analyst

   C. Application developer

   D. End user

☑ **A.** As the party who is responsible for the ongoing operations and success of business operations and business processes, a business department head is the best party to determine the behavior of business applications supporting business processes.

☒ **B, C,** and **D** are incorrect. **B** is incorrect because IT business analysts are not responsible for decisions about business unit operations. That said, the IT business analyst's role may include facilitation of discussions concerning the configuration and function of business applications, and in some cases, he or she may make configuration changes. **C** is incorrect because application developers are not responsible for decisions about business unit operations. In some cases, however, application developers may have intimate knowledge of the internal workings of business applications and may provide insight into the function of applications. Thus, they may provide information in support of decisions made by business department heads. **D** is incorrect because end users are generally not responsible for decisions about business unit operations.

9. Which of the following is the best definition of custodial responsibility?

   A. A custodian protects assets based on the customer's defined interests.

   B. A custodian protects assets based on the custodian's own defined interests.

   C. A custodian makes decisions based on the custodian's own defined interests.

   D. A custodian makes decisions based on the customer's defined interests.

   ☑ **D.** A custodian is charged with a potentially wide range of decisions regarding the care of an asset. Decisions are based upon the customer's defined interests. A germane example is an IT department that builds and maintains information systems on behalf of internal customers; the IT department will make various decisions about the design and operation of an information system so that the system will best meet customers' needs.

   ☒ **A, B,** and **C** are incorrect. **A** is incorrect because protection of an asset is only a part of the scope of responsibility of a custodian. **B** is incorrect because a custodian does not protect assets based on the custodian's own interests, but rather on the customer's interest. **C** is incorrect because a custodian does not make decisions based on the custodian's own interests, but rather on the customer's interest.

10. What is the primary risk of IT acting as custodian for a business owner?

   A. IT may not have enough interest to provide quality care for business applications.

   B. IT may not have sufficient staffing to care for business applications properly.

   C. IT may have insufficient knowledge of business operations to make good decisions.

   D. Business departments might not give IT sufficient access to manage applications properly.

   ☑ **C.** IT personnel tend to focus their thoughts on the technology supporting business departments rather than on the business operations occurring in the business departments they support. Often, IT departments are observed to make too many assumptions about the needs of their customers, and they do not work hard enough to understand their users' needs to ensure that business applications will support them properly.

   ☒ **A, B,** and **D** are incorrect. **A** and **B** are incorrect because they are not the best answers regarding the primary risk of IT acting as custodian for a business owner. **D** is incorrect because business units are not generally in a position to restrict IT departments from administrative access to business applications.

11. An organization needs to hire an executive who will build a management program that will consider threats and vulnerabilities and determine controls needed to protect systems and work centers. What is the best job title for this position?

   A. CSO

   B. CRO

   C. CISO

   D. CIRO

☑ **B.** The CRO (chief risk officer) is responsible for managing risk for multiple types of assets, commonly information assets, as well as physical assets and/or workplace safety. In financial services organizations, the CRO will also manage risks associated with financial transactions or financial asset portfolios.

☒ **A, C,** and **D** are incorrect. **A** is incorrect because the CSO (chief security officer) is not necessarily responsible for risk management, but is instead responsible for the design, deployment, and operation of protective controls, commonly for information systems as well as other assets such as equipment or work centers. **C** is incorrect because the CISO (chief information security officer) is typically responsible for protection of only information assets and not other types of assets such as property, plant, and equipment. **D** is incorrect because the CIRO (chief information risk officer) is typically responsible for risk management and protection of information assets but not other types of assets, such as property, plant, and equipment.

12. An organization needs to hire an executive who will be responsible for ensuring that the organization's policies, business processes, and information systems are compliant with laws and regulations concerning the proper collection, use, and protection of personally identifiable information. What is the best job title for the organization to use for this position?

A. CSO

B. CIRO

C. CISO

D. CPO

☑ **D.** The chief privacy officer (CPO) is the best title for a position in which the executive ensures that the organization's policies, practices, controls, and systems ensure the proper collection, use, and protection of personally identifiable information (PII).

☒ **A, B,** and **C** are incorrect. **A** is incorrect because the chief security officer (CSO) is typically not responsible for privacy-related activities concerning the collection and use of PII. **B** is incorrect because the chief information risk officer (CIRO) is typically not responsible for privacy-related activities concerning the collection and use of PII. **C** is incorrect because the chief information security officer (CISO) is typically not responsible for privacy-related activities concerning the collection and use of PII.

13. The Big Data Company is adjusting several position titles in its IT department to reflect industry standards. Included in consideration are two individuals: The first is responsible for the overall relationships and data flows among its internal and external information systems. The second is responsible for the overall health and management of systems containing information. Which two job titles are most appropriate for these two roles?

A. Systems architect and database administrator

B. Data architect and data scientist

C. Data scientist and database administrator

D. Data architect and database administrator

☑ **D.** Data architect is the best position title for someone who is responsible for the overall relationships and data flows among the organization's information systems. Database administrator (DBA) is the best position title for someone who is responsible for maintaining the database management systems (DBMSs) throughout the organization.

☒ **A**, **B**, and **C** are incorrect. **A** is incorrect because systems architect is not the best title for someone who is responsible for the overall relationships and data flows among the organization's information systems. **B** is incorrect because data scientist is not the best title for someone who is responsible for the overall health and management of systems containing information. **C** is incorrect because data scientist is not the best title for someone who is responsible for the overall relationships and data flows among its internal and external information systems.

14. What is the primary distinction between a network engineer and a telecom engineer?

   A. A network engineer is primarily involved with networks and internal network media, while a telecom engineer is primarily involved with networks and external (carrier) network media.

   B. A network engineer is primarily involved with networks and external (carrier) network media, while a telecom engineer is primarily involved with networks and internal network media.

   C. A network engineer is primarily involved with layer 3 protocols and above, while a telecom engineer is primarily involved with layer 1 and layer 2 protocols.

   D. There is no distinction, as both are involved in all aspects of an organization's networks.

   ☑ **A.** A network engineer is primarily involved with networks and internal network media (including cabling and internal wireless networks such as Wi-Fi), while a telecom engineer is primarily involved with networks and external (carrier) network media such as Multiprotocol Label Switching (MPLS), Frame Relay, and dark fiber in support of services such as data transport, phone systems, conferencing systems, and voicemail systems.

   ☒ **B**, **C**, and **D** are incorrect. **B** is incorrect because the definitions in this answer are swapped. **C** is incorrect because the distinction between a network engineer and a telecom engineer is not strictly about protocol layers. **D** is incorrect because there *is* a distinction between the network engineer and telecom engineer position titles.

15. An organization that is a U.S. public company is redesigning its access management and access review controls. What is the best role for internal audit in this redesign effort?

   A. Develop procedures

   B. Design controls

   C. Provide feedback on control design

   D. Develop controls and procedures

☑ **C.** Any internal audit function should not design or implement controls or procedures other than those in their own department. Internal audit cannot play a design role in any process or control that it may later be required to audit.

☒ **A, B,** and **D** are incorrect. **A** is incorrect because internal audit should not develop procedures that it may later be required to audit. Instead, internal audit can provide feedback on procedures developed by others. Internal audit can never be in a position to audit its own work. **B** is incorrect because internal audit should not design controls that it may later be required to audit. Internal audit can provide feedback on controls designed by others. Internal audit can never be in a position to audit its own work. **D** is incorrect because internal audit should not develop controls or procedures. This is because internal audit may be required to audit these controls and/or procedures; internal audit can never be in a position to audit its own work.

16. A security operations manager is proposing that engineers who design and manage information systems play a role in monitoring those systems. Are design and management compatible with monitoring? Why or why not?

   A. Personnel who design and manage systems should not perform a monitoring role because this is a conflict of interest.

   B. Personnel who design and manage systems will be more familiar with the reasons and steps to take when alerts are generated.

   C. Personnel who design and manage systems will not be familiar with response procedures when alerts are generated.

   D. Personnel who design and manage systems are not permitted access to production environments and should not perform monitoring.

   ☑ **B.** Personnel who design and manage information systems are more likely to be familiar with the nature of alerts as well as procedures for responding to them.

   ☒ **A, C,** and **D** are incorrect. **A** is incorrect because there would normally not be any conflict of interest between design, management, and monitoring. **C** is incorrect because personnel who design and manage information systems are in a position to understand how those systems work and would be more likely to know how to respond to alerts. **D** is incorrect because personnel who manage information systems would be permitted to access them in production environments.

17. The statement "Complete migration of flagship system to latest version of vendor-supplied software" is an example of what?

   A. Mission statement

   B. Vision statement

   C. Purpose statement

   D. Objective statement

☑ **D.** The statement is a strategic objective.

☒ **A, B,** and **C** are incorrect. **A** is incorrect because the statement is too specific to be a mission statement. **B** is incorrect because the statement is not typical of a vision statement. **C** is incorrect because the statement is not typical of a purpose statement.

18. Ernie, a CISO who manages a large security group, wants to create a mission statement for the CISO group. What is the best approach for creating this mission statement?

    A. Start with the organization's mission statement.

    B. Start with Ernie's most recent performance review.

    C. Start with the results of the most recent risk assessment.

    D. Start with the body of open items in the risk register.

    ☑ **A.** The best way to manage a security organization is to align it with the business it is supporting. When creating a security organization mission statement, a good start is to look at the overall organization's mission statement; this way, the security team's mission is more likely to align with the overall organization. If the overall organization lacks a mission statement, the CISO can use what he or she knows about the organization's purpose to build a security team mission statement that is sure to support the organization.

    ☒ **B, C,** and **D** are incorrect. **B** is incorrect because it is not the best answer. Still, it is possible that the CISO's performance review may be well aligned with the overall business and may be a useful reference for creating a CISO team mission statement. **C** is incorrect because, by itself, a risk assessment report, though it may be an indicator of the nature of the work that the CISO organization may be undertaking in the future, will not provide much information about the overall business's purpose. **D** is incorrect because the risk register's open items will not provide much information about the organization's overall purpose. Although the risk register's open items may be an indicator of the types of work that the CISO organization will be working on, this does not provide sufficient information to develop the CISO organization's mission, because the CISO's mission is more than just solving short-term problems.

19. Samuel is the CISO in an organization that is a U.S. public company. Samuel has noted that the organization's internal audit function concentrates its auditing efforts on "financially relevant" applications and underlying IT systems and infrastructure. As an experienced CISO, what conclusion can Samuel draw from this?

    A. The audits performed by internal audit on underlying IT systems and infrastructure are value-added activities.

    B. Internal audit's scope is too narrow and must include all applications and IT systems.

    C. The scope of internal audit is of no consequence or value to the CISO.

    D. The scope of internal audit's auditing activities is as expected for a U.S. public company.

☑ **D.** In a U.S. public company, an internal audit function is required to audit the financially relevant business processes and their supporting business applications and IT infrastructure to provide reasonable assurances about the integrity of financial reports produced by the organization to its shareholders. This is required because in 2002, Congress passed the Sarbanes–Oxley Act (SOX) to protect shareholders and the general public from accounting errors and fraudulent practices in enterprises and to improve the accuracy of corporate disclosures. The act sets deadlines for compliance and publishes rules on requirements.

☒ **A, B,** and **C** are incorrect. **A** is incorrect because internal audits in a U.S. public company are required to audit the systems and infrastructures that support financially relevant business applications. This is not a value-added (not required) activity. **B** is incorrect because internal audit is not required to audit all of an organization's applications and IT systems. However, in some organizations, internal audit's scope surpasses what is required of U.S. public companies to provide assurances of the integrity of other processes and systems. **C** is incorrect because internal audit would be considered a business partner of a CISO in most organizations. This is because internal audit analyzes security controls in parts of IT, and this provides the CISO with valuable information on the effectiveness of at least some of the security controls in the organization.

20. What is the purpose of metrics in an information security program?

    A. To measure the performance and effectiveness of security controls

    B. To measure the likelihood of an attack on the organization

    C. To predict the likelihood of an attack on an organization

    D. To predict the method of an attack on an organization

    ☑ **A.** The purpose of metrics is to measure the performance and effectiveness of security controls. The meaning and usefulness of specific metrics will depend upon the context and measurement method of specific controls.

    ☒ **B, C,** and **D** are incorrect. **B** is incorrect because metrics do not necessarily foretell of an attack on an organization. **C** is incorrect because metrics are not always used to predict an attack on an organization. **D** is incorrect because metrics do not necessarily predict the method used for an attack on an organization.

21. Of what value is a third-party risk management (TPRM) process for a CISO who is developing a long-term security strategy for an organization?

    A. TPRM provides valuable insight into the security capabilities of critical service providers.

    B. TPRM provides valuable insight into the organization's procurement process.

    C. TPRM provides a list of all service providers used by the organization.

    D. TPRM does not provide value to the CISO because it is concerned only with business processes.

☑ **A.** An effective TPRM program captures and archives detailed information about security controls in third-party service-provider organizations. This helps a CISO better understand the overall world of risk with regard to the protection of critical data and capabilities.

☒ **B, C,** and **D** are incorrect. **B** is incorrect because TPRM provides little, if any, insight into procurement. This is because TPRM does not include activities such as competitive analysis, suitability of services, or pricing, which are among the matters of focus by procurement. **C** is incorrect because a TPRM process does not necessarily provide a list of *all* of an organization's service providers. This is because individuals and groups may still procure low-cost or free services and "fly under the radar" of IT, security, legal, and procurement processes and put the organization at risk. **D** is incorrect because a TPRM process focuses on information security risk in third-party service-provider organizations, which is a high-value concern for a CISO.

22. Joseph, a new security leader in an online retail organization, is developing a long-term security strategy. Joseph has developed a detailed description of the future state of the security organization. What must Joseph do before developing a strategy to realize the future state?

   A. Perform an audit of existing security controls to understand their effectiveness.

   B. Understand the current state and perform a gap analysis to identify the differences.

   C. Perform a risk assessment to identify potential pitfalls in the strategy.

   D. Commission a penetration test to identify unknown vulnerabilities in critical systems.

   ☑ **B.** When developing a strategy, it is first necessary to develop the desired end state, understand the current state, and understand the gaps between the two. The strategy, then, will consist of work required to close those gaps, transforming the organization into the desired end state.

   ☒ **A, C,** and **D** are incorrect. **A** is incorrect because, although it is important to perform audits of controls to understand their effectiveness, this question is focused on the proper method for developing a strategy: develop the desired end state, determine the current state, and perform a gap analysis to determine the work required to realize the end state. **C** is incorrect because, although it is important to perform risk assessments, this question is focused on the proper method for developing a strategy: develop the desired end state, determine the current state, and perform a gap analysis to determine the work required to realize the end state. **D** is incorrect because, although it is important to perform penetration tests to identify potentially critical vulnerabilities in information systems and applications, this question is focused on the proper method for developing a strategy: develop the desired end state, determine the current state, and perform a gap analysis to determine the work required to realize the end state.

23. Joseph, a new security leader in an online retail organization, is developing a long-term security strategy. In his research, Joseph is seeking documents describing the current security program. Which of the following documents would *not* provide the best value in this analysis?

A. Security program charter

B. Security team job descriptions

C. Information security policy

D. Meeting minutes for the cybersecurity steering committee

☑ **B.** Of these four sets of information, job descriptions for security team members would provide the least valuable insight. In part this is because workers' regular activities sometimes stray away from statements in a job description. At best, a job description describes desired or expected activities at a point in time in the past.

☒ **A, C,** and **D** are incorrect. **A** is incorrect because a security program charter would provide considerable insight into the mission and vision for an information security program. **C** is incorrect because an information security policy would provide insight into the security-related expectations in an organization. That said, a security leader would need to explore the policy further to determine the degree of compliance. **D** is incorrect because meeting minutes for a cybersecurity steering committee are of potentially high value to a security leader. This, of course, depends upon the purpose of the steering committee and the nature of its proceedings and decisions.

24. Quincy is a security leader who wants to formalize information security in his organization. What is the best first step to formalizing the program?

A. Start an information security intranet site.

B. Start an information security newsletter.

C. Develop an information security policy.

D. Develop an information security program charter.

☑ **D.** An information security program charter describes the mission and vision for an information security program, defines roles and responsibilities, and describes its engagement with others in the organization as well as external parties such as customers or regulators.

☒ **A, B,** and **C** are incorrect. **A** is incorrect because, although an intranet site can help others in the organization be better informed about the information security program, a charter is the best choice. **B** is incorrect because, although a newsletter can help others in the organization be better informed about the information security program, a charter is the best choice. **C** is incorrect because an organization needs to have an information security policy, whether its information security program is formal or not.

25. Ravila, a security leader, has assessed the maturity of the information security capabilities in the organization using the CMMI model. The average maturity of business processes in the organization is 3.2. What should Ravila do next?

   A. Compare the current maturity levels to desired maturity levels and develop a strategy to achieve desired levels.

   B. Determine the steps necessary to raise process maturity to 5.

   C. Identify the processes with the lowest maturity and develop a strategy to raise them to the level of other processes.

   D. Perform a root cause analysis (RCA) to determine why business process maturity has fallen to this level.

   ☑ **A.** The best answer here is to determine any gaps between current and future maturity levels so that any processes needing improvement can be improved and measured.

   ☒ **B**, **C**, and **D** are incorrect. **B** is incorrect because level 5 is not necessarily a realistic goal for maturity in an organization. An average maturity between 2.5 and 4 is acceptable and appropriate in many organizations. **C** is incorrect because it is normal and acceptable for some processes to have lower maturity levels than others. **D** is incorrect because there is no indication here that the maturity of any processes has declined. RCA, however, may be a reasonable activity to undertake if the maturity of a specific process has declined in order to understand how to mitigate it.

Information Security Strategy

This domain includes questions from the following topics:

- Business alignment
- Security strategy development
- Security governance activities
- Information security strategy development
- Resources needed to develop and execute a security strategy
- Obstacles to strategy development and execution

This chapter covers Certified Information Security Manager (CISM) job practice 1, "Information Security Governance," part B, "Information Security Strategy." The entire Information Security Governance domain represents 17 percent of the CISM examination.

Supporting Tasks in the CISM job practice that align with the Information Security Governance / Information Security Strategy domain include

1. Identify internal and external influences to the organization that impact the information security strategy.

2. Establish and/or maintain an information security strategy in alignment with organizational goals and objectives.

3. Establish and/or maintain an information security governance framework.

6. Develop business cases to support investments in information security.

7. Gain ongoing commitment from senior leadership and other stakeholders to support the successful implementation of the information security strategy.

If for no other reason than cyber threats are ever-changing and increasingly dangerous, all organizations need to reassess their information security programs and develop strategies for key improvements.

A strategy is a plan to achieve a defined set of objectives to enable the vision of the organization to be successfully achieved. Objectives are the desired future states in an organization and, in the context of information security, in the organization's information security program.

A strategy should be business aligned, and it should deliver value, optimize resources, and be measurable.

Security managers can build a security program around a security governance standard framework (not to be confused with control frameworks) such as NIST CSF or ISO/IEC 27001.

Often it is necessary to build a business case so that executive management will agree to support and fund a strategy. A business case typically includes a problem statement, followed by a description of the current state, the desired future state, requirements, an approach, and a plan to achieve the strategy. Often a business case is reviewed by a business or IT steering committee consisting of business stakeholders.

1. What is the best method for ensuring that an organization's security program achieves adequate business alignment?

   A. Find and read the organization's articles of incorporation.

   B. Understand the organization's vision statement, mission statement, and objectives.

   C. Study the organization's chart of management reporting (the "org chart").

   D. Study the organization's financial chart of accounts.

2. Robert has located his organization's mission statement and a list of strategic objectives. What should Robert do to ensure that the information security program aligns with the business?

   A. Discuss strategic objectives with business leaders to understand better what they want to accomplish and what steps are being taken to achieve them.

   B. Develop a list of activities that will support the organization's strategic objectives, and determine the cost of each.

   C. Select those controls from the organization's control framework that align to each objective, and then ensure that those controls are effective.

   D. Select the policies from the organization's information security policy that are relevant to each objective, and ensure that those policies are current.

3. Michael wants to improve the risk management process in his organization by creating guidelines that will help management understand when certain risks should be accepted and when certain risks should be mitigated. The policy that Michael needs to create is known as what?

   A. Security policy

   B. Control framework

   C. Risk appetite statement

   D. Control testing procedure

4. Two similar-sized organizations are merging. Paul will be the CISO of the new combined organization. What is the greatest risk that may occur as a result of the merger?

   A. Differences in practices that may not be understood

   B. Duplication of effort

   C. Gaps in coverage of key processes

   D. Higher tooling costs

5. Which of the following is the best description of the Business Model for Information Security (BMIS)?

    A. It describes the relationships (as dynamic interconnections) between policy, people, process, and technology.

    B. It describes the relationships (as dynamic interconnections) between people, process, technology, and the organization.

    C. It describes the primary elements (people, process, and technology) in an organization.

    D. It describes the dynamic interconnections (people, process, and technology) in an organization.

6. What is the correct name for the following illustration?

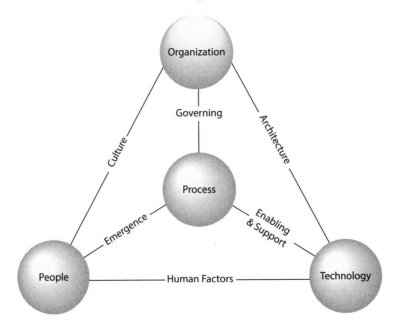

    A. COBIT Model for Information Technology

    B. COBIT Model for Information Security

    C. Business Model for Information Security

    D. Business Model for Information Technology

7. Jacqueline, an experienced CISO, is reading the findings in a recent risk assessment that describes deficiencies in the organization's vulnerability management process. How would Jacqueline use the Business Model for Information Security (BMIS) to analyze the deficiency?

    A. Identify the elements connected to the process DI.

    B. Identify the dynamic interconnections (DIs) connected to the process element.

C. Identify the dynamic elements connected to human factors.

D. Identify the dynamic elements connected to technology.

8. Which of the following would constitute an appropriate use of the Zachman enterprise framework?

    A. An IT service management model as an alternative to ITIL

    B. Identifying system components, followed by high-level design and business functions

    C. Development of business requirements, translated top-down into technical architecture

    D. IT systems described at a high level and then in increasing levels of detail

9. An IT architect needs to document the flow of data from one system to another, including external systems operated by third-party service providers. What kind of documentation does the IT architect need to develop?

    A. Data flow diagrams (DFDs)

    B. Entity relationship diagrams (ERDs)

    C. A Zachman architecture framework

    D. Visio diagrams showing information systems and data flows

10. Carole is a CISO in a new organization with a fledgling security program. Carole needs to identify and develop mechanisms to ensure desired outcomes in selected business processes. What is a common term used to define these mechanisms?

    A. Checkpoints

    B. Detective controls

    C. Controls

    D. Preventive controls

11. What is the best approach to developing security controls in a new organization?

    A. Start with a standard control framework and make risk-based adjustments as needed.

    B. Start from scratch and develop controls based on risk as needed.

    C. Start with NIST CSF and move up to ISO/IEC 27001, and then NIST SP 800-53 as the organization matures.

    D. Develop controls in response to an initial risk assessment.

12. Name one distinct disadvantage of the ISO/IEC 27001 standard.

    A. The standard is costly (more than 100 U.S. dollars per copy).

    B. The standard is costly (a few thousand U.S. dollars per copy).

    C. The standard is available only for use in the United States.

    D. The standard is suitable only in large organizations.

13. Which of the following statements about ISO/IEC 27001 is correct?

  A. ISO/IEC 27001 consists primarily of a framework of security controls, followed by an appendix of security requirements for running a security management program.

  B. ISO/IEC 27001 consists primarily of a body of requirements for running a security management program, along with an appendix of security controls.

  C. ISO/IEC 27001 consists of a framework of information security controls.

  D. ISO/IEC 27001 consists of a framework of requirements for running a security management program.

14. What is the best explanation for the Implementation Tiers in the NIST Cybersecurity Framework?

  A. Implementation Tiers are levels of risk as determined by the organization.

  B. Implementation Tiers are stages of implementation of controls in the framework.

  C. Implementation Tiers are likened to maturity levels.

  D. Implementation Tiers are levels of risk as determined by an external auditor or regulator.

15. What are three factors that a risk manager may consider when developing an information security strategy?

  A. Threats, risks, and solutions

  B. Prevention, detection, and response

  C. Risk levels, staff qualifications, and security tooling

  D. Risk levels, operating costs, and compliance levels

16. Jerome, a new CISO in a SaaS organization, has been asked to develop a long-term information security strategy. Which is the best first step for understanding the present state of the organization's existing information security program?

  A. Perform a code review of the organization's SaaS offerings.

  B. Study the contents of the risk register.

  C. Perform a baseline risk assessment.

  D. Commission a penetration test of internal and external networks.

17. Jerome, a new CISO in a SaaS organization, has been asked to develop a long-term information security strategy. Why would Jerome choose to perform a threat assessment prior to producing the strategy?

  A. To ensure that the organization is aware of everything that could reasonably go wrong.

  B. To ensure that preventive controls are effective.

  C. To ensure that there are no unidentified vulnerabilities.

  D. To ensure that there are no unidentified risks.

18. Jerome, a new CISO in a SaaS organization, has been asked to develop a long-term information security strategy. While examining the organization's information security policy, and together with knowledge of the organization's practices and controls, Jerome now realizes that the organization's security policy is largely aspirational. What is the most important consequence of this on the organization?

   A. Confusion on the part of end users

   B. Appearance that the organization is not in control of its security practices

   C. Fines and sanctions from regulators

   D. Unmitigated risks and vulnerabilities

19. Jerome, a new CISO in a SaaS organization, has been asked to develop a long-term information security strategy. While examining the organization's information security policy, and together with knowledge of the organization's practices and controls, Jerome now realizes that the organization's security policy is largely aspirational. What is the best first step Jerome should take next?

   A. Create an entry in the organization's risk register.

   B. Withdraw the security policy and write a new one that's closer to reality.

   C. Perform a gap analysis and determine actions to take to close the policy gaps.

   D. Consult with the organization's general counsel to develop a plan of action.

20. Jerome, a new CISO in a SaaS organization, has identified a document that describes acceptable encryption protocols. What type of document is this?

   A. Policy

   B. Standard

   C. Practice

   D. Guideline

21. Jerome, a new CISO in a SaaS organization, has identified a document that describes suggested techniques for implementing encryption protocols. What type of document is this?

   A. Policy

   B. Standard

   C. Guideline

   D. Procedure

22. Which of the following is the most likely result of an organization that lacks a security architecture function?

   A. Inconsistent security-related procedures

   B. Inconsistent application of standards

   C. Lower process maturity

   D. Added complication in vulnerability management tools

23. What is the main advantage of a security architecture function in a larger, distributed organization?

   A. Greater employee satisfaction

   B. Better results in vulnerability assessments

   C. Greater consistency in the use of tools and configurations

   D. Lower cost of operations

24. A new CISO in a manufacturing company is gathering artifacts to understand the state of security in the organization. Which of the following would be the *least* valuable for determining risk posture?

   A. Security incident log

   B. Security awareness training records

   C. Penetration test results

   D. Report to the board of directors

25. Of what value is a business impact analysis (BIA) for a security leader in an organization?

   A. It provides a view of the criticality of IT systems in an organization.

   B. It provides a view of the criticality of business processes in an organization.

   C. It provides a view of the criticality of software applications in an organization.

   D. It provides no value to a security leader because it focuses on business continuity, not security.

26. A security leader has been asked to justify the need to implement a new strategy for information security. How should the security leader respond?

   A. Develop a project plan showing the personnel, tasks, timelines, and dependencies.

   B. Develop a risk matrix that includes the potential consequences if the strategy is not implemented.

   C. Develop a SWOT diagram showing strengths, weaknesses, opportunities, and threats.

   D. Develop a business case that includes success criteria, requirements, costs, and action plan.

1. B	**14.** C
2. A	**15.** D
3. C	**16.** C
4. A	**17.** A
5. B	**18.** B
6. C	**19.** D
7. B	**20.** B
8. D	**21.** C
9. A	**22.** B
10. C	**23.** C
11. A	**24.** D
12. A	**25.** B
13. B	**26.** D

1. What is the best method for ensuring that an organization's security program achieves adequate business alignment?

   A. Find and read the organization's articles of incorporation.

   B. Understand the organization's vision statement, mission statement, and objectives.

   C. Study the organization's chart of management reporting (the "org chart").

   D. Study the organization's financial chart of accounts.

   ☑ **B.** The best way to align an information security program to the business is to find and understand the organization's vision statement, mission statement, goals, and objectives. Many organizations develop and publish one or more of these statements. Others take a simpler approach and develop strategic objectives for a calendar or fiscal year. Whatever can be found is valuable: once a security manager understands these statements, then he or she can prioritize resources and activities in the information security program to support the vision, mission, goals, or other strategic statements.

   ☒ **A, C,** and **D** are incorrect. **A** is incorrect because an organization's articles of incorporation do not provide sufficient information about an organization's mission or objectives. **C** is incorrect because the org chart reveals little about what the organization wants to accomplish. **D** is incorrect because the organization's financial chart of accounts reveals little or nothing about the organization's strategic objectives.

2. Robert has located his organization's mission statement and a list of strategic objectives. What should Robert do to ensure that the information security program aligns with the business?

   A. Discuss strategic objectives with business leaders to understand better what they want to accomplish and what steps are being taken to achieve them.

   B. Develop a list of activities that will support the organization's strategic objectives, and determine the cost of each.

   C. Select those controls from the organization's control framework that align to each objective, and then ensure that those controls are effective.

   D. Select the policies from the organization's information security policy that are relevant to each objective, and ensure that those policies are current.

   ☑ **A.** The best first step to aligning an information security program to the organization's strategic objectives is to understand those objectives fully, including the resources and activities that will be employed to achieve them.

☒ **B**, **C**, and **D** are incorrect. **B** is incorrect because, without a dialogue with business leaders, simply identifying supporting activities is likely to miss important details. **C** is incorrect because proper alignment of an information security program does not generally begin with the selection or implementation of controls. In fact, the implementation of controls may play only a minor part (if any) in support of strategic objectives. **D** is incorrect because proper alignment of an information security program does not generally involve identifying relevant security policies. This may be a minor supporting activity but would not be a primary activity when aligning a program to the business.

3. Michael wants to improve the risk management process in his organization by creating guidelines that will help management understand when certain risks should be accepted and when certain risks should be mitigated. The policy that Michael needs to create is known as what?

   A. Security policy

   B. Control framework

   C. Risk appetite statement

   D. Control testing procedure

   ☑ **C.** A risk appetite statement (sometimes known as a risk tolerance statement or risk capacity statement) provides guidance on the types of risk and the amount of risk that an organization may be willing to accept, versus what risks an organization may instead prefer to mitigate, avoid, or transfer. Risk appetite statements are most often created in financial services organizations, although they are used in other types of organizations as well. They help management seek a more consistent approach to risk treatment decisions. In part, this can help management avoid the appearance of being biased or preferential through the use of objective or measurable means for risk treatment decisions.

   ☒ **A**, **B**, and **D** are incorrect. **A** is incorrect because a security policy is not a primary means for making risk treatment decisions. **B** is incorrect because an organization's controls framework is not typically used for making risk treatment decisions. **D** is incorrect because control testing procedures are not related to risk treatment decisions.

4. Two similar-sized organizations are merging. Paul will be the CISO of the new combined organization. What is the greatest risk that may occur as a result of the merger?

   A. Differences in practices that may not be understood

   B. Duplication of effort

   C. Gaps in coverage of key processes

   D. Higher tooling costs

☑ **A.** A merger of two organizations typically results in the introduction of new practices that are not always understood. The CISO may specify directives to the new combined security organization that could result in an increase in one or more risks. For example, the combining of two different organizations' device hardening standards could result in a new standard that results in new and unforeseen vulnerabilities.

☒ **B, C,** and **D** are incorrect. **B** is incorrect because duplication of effort is not the greatest risk. **C** is incorrect because coverage gaps are a potential risk, but they are not the greatest risk. **D** is incorrect because higher tooling costs, if managed properly, are a short-term spending matter that should not result in increased risk.

5. Which of the following is the best description of the Business Model for Information Security (BMIS)?

   A. It describes the relationships (as dynamic interconnections) between policy, people, process, and technology.

   B. It describes the relationships (as dynamic interconnections) between people, process, technology, and the organization.

   C. It describes the primary elements (people, process, and technology) in an organization.

   D. It describes the dynamic interconnections (people, process, and technology) in an organization.

   ☑ **B.** The Business Model for Information Security (BMIS) describes the dynamic interconnections between the four elements of an organization: people, process, technology, and the organization itself. The dynamic interconnections describe the relationship between each of the relationship pairs. For example, the dynamic interconnection between people and technology, known as human factors, describes the relationship between people and technology.

   ☒ **A, C,** and **D** are incorrect. **A** is incorrect because the organization element of BMIS is missing in this answer. **C** is incorrect because there are four primary elements in an organization: people, process, technology, and the organization itself. **D** is incorrect because people, process, and technology are not the labels for the dynamic interconnections. Instead, the dynamic interconnections are human factors (between people and technology), emergence (between people and process), enabling and support (between process and technology), culture (between people and organization), architecture (between technology and organization), and governing (between process and organization).

6. What is the correct name for the following illustration?

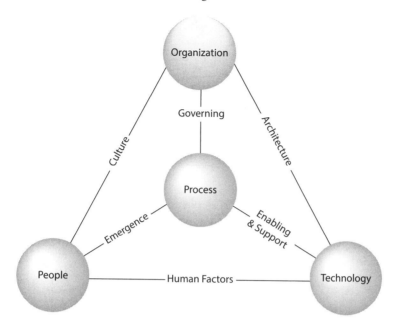

A. COBIT Model for Information Technology

B. COBIT Model for Information Security

C. Business Model for Information Security

D. Business Model for Information Technology

☑ **C.** This illustration depicts the Business Model for Information Security (BMIS), which was developed by ISACA to help individuals better understand the nature of the relationships between people, process, technology, and the organization itself.

☒ **A**, **B**, and **D** are incorrect. These answers are all distractors.

7. Jacqueline, an experienced CISO, is reading the findings in a recent risk assessment that describes deficiencies in the organization's vulnerability management process. How would Jacqueline use the Business Model for Information Security (BMIS) to analyze the deficiency?

A. Identify the elements connected to the process DI.

B. Identify the dynamic interconnections (DIs) connected to the process element.

C. Identify the dynamic elements connected to human factors.

D. Identify the dynamic elements connected to technology.

☑ **B.** The deficiency was identified in the vulnerability management process. The CISO would see what dynamic interconnections (DIs) are connected to the process element. They are emergence (connecting to people), enabling and support (connecting to technology), and governing (connecting to organization). A description of the deficiency in the vulnerability management process should lead Jacqueline to one of the dynamic interconnections, emergence, enabling and support, and governing. In this case, the process deficiency is related to the frequency of scans, which is most likely the governing DI. Further investigation reveals that policy permits vulnerability scans only during small service windows, which are not enough time for scans to be completed. The solution to this deficiency is likely a process or policy change so that scans will be permitted to run through to completion.

☒ **A, C,** and **D** are incorrect. They are all improper uses of the BMIS.

8. Which of the following would constitute an appropriate use of the Zachman enterprise framework?

   A. An IT service management model as an alternative to ITIL

   B. Identifying system components, followed by high-level design and business functions

   C. Development of business requirements, translated top-down into technical architecture

   D. IT systems described at a high level and then in increasing levels of detail

   ☑ **D.** Zachman is an IT enterprise framework that describes IT systems at a high level and in increasing levels of detail, down to individual components.

   ☒ **A, B,** and **C** are incorrect. **A** is incorrect because Zachman is not an IT service management framework. **B** is incorrect because Zachman is a top-down framework, not a bottom-up framework as described. **C** is incorrect because Zachman does not start with business requirements, but rather describes only the IT architecture itself.

9. An IT architect needs to document the flow of data from one system to another, including external systems operated by third-party service providers. What kind of documentation does the IT architect need to develop?

   A. Data flow diagrams (DFDs)

   B. Entity relationship diagrams (ERDs)

   C. A Zachman architecture framework

   D. Visio diagrams showing information systems and data flows

   ☑ **A.** The IT architect needs to develop data flow diagrams, which are visual depictions showing information systems (and information system components, optionally) and the detailed nature of data flowing among them. DFDs are sometimes accompanied by documents that describe metadata, such as system specifications and descriptions.

   ☒ **B, C,** and **D** are incorrect. **B** is incorrect because an entity relationship diagram (ERD) does not depict data flows among and between information systems. Instead, ERDs describe entities (for instance, information systems) and the relationships between them. ERDs are often depicted visually. **C** is incorrect because a Zachman framework describes the architecture of an IT environment in detail, but not necessarily the flows of data between systems in an environment. **D** is incorrect because this is a vague description. Although it is true that a DFD may be composed in Visio (or other graphical drawing tool), this is not the best answer because it is unspecific.

10. Carole is a CISO in a new organization with a fledgling security program. Carole needs to identify and develop mechanisms to ensure desired outcomes in selected business processes. What is a common term used to define these mechanisms?

    A. Checkpoints

    B. Detective controls

    C. Controls

    D. Preventive controls

    ☑ **C.** "Controls" is the best term describing the mechanisms designed to ensure desired outcomes in business processes.

    ☒ **A, B,** and **D** are incorrect. **A** is incorrect because "checkpoints" is not the term that describes these mechanisms. **B** is incorrect because there will be not only detective controls but also preventive controls, administrative controls, and perhaps even compensating and recovery controls. **D** is incorrect because there will be not only preventive controls but also detective controls, administrative controls, and perhaps even compensating and recovery controls.

11. What is the best approach to developing security controls in a new organization?

    A. Start with a standard control framework and make risk-based adjustments as needed.

    B. Start from scratch and develop controls based on risk as needed.

    C. Start with NIST CSF and move up to ISO/IEC 27001, and then NIST SP 800-53 as the organization matures.

    D. Develop controls in response to an initial risk assessment.

    ☑ **A.** Starting with a standard control framework is the best approach, particularly if an appropriate, business-relevant framework is selected. In a proper risk management framework, risk assessment and risk treatment will result in adjustments to the framework (removing, improving, and adding controls) over time.

    ☒ **B, C,** and **D** are incorrect. **B** is incorrect because, although technically this approach will work, too much time may elapse while waiting for the initial set of controls to be developed. In most organizations, over several years, the resulting control framework will not be that different from a standard, industry-relevant framework. **C** is incorrect because there is little to be gained by changing from one control framework to another. Because this approach is not risk based, there is a chance that some risks will result in never having appropriate controls developed to compensate for those risks. **D** is incorrect because this approach implies that only an initial risk assessment takes place. Instead, the accepted approach is one where risk assessments are performed periodically, resulting in periodic adjustments to the control framework in response to newly discovered risks.

12. Name one distinct disadvantage of the ISO/IEC 27001 standard.

   A. The standard is costly (more than 100 U.S. dollars per copy).

   B. The standard is costly (a few thousand U.S. dollars per copy).

   C. The standard is available only for use in the United States.

   D. The standard is suitable only in large organizations.

   ☑ **A.** Single copies of the ISO/IEC 27001 standard (as well as virtually all other ISO standards) cost more than U.S. $100 each. This prevents widespread adoption of the standard, as organizations are somewhat less likely to implement it, since the standard is expensive to download and difficult to understand. Further, students are unlikely to learn about the standard in school because of its cost. Contrast this with most other standards, which are free to download and use.

   ☒ **B, C,** and **D** are incorrect. **B** is incorrect because the ISO/IEC 27001 standard does not cost thousands of dollars per copy. **C** is incorrect because there are no restrictions on where ISO/IEC 27001 (and virtually all other standards) can be used. **D** is incorrect because ISO/IEC 27001 is suitable for organizations of all sizes, from very large to very small and everything in between.

13. Which of the following statements about ISO/IEC 27001 is correct?

   A. ISO/IEC 27001 consists primarily of a framework of security controls, followed by an appendix of security requirements for running a security management program.

   B. ISO/IEC 27001 consists primarily of a body of requirements for running a security management program, along with an appendix of security controls.

   C. ISO/IEC 27001 consists of a framework of information security controls.

   D. ISO/IEC 27001 consists of a framework of requirements for running a security management program.

   ☑ **B.** ISO/IEC 27001's main focus is the body of requirements (sometimes known as clauses) that describe all of the required activities and business records needed to run an information security management program. ISO/IEC 27001 also includes an Annex A, containing a list of information security controls. The controls here are described briefly; the ISO/IEC 27002 standard contains the same control framework, but with longer explanations, as well as implementation guidance for each control.

   ☒ **A, C,** and **D** are incorrect. **A** is incorrect because the main focus of ISO/IEC 27001 is the requirements for running a security management program, not the security controls. **C** is incorrect because ISO/IEC 27001's main focus is the requirements for running a security management program. **D** is incorrect because ISO/IEC 27001 does not contain *only* the requirements for running a security management program but also includes an appendix of security controls also contained in ISO/IEC 27002, where they are fully explained.

14. What is the best explanation for the Implementation Tiers in the NIST Cybersecurity Framework?

   A. Implementation Tiers are levels of risk as determined by the organization.

   B. Implementation Tiers are stages of implementation of controls in the framework.

   C. Implementation Tiers are likened to maturity levels.

   D. Implementation Tiers are levels of risk as determined by an external auditor or regulator.

   ☑ **C.** Although the CSF states that Implementation Tiers are not strictly maturity levels, they are very similar to maturity levels.

   ☒ **A, B,** and **D** are incorrect. **A** and **D** are incorrect because Implementation Tiers are not risk levels. **B** is incorrect because Implementation Tiers are not related to the progress of implementation of controls.

15. What are three factors that a risk manager may consider when developing an information security strategy?

   A. Threats, risks, and solutions

   B. Prevention, detection, and response

   C. Risk levels, staff qualifications, and security tooling

   D. Risk levels, operating costs, and compliance levels

   ☑ **D.** When developing a long-term strategy for an information security program, the best three factors are risk levels, operating costs, and compliance levels. One of these factors may be more important than others in any given organization and for a variety of reasons. Generally, a long-term strategy is being developed to improve the state of one of these: reduction of risk, reduction of cost, or improvement of compliance.

   ☒ **A, B,** and **C** are incorrect. **A** is incorrect because this is not the best answer. These are factors that may be considered in some circumstances. **B** is incorrect because these are information security program capabilities. **C** is incorrect because this answer does not include budget (operating costs), which is among the most important considerations, as budget enables the security manager to acquire staff and tooling to address risks.

16. Jerome, a new CISO in a SaaS organization, has been asked to develop a long-term information security strategy. Which is the best first step for understanding the present state of the organization's existing information security program?

   A. Perform a code review of the organization's SaaS offerings.

   B. Study the contents of the risk register.

   C. Perform a baseline risk assessment.

   D. Commission a penetration test of internal and external networks.

☑ **C.** The best first step for understanding the current state of an organization's information security program is to perform a comprehensive baseline risk assessment. This is the best answer because a risk assessment takes the broadest assessment of the state of information risk, along with the state of any existing controls.

☒ **A, B, and D are incorrect. A** is incorrect because a code review is a consideration of a very narrow portion of the overall state of the organization's information security program. At best, a code review will assess the state of the organization's secure-by-design practices, as well as the effectiveness of safe development training for its developers. Virtually every other aspect of the organization's information security program is ignored. **B** is incorrect because, although the risk register may indeed contain valuable information about many risks in the organization, it is not a good indicator of the state of existing security tooling and processes in the organization. Indeed, the risk register itself may be woefully incomplete, it may be out of date, or it may be inaccurate. **D** is incorrect because a penetration test provides a narrow viewpoint of the overall state of the organization's information security program. Although a penetration test may be a good assessment of an organization's vulnerability management and system hardening practices, it completely overlooks the majority of activities needed in today's information security programs.

17. Jerome, a new CISO in a SaaS organization, has been asked to develop a long-term information security strategy. Why would Jerome choose to perform a threat assessment prior to producing the strategy?

   A. To ensure that the organization is aware of everything that could reasonably go wrong.

   B. To ensure that preventive controls are effective.

   C. To ensure that there are no unidentified vulnerabilities.

   D. To ensure that there are no unidentified risks.

   ☑ **A.** The purpose of a threat assessment is to identify and study internal and external threat scenarios involving key assets, including threats from any and all types of threat actors that can have the most significant impact to the organization based on the most likely scenarios that could reasonably occur.

   ☒ **B, C, and D are incorrect. B** is incorrect because a threat assessment takes a different, and broader, view than preventive controls. For instance, it's possible that there are reasonable threat scenarios for which no controls exist to reduce those threats' impact or probability of occurrence. **C** is incorrect because a threat assessment does not take a vulnerability-centric approach. A threat assessment starts with threat actors and various scenarios. Once a threat assessment has been completed, the vulnerabilities can be identified and remediated. **D** is incorrect because this is not the best answer. Although it is true that a threat assessment's role is to identify risks, a threat assessment does not identify *all* risks.

18. Jerome, a new CISO in a SaaS organization, has been asked to develop a long-term information security strategy. While examining the organization's information security policy, and together with knowledge of the organization's practices and controls, Jerome now realizes that the organization's security policy is largely aspirational. What is the most important consequence of this on the organization?

A. Confusion on the part of end users

B. Appearance that the organization is not in control of its security practices

C. Fines and sanctions from regulators

D. Unmitigated risks and vulnerabilities

☑ **B.** An organization with a largely aspirational security policy (that is, the organization is not in compliance with most of its security policies) will have the appearance of not being in control of its practices. Were the organization to enter into cybersecurity-related legal proceedings in such a state, the organization's information security policy would be a liability and would give the appearance that the organization does not take information security seriously.

☒ **A, C,** and **D** are incorrect. **A** is incorrect because it is not the best answer. Though end users may indeed be confused by the dichotomy between stated policies and actual practices, this is an important consequence, but not the *most* important one. **C** is incorrect because it is not the best answer. There may be cases where fines may be levied by regulators because of an organization not being in compliance with its policies, but this is not the most important consequence. **D** is incorrect because it is not the best answer. It may, however, be true that the aspirational policy may result in unmitigated risks, but this is not the *most* important consequence.

19. Jerome, a new CISO in a SaaS organization, has been asked to develop a long-term information security strategy. While examining the organization's information security policy, and together with knowledge of the organization's practices and controls, Jerome now realizes that the organization's security policy is largely aspirational. What is the best first step Jerome should take next?

A. Create an entry in the organization's risk register.

B. Withdraw the security policy and write a new one that's closer to reality.

C. Perform a gap analysis and determine actions to take to close the policy gaps.

D. Consult with the organization's general counsel to develop a plan of action.

☑ **D.** Consulting counsel is the best first step. A security policy that is largely aspirational (meaning the organization is not in compliance with the majority of its policies) introduces legal liability upon the organization, which is best handled by the organization's general counsel. Although a CISO is in the best position to describe the nature and type of gaps in an organization's security policy, the precise course of action is best decided by the general counsel.

   ☒ **A**, **B**, and **C** are incorrect. **A** is incorrect because this is not the best answer. Although putting an entry in the risk register is appropriate, this answer does not indicate the best substantial step to take. **B** is incorrect because withdrawing the information security policy would leave the organization in a state of having no information security policy at all. If an organization were to change its policy, it should keep the existing policy in place, then fully develop a new policy, and then "switch" the policies. **C** is incorrect because this is not the best answer. This is, however, a step that may need to be taken so that the organization's security policy may eventually be corrected.

20. Jerome, a new CISO in a SaaS organization, has identified a document that describes acceptable encryption protocols. What type of document is this?

   A. Policy

   B. Standard

   C. Practice

   D. Guideline

   ☑ **B.** A document that describes tools, products, or protocols is a standard.

   ☒ **A**, **C**, and **D** are incorrect. **A** is incorrect because a policy would not typically specify tools or protocols. **C** is incorrect because a list of tools, products, or protocols is not a practice. **D** is incorrect because a guideline is a document that provides suggestions on the implementation of policies and standards.

21. Jerome, a new CISO in a SaaS organization, has identified a document that describes suggested techniques for implementing encryption protocols. What type of document is this?

   A. Policy

   B. Standard

   C. Guideline

   D. Procedure

   ☑ **C.** A document that provides suggestions on the implementation or use of a policy or standard is known as a guideline.

   ☒ **A**, **B**, and **D** are incorrect. **A** is incorrect because a policy document does not specify tools, techniques, protocols, or implementation guidance for any of these. **B** is incorrect because a standard is typically used to specify protocols to use, not how to implement them. **D** is incorrect because a procedure is a document that describes the steps to take to accomplish a task.

22. Which of the following is the most likely result of an organization that lacks a security architecture function?

   A. Inconsistent security-related procedures

   B. Inconsistent application of standards

C. Lower process maturity

D. Added complication in vulnerability management tools

☑ **B.** In an organization lacking a security architecture function, there is a greater likelihood that standards are going to be applied inconsistently. A security architecture function would likely include "reference architectures," which are documents that define in detail how technology is implemented, configured, and even managed in an organization.

☒ **A, C,** and **D** are incorrect. **A** is incorrect because, although inconsistent technology might also drive inconsistency in procedures, this is not the most direct result. **C** is incorrect because the lack of security architecture may or may not be a bellwether indicator of process maturity overall. **D** is incorrect because, although it may be true that lack of security architecture will result in complication in vulnerability management tools (because of inconsistencies in the environment), this is not the best answer.

23. What is the main advantage of a security architecture function in a larger, distributed organization?

A. Greater employee satisfaction

B. Better results in vulnerability assessments

C. Greater consistency in the use of tools and configurations

D. Lower cost of operations

☑ **C.** The main benefit of a security architecture is consistency in approach for all instances in the organization. For example, in a retail organization with dozens, hundreds, or thousands of locations, the use of a "reference architecture" as a part of a security architecture function would help ensure that equipment in all locations was configured identically. In another example, a reference architecture for access management would specify that SAML 2.0 would be used for single sign-on for all business applications. In the absence of a security architecture function, security tools and protocols might be inconsistently implemented and configured. Complexity is the enemy of security, it is said, and a large environment implemented inconsistently would be unnecessarily complex.

☒ **A, B,** and **D** are incorrect. **A** is incorrect because employee satisfaction has little to do with security architecture, other than the consideration of engineers' workloads in large environments that are inconsistent and unnecessarily complex. **B** is incorrect because this is not the best answer. However, in an environment with a security architecture function, it may be expected that vulnerability assessment results would be more consistent. **D** is incorrect because this is not the best answer. Still, in an environment that is highly consistent, there could be a somewhat lower cost incurred to operate it.

24. A new CISO in a manufacturing company is gathering artifacts to understand the state of security in the organization. Which of the following would be the *least* valuable for determining risk posture?

A. Security incident log

B. Security awareness training records

C. Penetration test results

D. Report to the board of directors

☑ **D.** A report to the board of directors is the only one of the answers that represents secondary information that may have been filtered, edited, and/or biased. The other answers (security incident log, security awareness training records, and penetration test results) are more valuable records that are less subject to bias.

☒ **A, B,** and **C** are incorrect. **A** is incorrect because a security incident log would be of particular value to a new CISO, particularly if this record contains data generated by a security information and event management system (SIEM). **B** is incorrect because security awareness training records would indicate the degree of participation in security awareness training (itself an indicator of executive commitment to security awareness training and security overall), as well as competency test scores if they are a part of the record. **C** is incorrect because penetration test results are useful indicators of certain aspects of security in the organization. The number and type of vulnerabilities identified would be indicators of maturity in a secure systems development life cycle (whether the penetration test targeted software applications or infrastructure) as well as the organization's vulnerability management process.

25. Of what value is a business impact analysis (BIA) for a security leader in an organization?

A. It provides a view of the criticality of IT systems in an organization.

B. It provides a view of the criticality of business processes in an organization.

C. It provides a view of the criticality of software applications in an organization.

D. It provides no value to a security leader because it focuses on business continuity, not security.

☑ **B.** The purpose of a business impact analysis (BIA) is to provide a concise view of the criticality of business processes in an organization. From there, dependencies on information systems (that is, software applications and supporting infrastructure) can be determined.

☒ **A, C,** and **D** are incorrect. **A** is incorrect because the primary purpose of a BIA is to determine critical business processes. The criticality of IT systems can be derived from a BIA after further analysis. **C** is incorrect because the primary purpose of a BIA is to determine critical business processes. The criticality of software applications can be derived from a BIA after further analysis. **D** is incorrect because the BIA does provide value to a security leader by indicating which business processes are most important in an organization. This knowledge has several benefits: it helps prioritize IT disaster recovery planning efforts, and it helps security understand which information systems warrant the most protection.

26. A security leader has been asked to justify the need to implement a new strategy for information security. How should the security leader respond?

   A. Develop a project plan showing the personnel, tasks, timelines, and dependencies.

   B. Develop a risk matrix that includes the potential consequences if the strategy is not implemented.

   C. Develop a SWOT diagram showing strengths, weaknesses, opportunities, and threats.

   D. Develop a business case that includes success criteria, requirements, costs, and action plan.

   ☑ **D.** A business case is the best method for justifying a project or initiative to support the company's strategy. A well-formed business case includes a problem statement, current and desired states, resources required, requirements, a plan, and success criteria.

   ☒ **A**, **B**, and **C** are incorrect. **A** is incorrect because a project plan is not designed to justify the need for a strategy. Instead, a project plan is used to document how a plan will be executed and by whom. **B** is incorrect because a risk matrix is not designed to justify the need for a strategy. It may, however, be useful to understand the risks involved in current and desired future states. **C** is incorrect because a SWOT (strengths, weaknesses, opportunities, and threats) diagram is not used to justify a strategy.

PART II

Information Security Risk Management

Information Security Risk Assessment

This domain includes questions from the following topics:

- Benefits and outcomes of an information risk management program
- Developing a risk management strategy
- Risk assessment and risk management standards and frameworks
- The risk management life-cycle process
- Vulnerability and threat analysis
- Integrating risk management into an organization's practices and culture
- The components of a risk assessment: asset value, vulnerabilities, threats, and probability and impact of occurrence
- Qualitative and quantitative risk analysis
- The risk register
- Risk management in other business processes

This chapter covers Certified Information Security Manager (CISM) Domain 2, "Information Security Risk Management," part A, "Information Security Risk Assessment." The entire Information Security Risk Management domain represents 20 percent of the CISM examination.

Supporting Tasks in the CISM job practice that align with the Information Security Risk Management / Information Security Risk Assessment domain include

22. Participate in and/or oversee the risk identification, risk assessment, and risk treatment process.

23. Participate in and/or oversee the vulnerability assessment and threat analysis process.

26. Facilitate the integration of information risk management into business and IT processes.

Information security risk management is the practice of balancing business opportunities with potential information security–related losses or negative impacts to business operations. Information security risk management is largely a qualitative effort, because it is difficult to know the probability and costs of significant loss events. Still, several methods for measuring risk have been established that help organizations better understand risks and how they can be handled. These methods include qualitative and quantitative techniques used to contribute to business decisions.

1. An organization has a process whereby security-related hazards are identified, followed by analysis and decisions about what to do about these hazards. What kind of a business process is this?

    A. Vulnerability management

    B. Risk treatment

    C. Risk management

    D. Risk assessment

2. What is the purpose of a cyber-risk management program in an organization?

    A. Consume information from a centralized risk register

    B. Identify and make decisions about information security risks

    C. Plan for future cybersecurity projects and initiatives

    D. Develop mitigating controls

3. All of the following activities are typical inputs into a risk management process *except* which one?

    A. Code reviews

    B. Risk assessments

    C. Threat assessments

    D. Internal audits

4. What should be the primary objective of a risk management strategy?

    A. Determine the organization's risk appetite.

    B. Identify credible risks and transfer them to an external party.

    C. Identify credible risks and reduce them to an acceptable level.

    D. Eliminate credible risks.

5. Marie, a CISO at a manufacturing company, is building a new cyber-risk governance process. For this process to be successful, what is the best first step for Marie to take?

    A. Develop a RACI matrix that defines executive roles and responsibilities.

    B. Charter a security steering committee consisting of IT and cybersecurity leaders.

    C. Develop a risk management process similar to what is found in ISO/IEC 27001.

    D. Charter a security steering committee consisting of IT, security, and business leaders.

6. An organization's internal audit department is assessing the organization's compliance with PCI DSS. Internal audit finds that the organization is not compliant with a PCI DSS control regarding workers' annual acknowledgement of security policy. What kind of a risk has been identified?

    A. Insider threat risk

    B. Disclosure risk

C. Compliance risk

D. Administrative risk

7. Which of the following statements is correct regarding applicable regulation and the selection of a security controls framework?

   A. An appropriate framework will make it easier to map regulatory details to required activities.

   B. It makes no difference which controls framework is selected for regulatory compliance matters.

   C. Applicable laws and security control framework have little to do with each other.

   D. For regulated organizations, wise selection of control frameworks will result in lower cyber-insurance premiums.

8. In the use of FAIR (Factor Analysis of Information Risk), how does a risk manager determine the potential types of loss?

   A. A risk assessment is used to determine what types of loss may occur.

   B. The record of prior losses is used.

   C. Losses in similar companies are used.

   D. Loss types are defined by the FAIR method.

9. Dawn, a CISO in a pharmaceutical organization, is partnering with the company's legal department on the topic of new applicable regulations. Which of the following approaches is most likely to be successful?

   A. Examine each new regulation for impact to the organization. Confirm applicability if impact is significant.

   B. Examine each new regulation for impact to the organization. Confirm applicability for regulations from other countries.

   C. Examine each new regulation for applicability. If applicable, analyze for impact to the organization.

   D. Subscribe to a service that informs the organization of new laws. Implement them in the following budget year.

10. What steps must be completed prior to the start of a risk assessment in an organization?

   A. Determine the qualifications of the firm that will perform the audit.

   B. Determine scope, purpose, and criteria for the audit.

   C. Determine the qualifications of the person(s) who will perform the audit.

   D. Determine the framework for reporting audit results.

11. Which of the following is *not* a risk management methodology?

    A. Risk-IT

    B. ISO/IEC 27005

    C. NIST Special Publication 800-39

    D. FAIR

12. What is the primary objective of the Factor Analysis of Information Risk (FAIR) methodology?

    A. Determine the probability of a threat event.

    B. Determine the impact of a threat event.

    C. Determine the cost of a threat event.

    D. Determine the type of a threat event.

13. A new CISO in a financial service organization is working to get asset inventory processes under control. The organization uses on-premises and IaaS-based virtualization services. What approach will most effectively identify all assets in use?

    A. Perform discovery scans on all networks.

    B. Obtain a list of all assets from the patch management platform.

    C. Obtain a list of all assets from the security information and event management system (SIEM).

    D. Count all of the servers in each data center.

14. Russ, a security manager at a small online retailer, learned recently about the European General Data Protection Regulation (GDPR). The retailer has customers all over the world. The organization has outsourced its online catalog, order acceptance, and payment functions to a cloud-based e-commerce platform. Russ is unaware of any efforts that the retailer may have made to be compliant with GDPR. What should Russ do about this?

    A. Ask senior management or the legal department about this matter.

    B. Assume that the organization is compliant with GDPR.

    C. Nothing, because the cloud-based e-commerce platform is required to be GDPR compliant.

    D. Contact the cloud-based e-commerce platform and confirm its compliance to GDPR.

15. Dylan is an executive security consultant who is assessing a client organization for compliance to various applicable information security and privacy regulations. Dylan has identified compliance issues and recommends that these issues be documented in the client organization's business. How should these issues be documented?

    A. Separate entries for each regulation should be made in the organization's risk register.

    B. A single entry should be made in the organization's risk register.

    C. Separate entries for each regulation should be made in the organization's security incident log.

    D. A single entry should be made in the organization's security incident log.

16. A security analyst has identified a critical server that is missing an important security-related operating system patch. What has the security analyst identified?

   A. A vulnerability

   B. A threat

   C. A risk

   D. An incident

17. A security analyst has identified a new technique that cybercriminals are using to break into server operating systems. What has the security analyst identified?

   A. A vulnerability

   B. A threat

   C. A risk

   D. An incident

18. Threat actors consist of all of the following *except* which one?

   A. Trojans

   B. Hacktivists

   C. Cybercriminal organizations

   D. Employees

19. NotPetya is an example of what?

   A. Threat

   B. Spyware

   C. Mass-mailing worm

   D. Password-cracking tool

20. Which European law enforces users' rights to privacy?

   A. GLBA

   B. GDPR

   C. 95/46/EC

   D. SB-1386

21. Which mechanism does GDPR provide for multinational organizations to make internal transfers of PII?

   A. Model clauses

   B. Privacy Shield

   C. Safe Harbor

   D. Binding corporate rules

22. The internal audit department in a public company recently audited key controls in the vulnerability management process and found that the control "Production servers will be patched within 30 days of receipt of critical patches" fails 30 percent of the time. What finding should the internal audit make?

   A. A new control is needed for vulnerability management.

   B. The control is ineffective and needs to be corrected.

   C. The control should be changed from 30 days to 45 days.

   D. The control should be changed from 30 days to 21 days.

23. Upon examining the change control process in a SaaS provider organization, a new security manager has discovered that the change control process lacks a security impact procedure. What should the security management recommend for this matter?

   A. Systems impacted by a change should be scanned before and after changes are made.

   B. A post-change security review should be added to the change control process.

   C. No change is needed because security is not needed in change control processes.

   D. Add a security impact procedure to the change control process so that the security impact of each proposed change can be identified.

24. The term "insider threat" includes all of the following *except* which one?

   A. End users who are ignorant and make unwise decisions

   B. Employees who have a grudge against their employer

   C. Customers who attempt to break into systems while onsite

   D. End users who are doing the right thing but make mistakes

25. Examples of employees gone rogue include all of the following *except* which one?

   A. A developer who inserts a time bomb in application source code

   B. A securities trader who makes unauthorized trades resulting in huge losses

   C. An engineer who locks co-workers out of the network because they are not competent

   D. A systems engineer who applies security patches that cause applications to malfunction

26. Janice, a new CISO in a healthcare delivery organization, has discovered that virtually all employees are local administrators on their laptop/desktop computers. This is an example of what?

   A. Insider threat

   B. Vulnerability

   C. Threat

   D. Incident

27. A campaign by a cybercriminal to perform reconnaissance on a target organization and develop specialized tools to build a long-term presence in the organization's environment is known as what?

    A. Watering hole attack

    B. Hacktivism

    C. Advanced persistent campaign (APC)

    D. Advanced persistent threat (APT)

28. Which of the following factors in risk analysis is the most difficult to determine?

    A. Exposure factor

    B. Single-loss expectancy

    C. Event probability

    D. Event impact

29. An estimate on the number of times that a threat might occur in a given year is known as what?

    A. Annualized loss expectancy (ALE)

    B. Annualized rate of occurrence (ARO)

    C. Exposure factor (EF)

    D. Annualized exposure factor (AEF)

30. Joel is a security manager in a large manufacturing company. The company uses primarily Microsoft, Cisco, and Oracle products. Joel subscribes to security bulletins from these three vendors. Which of the following statements best describes the adequacy of these advisory sources?

    A. Joel should also subscribe to nonvendor security sources such as US-CERT and InfraGard.

    B. Joel's security advisory sources are adequate.

    C. Joel should discontinue vendor sources and subscribe to nonvendor security sources such as US-CERT and InfraGard.

    D. Joel should focus on threat hunting in the dark web.

1. C		**16.** A	
2. B		**17.** B	
3. A		**18.** A	
4. C		**19.** A	
5. D		**20.** B	
6. C		**21.** D	
7. A		**22.** B	
8. D		**23.** D	
9. C		**24.** C	
10. B		**25.** D	
11. D		**26.** B	
12. A		**27.** D	
13. A		**28.** C	
14. A		**29.** B	
15. B		**30.** A	

1. An organization has a process whereby security-related hazards are identified, followed by analysis and decisions about what to do about these hazards. What kind of a business process is this?

   A. Vulnerability management

   B. Risk treatment

   C. Risk management

   D. Risk assessment

   ☑ **C.** The risk management process consists of risk assessments, analysis about risks that are identified by risk assessment, followed by discussions, and finally decisions about what to do about these risks.

   ☒ **A, B,** and **D** are incorrect. **A** is incorrect because the steps in the question do not describe a vulnerability management process. **B** is incorrect because the steps in the question do not describe a risk treatment process. However, risk treatment is a part of the risk management process. **D** is incorrect because the steps in the question do not describe a risk management process. Risk assessment is a part of the risk management process.

2. What is the purpose of a cyber-risk management program in an organization?

   A. Consume information from a centralized risk register

   B. Identify and make decisions about information security risks

   C. Plan for future cybersecurity projects and initiatives

   D. Develop mitigating controls

   ☑ **B.** The purpose of a cyber-risk management program is to use various means to identify information- and technology-related risks in an organization and then study and make decisions about those risks through a process known as risk treatment.

   ☒ **A, C,** and **D** are incorrect. **A** is incorrect because the purpose of a risk management program is not to consume information from the risk register, but instead to populate it and manage information there. **C** is incorrect because the core purpose of risk management is not long-term planning, but the management of risk. An *output* of the risk treatment process is a series of decisions that may result in one or more initiatives and projects to take place in the future. **D** is incorrect because this is too narrow a definition of risk management; while mitigating controls will sometimes be developed as a result of risk management, there are other outcomes as well.

3. All of the following activities are typical inputs into a risk management process *except* which one?

   A. Code reviews

   B. Risk assessments

   C. Threat assessments

   D. Internal audits

☑ **A.** A code review is not a typical input to a risk management process, primarily because a code review represents a narrow, tactical examination of a program's source code. Output from a code review would likely be fed into a software defect tracking process or a vulnerability management process.

☒ **B**, **C**, and **D** are incorrect. They are incorrect because risk assessments, threat assessments, and internal audits *would* typically result in issues being processed by a risk management process. The distinction is this: A standard risk management process is designed to tackle cyber risks that are systemic in an organization. Examples of such risks include weaknesses in business processes and overarching design problems in complex information systems. Issues such as missing patches, security configuration problems, and software vulnerabilities are instead handled by tactical vulnerability management and software defect management processes.

4. What should be the primary objective of a risk management strategy?

   A. Determine the organization's risk appetite.

   B. Identify credible risks and transfer them to an external party.

   C. Identify credible risks and reduce them to an acceptable level.

   D. Eliminate credible risks.

   ☑ **C.** The primary objective of a risk management strategy is the identification of risks, followed by the reduction of those risks to levels acceptable to executive management.

   ☒ **A**, **B**, and **D** are incorrect. **A** is incorrect because the determination of risk appetite, while important—and essential to the proper functioning of a risk management program—is not the main purpose of a risk management strategy. **B** is incorrect because transferring risks to external parties is but one of several possible outcomes for risks that are identified. **D** is incorrect because risks cannot be eliminated, only reduced to acceptable levels.

5. Marie, a CISO at a manufacturing company, is building a new cyber-risk governance process. For this process to be successful, what is the best first step for Marie to take?

   A. Develop a RACI matrix that defines executive roles and responsibilities.

   B. Charter a security steering committee consisting of IT and cybersecurity leaders.

   C. Develop a risk management process similar to what is found in ISO/IEC 27001.

   D. Charter a security steering committee consisting of IT, security, and business leaders.

   ☑ **D.** The best course of action is the formation of a chartered information security steering committee that consists of IT and security leaders, as well as business leaders. For security governance to succeed, business leaders need to be involved and participate in discussions and decisions.

   ☒ **A**, **B**, and **C** are incorrect. **A** is incorrect because a RACI matrix, while important, is but a small part of a chartered information security steering committee. **B** is incorrect because a security steering committee must include business leaders. **C** is incorrect because this question is about security governance, which is more than just a risk management process.

6. An organization's internal audit department is assessing the organization's compliance with PCI DSS. Internal audit finds that the organization is not compliant with a PCI DSS control regarding workers' annual acknowledgement of security policy. What kind of a risk has been identified?

A. Insider threat risk

B. Disclosure risk

C. Compliance risk

D. Administrative risk

☑ **C.** This is primarily a matter of compliance risk. Organizations handling credit card data are required to comply with all controls in PCI DSS, whether they represent actual risks or not.

☒ **A**, **B**, and **D** are incorrect. These are not the appropriate terms for this type of risk. In addition to risks related to information theft, disclosure, and destruction, organizations need to understand matters of compliance risk, which may result in fines or sanctions and may become public matters in some circumstances.

7. Which of the following statements is correct regarding applicable regulation and the selection of a security controls framework?

A. An appropriate framework will make it easier to map regulatory details to required activities.

B. It makes no difference which controls framework is selected for regulatory compliance matters.

C. Applicable laws and security control framework have little to do with each other.

D. For regulated organizations, wise selection of control frameworks will result in lower cyber-insurance premiums.

☑ **A.** Applicable regulations may or may not be specific to required activities. In some cases, control frameworks are available that closely resemble required activities. Selection of a control framework that corresponds to an applicable law or regulation may help an organization to better align regulatory requirements with required activities.

☒ **B**, **C**, and **D** are incorrect. **B** is incorrect because there are cases where specific frameworks have coverage for specific regulations. For example, U.S. federal government agencies, as well as service providers that provide information-related services to one or more of those agencies, often follow NIST SP 800-53, as the controls in NIST SP 800-53 are required of these organizations. Similarly, organizations that manage credit card payment information often adopt PCI DSS as a control framework because they are specifically required to comply with all PCI DSS requirements. (Note that PCI DSS is not actually a law, but its position in the payments ecosystem gives it strong resemblance to a regulation.) **C** is incorrect since this blanket statement is not true. **D** is incorrect because the question is not addressing cyber-risk insurance.

8. In the use of FAIR (Factor Analysis of Information Risk), how does a risk manager determine the potential types of loss?

   A. A risk assessment is used to determine what types of loss may occur.

   B. The record of prior losses is used.

   C. Losses in similar companies are used.

   D. Loss types are defined by the FAIR method.

   ☑ **D.** The FAIR analysis method contains six types of loss, which are productivity, response, replacement, fines and judgments, competitive advantage, and reputation. According to the FAIR method, any cybersecurity incident would result in one or more of these losses.

   ☒ **A, B,** and **C** are incorrect because the FAIR methodology does not employ these means. Instead, FAIR uses six types of loss: productivity, response, replacement, fines and judgments, competitive advantage, and reputation. The FAIR method does not accommodate any other types of loss.

9. Dawn, a CISO in a pharmaceutical organization, is partnering with the company's legal department on the topic of new applicable regulations. Which of the following approaches is most likely to be successful?

   A. Examine each new regulation for impact to the organization. Confirm applicability if impact is significant.

   B. Examine each new regulation for impact to the organization. Confirm applicability for regulations from other countries.

   C. Examine each new regulation for applicability. If applicable, analyze for impact to the organization.

   D. Subscribe to a service that informs the organization of new laws. Implement them in the following budget year.

   ☑ **C.** Because there are so many regulations of different kinds, it is first necessary to determine which ones are applicable to the organization. For regulations that are applicable, the next best course of action is to understand the impact of the regulation on business processes and costs and then develop an action plan for complying with the regulation.

   ☒ **A, B,** and **D** are incorrect. **A** and **B** are incorrect because these approaches will cause unnecessary burden on the organization. Regulations should first be vetted for applicability; if they are not applicable, no further work needs to be done. **D** is incorrect because this answer does not include the vital step of determining applicability. That said, a subscription service for new and emerging laws and regulations may be cost-effective for many organizations.

10. What steps must be completed prior to the start of a risk assessment in an organization?

   A. Determine the qualifications of the firm that will perform the audit.

   B. Determine scope, purpose, and criteria for the audit.

C. Determine the qualifications of the person(s) who will perform the audit.

D. Determine the framework for reporting audit results.

☑ **B.** According to ISO/IEC 27005 and other risk management frameworks, it is first necessary to establish the context of an audit. This means making a determination of the scope of the audit—which parts of the organization are to be included. Also, it is necessary to determine the purpose of the risk assessment; for example, determining control coverage, control effectiveness, or business process effectiveness. Finally, the criteria for the audit need to be determined.

☒ **A, C,** and **D** are incorrect. **A** and **C** are incorrect because any confirmation of qualifications would be determined prior to this point. **D** is incorrect because the framework for reporting results does not need to be completed prior to the start of the assessment.

11. Which of the following is *not* a risk management methodology?

A. Risk-IT

B. ISO/IEC 27005

C. NIST Special Publication 800-39

D. FAIR

☑ **D.** FAIR (Factor Analysis of Information Risk) is not a risk management framework, but a risk *assessment* methodology. Though closely related, a risk management framework is concerned with the outcomes of risk assessments, but not the performance of the risk assessments themselves.

☒ **A, B,** and **C** are incorrect because Risk-IT, ISO/IEC 27005, and NIST SP 800-39 are examples of risk management frameworks.

12. What is the primary objective of the Factor Analysis of Information Risk (FAIR) methodology?

A. Determine the probability of a threat event.

B. Determine the impact of a threat event.

C. Determine the cost of a threat event.

D. Determine the type of a threat event.

☑ **A.** The primary objective of FAIR is to determine the probability of an event using "what if" analysis, which cannot be easily done using maturity models or checklists.

☒ **B, C,** and **D** are incorrect because FAIR is not used to determine the impact, cost, or type of a threat or threat event.

13. A new CISO in a financial service organization is working to get asset inventory processes under control. The organization uses on-premises and IaaS-based virtualization services. What approach will most effectively identify all assets in use?

A. Perform discovery scans on all networks.

B. Obtain a list of all assets from the patch management platform.

C. Obtain a list of all assets from the security information and event management system (SIEM).

D. Count all of the servers in each data center.

☑ **A.** Although none of these approaches is ideal, performing discovery scans on all networks is the best first step. Even so, it will be necessary to consult with network engineers to ensure that discovery scans will scan all known networks in on-premises and IaaS environments. Other helpful steps include interviewing system engineers to understand virtual machine management systems and obtain inventory information from them.

☒ **B, C,** and **D** are incorrect. **B** is incorrect because patch management systems may not be covering all assets in the organization's environment. **C** is incorrect because the SIEM may not be receiving log data from all assets in the organization's environment. **D** is incorrect because the organization is using virtualization technology, as well as IaaS-based platforms; counting servers in an on-premises data center will fail to discover virtual assets and IaaS-based assets.

14. Russ, a security manager at a small online retailer, learned recently about the European General Data Protection Regulation (GDPR). The retailer has customers all over the world. The organization has outsourced its online catalog, order acceptance, and payment functions to a cloud-based e-commerce platform. Russ is unaware of any efforts that the retailer may have made to be compliant with GDPR. What should Russ do about this?

A. Ask senior management or the legal department about this matter.

B. Assume that the organization is compliant with GDPR.

C. Nothing, because the cloud-based e-commerce platform is required to be GDPR compliant.

D. Contact the cloud-based e-commerce platform and confirm its compliance to GDPR.

☑ **A.** A responsible security manager would always reach out to the legal department or another member of senior management to inquire about the organization's state of compliance to a law or regulation.

☒ **B, C,** and **D** are incorrect. **B** is incorrect because it is unwise to assume that others in an organization have all matters taken care of. **C** is incorrect because the retailer itself must be GDPR compliant, regardless of whether any part of its operations is outsourced. **D** is incorrect because the organization itself must be GDPR compliant. That said, the outsourcing organization must also be GDPR compliant.

15. Dylan is an executive security consultant who is assessing a client organization for compliance to various applicable information security and privacy regulations. Dylan has identified compliance issues and recommends that these issues be documented in the client organization's business. How should these issues be documented?

A. Separate entries for each regulation should be made in the organization's risk register.

B. A single entry should be made in the organization's risk register.

C. Separate entries for each regulation should be made in the organization's security incident log.

D. A single entry should be made in the organization's security incident log.

☑ **B.** The best way to document these findings is to create a single risk register entry for the matter. There could be dozens of similar issues that have common remedies, making it impractical to create potentially dozens of similar entries.

☒ **A, C,** and **D** are incorrect. **A** is incorrect because there could be numerous similar entries that would create unnecessary clutter in the risk register. **C** and **D** are incorrect because the security incident log is not the best place to record this matter.

16. A security analyst has identified a critical server that is missing an important security-related operating system patch. What has the security analyst identified?

A. A vulnerability

B. A threat

C. A risk

D. An incident

☑ **A.** The security analysist has identified a vulnerability, which is a weakness that could more easily permit one or more types of threats to occur.

☒ **B, C,** and **D** are incorrect. **B** is incorrect because the missing patch is not a threat, but a vulnerability that could permit a threat to occur. **C** is incorrect because this is not the most specific answer. **D** is incorrect because the missing patch is not an incident, although it may permit an incident to occur.

17. A security analyst has identified a new technique that cybercriminals are using to break into server operating systems. What has the security analyst identified?

A. A vulnerability

B. A threat

C. A risk

D. An incident

☑ **B.** The security analyst has identified a threat that, if realized, could result in an intrusion into the organization's systems.

☒ **A, C,** and **D** are incorrect. **A** is incorrect because these techniques are not a vulnerability, but a threat. **C** is incorrect because this is not the most specific answer. **D** is incorrect because the new technique is not an incident, although it might be possible for an incident to occur because of the threat.

18. Threat actors consist of all of the following *except* which one?

A. Trojans

B. Hacktivists

C. Cybercriminal organizations

D. Employees

☑ **A.** Trojans are threats, but they are not threat actors. Threat actors consist of external parties such as hackers, cybercriminal organizations, hacktivists, and more; internal users are also considered threat actors in the context of "insider threat."

☒ **B, C,** and **D** are incorrect because hacktivists, employees, and cybercriminals are all considered threat actors.

19. NotPetya is an example of what?

   A. Threat

   B. Spyware

   C. Mass-mailing worm

   D. Password-cracking tool

   ☑ **A.** NotPetya is a threat. More specifically, NotPetya is malware that resembles ransomware but lacks the ability to decrypt data; thus, it is considered by many to be destructware, or software that destroys data files.

   ☒ **B, C,** and **D** are incorrect. **B** is incorrect because NotPetya is not spyware. **C** is incorrect because NotPetya is not a mass-mailing worm. **D** is incorrect because NotPetya is not a password cracker.

20. Which European law enforces users' rights to privacy?

   A. GLBA

   B. GDPR

   C. 95/46/EC

   D. SB-1386

   ☑ **B.** GDPR, or the European General Data Protection Regulation, which took effect in 2018, provides several means to improve privacy for European residents.

   ☒ **A, C,** and **D** are incorrect. **A** is incorrect because GLBA is a U.S. law that requires financial services organizations to protect information about its customers. **C** is incorrect because 95/46/EC, otherwise known as the European Privacy Directive, is the former European privacy law that has been superseded by GDPR. **D** is incorrect because SB-1386 is the original data breach disclosure law in the state of California.

21. Which mechanism does GDPR provide for multinational organizations to make internal transfers of PII?

   A. Model clauses

   B. Privacy Shield

   C. Safe Harbor

   D. Binding corporate rules

☑ **D.** Binding corporate rules were established by European privacy laws that permit multinational organizations to perform internal transfers of personally identifiable information (PII). Typically, this is applied to internal human resources information.

☒ **A**, **B**, and **C** are incorrect. **A** is incorrect because model clauses are used between organizations to legally obligate them to comply with GDPR and other privacy regulations. **B** is incorrect because Privacy Shield was used by organizations to register their obligation to comply with GDPR. **C** is incorrect because Safe Harbor is the now-defunct means for organizations to register their obligation to comply with the former European privacy directive, 95/46/EC.

22. The internal audit department in a public company recently audited key controls in the vulnerability management process and found that the control "Production servers will be patched within 30 days of receipt of critical patches" fails 30 percent of the time. What finding should the internal audit make?

   A. A new control is needed for vulnerability management.

   B. The control is ineffective and needs to be corrected.

   C. The control should be changed from 30 days to 45 days.

   D. The control should be changed from 30 days to 21 days.

   ☑ **B.** There is a control in place that is not effective. The best remedy is to fix the existing control, which is still reasonable and appropriate.

   ☒ **A**, **C**, and **D** are incorrect. **A** is incorrect because creating an additional control should not be considered until the existing control is fixed. **C** and **D** are incorrect because the SLA for critical patches does not necessarily need to be changed.

23. Upon examining the change control process in a SaaS provider organization, a new security manager has discovered that the change control process lacks a security impact procedure. What should the security management recommend for this matter?

   A. Systems impacted by a change should be scanned before and after changes are made.

   B. A post-change security review should be added to the change control process.

   C. No change is needed because security is not needed in change control processes.

   D. Add a security impact procedure to the change control process so that the security impact of each proposed change can be identified.

   ☑ **D.** The best remedy is the addition of a security impact procedure that is performed for each proposed change. This will help to identify any security-related issues associated with a proposed change that can be discussed prior to the change being made. This is preferable to the alternative: accepting a change that may have one or more security issues that may increase the risk of a security incident.

   ☒ **A**, **B**, and **C** are incorrect. **A** is incorrect because not all security-related issues will be manifested in a vulnerability scan. **B** is incorrect because a security review should be performed prior to a change being made so that an organization can consider modifying the nature of the change so that there is no increase in risk. **C** is incorrect because security *is* an important consideration in a change control process.

24. The term "insider threat" includes all of the following *except* which one?

    A. End users who are ignorant and make unwise decisions

    B. Employees who have a grudge against their employer

    C. Customers who attempt to break into systems while onsite

    D. End users who are doing the right thing but make mistakes

    ☑ **C.** Customers, even while onsite, are not usually considered insiders.

    ☒ **A, B,** and **D** are incorrect. Each of these is considered an insider threat.

25. Examples of employees gone rogue include all of the following *except* which one?

    A. A developer who inserts a time bomb in application source code

    B. A securities trader who makes unauthorized trades resulting in huge losses

    C. An engineer who locks co-workers out of the network because they are not competent

    D. A systems engineer who applies security patches that cause applications to malfunction

    ☑ **D.** The systems engineer who applies patches to fix feature or security defects is the best choice, because there is little or no sign of malice. In this example, the change control process should be improved so that there is an opportunity to test software applications in a nonproduction environment prior to applying patches to production.

    ☒ **A, B,** and **C** are incorrect. Each of these is an example of an employee who has gone rogue and is consequently harming the organization.

26. Janice, a new CISO in a healthcare delivery organization, has discovered that virtually all employees are local administrators on their laptop/desktop computers. This is an example of what?

    A. Insider threat

    B. Vulnerability

    C. Threat

    D. Incident

    ☑ **B.** The matter of end users being local administrators means that they have administrative control of the computers they use, namely their laptop and/or desktop computers. This means they can install software and security patches and change the configuration of the operating system. This also means that malware introduced by the user onto the system will probably be able to run with administrative privileges, which may result in significantly more harm to the system and the organization.

    ☒ **A, C,** and **D** are incorrect. **A** is incorrect because this configuration setting is not, by itself, an insider threat. However, an insider threat situation can be made worse through end users having local administrative privileges. **C** is incorrect because this is not a threat, but a vulnerability (these terms are often misused). **D** is incorrect because this is not an incident. However, an incident is somewhat more likely to occur and more likely to have greater impact because end users have local administrative privileges.

27. A campaign by a cybercriminal to perform reconnaissance on a target organization and develop specialized tools to build a long-term presence in the organization's environment is known as what?

    A. Watering hole attack

    B. Hacktivism

    C. Advanced persistent campaign (APC)

    D. Advanced persistent threat (APT)

    ☑ **D.** A long-term campaign of patient reconnaissance, development of tools, and establishment of a long-term quiet presence inside an organization's environment is known as an advanced persistent threat (APT). It is "advanced" on account of the reconnaissance and the development of an intrusion strategy with specialized tools; it is "persistent" by design, so that the intruder can maintain a long-term presence in the environment; it is a "threat" because the criminal actor is performing all of this to reach a long-term objective, whether the acquisition or destruction of sensitive information or the disruption of the organization's operations.

    ☒ **A**, **B**, and **C** are incorrect. **A** is incorrect because a watering hole attack is an attack on an organization via a compromised website that will automatically download malware onto visitors' systems. **B** is incorrect because hacktivism refers to an ideology wherein an attacker seeks to expose or disrupt an organization for ideological reasons. **C** is incorrect because the term "advanced persistent campaign" is not in use.

28. Which of the following factors in risk analysis is the most difficult to determine?

    A. Exposure factor

    B. Single-loss expectancy

    C. Event probability

    D. Event impact

    ☑ **C.** Event probability is the most difficult of these values to determine accurately, particularly for high-impact, low-frequency events. Because event probability is so difficult to determine, much risk analysis work performed is qualitative in nature.

    ☒ **A**, **B**, and **D** are incorrect. **A** is incorrect because exposure factor (which is calculated as a percentage of an asset's value) is relatively easy to determine. **B** is incorrect because single-loss expectancy (which is calculated as asset value times exposure factor) is relatively easy to determine. **D** is incorrect because event impact (formally known as event cost) is not altogether difficult to determine.

29. An estimate on the number of times that a threat might occur in a given year is known as what?

   A. Annualized loss expectancy (ALE)

   B. Annualized rate of occurrence (ARO)

   C. Exposure factor (EF)

   D. Annualized exposure factor (AEF)

   ☑ **B.** Annualized rate of occurrence (ARO) is defined as an estimate of the number of times that a threat will occur per year.

   ☒ **A, C,** and **D** are incorrect. **A** is incorrect because annualized loss expectancy (ALE) is defined as the annualized rate of occurrence (ARO) times the single loss expectancy (SLE). **C** is incorrect as exposure factor (EF) is the loss that represents a percentage of an asset's value (because in some cases, an asset is not completely destroyed). **D** is incorrect because there is no such term as annualized exposure factor (AEF).

30. Joel is a security manager in a large manufacturing company. The company uses primarily Microsoft, Cisco, and Oracle products. Joel subscribes to security bulletins from these three vendors. Which of the following statements best describes the adequacy of these advisory sources?

   A. Joel should also subscribe to nonvendor security sources such as US-CERT and InfraGard.

   B. Joel's security advisory sources are adequate.

   C. Joel should discontinue vendor sources and subscribe to nonvendor security sources such as US-CERT and InfraGard.

   D. Joel should focus on threat hunting in the dark web.

   ☑ **A.** The best set of security advisories includes those from all IT product vendors, as well as a number of nonvendor sources such as US-CERT and InfraGard.

   ☒ **B, C,** and **D** are incorrect. **B** is incorrect because Joel should also have at least one good nonvendor source such as US-CERT. **C** is incorrect because it is important to continue to receive vendor advisories. **D** is incorrect because "threat hunting on the dark web" is not a real activity.

Information Security Risk Response

This domain includes questions from the following topics:
- Risk response options and considerations
- Responding to risk via risk treatment
- Ownership of risks, risk treatment, and controls
- Monitoring and reporting on risk
- Key risk indicators

This chapter covers Certified Information Security Manager (CISM) Domain 2, "Information Security Risk Management," part B, "Information Security Risk Response." The entire Information Security Risk Management domain represents 20 percent of the CISM examination.

Supporting Tasks in the CISM job practice that align with the Information Security Risk Management / Information Security Risk Response domain include

9. Compile and present reports to key stakeholders on the activities, trends, and overall effectiveness of the information security program.

22. Participate in and/or oversee the risk identification, risk assessment, and risk treatment process.

24. Identify, recommend, or implement appropriate risk treatment and response options to manage risk to acceptable levels based on organizational risk appetite.

25. Determine whether information security controls are appropriate and effectively manage risk to an acceptable level.

27. Monitor for internal and external factors that may require reassessment of risk.

28. Report on information security risk, including noncompliance and changes in information risk, to key stakeholders to facilitate the risk management decision-making process.

Information security risk response is the entirety of actions undertaken once the organization becomes aware of a risk. The risk management life cycle specifies that when a risk is identified, it is first analyzed. Next, a business decision, known as risk treatment, determines what the organization will do about an identified risk. Each risk is assigned an owner who participates in risk treatment decisions. If a control must be created or modified to mitigate the risk, management assigns an owner to the control itself. Finally, each risk is monitored and reports are created to track any changes in risk over time.

1. All of the following activities are typical inputs into a risk reporting process *except* which one?

    A. Code reviews

    B. Risk assessments

    C. Threat assessments

    D. Internal audits

2. What are possible outcomes of a risk that has been identified and analyzed in a risk management process?

    A. Acceptance, avoidance, mitigation, transfer, residual

    B. Acceptance, elimination, reduction, transfer

    C. Acceptance, avoidance, elimination, mitigation, transfer

    D. Acceptance, avoidance, mitigation, transfer

3. Dawn, a new CISO in a pharmaceutical company, is reviewing an existing risk management process. The process states that the CISO alone makes all risk treatment decisions. What should Dawn conclude from this observation?

    A. The process should be changed so that other business leaders may collaborate on risk treatment decisions.

    B. The process is appropriate, as it is the CISO's responsibility to make risk treatment decisions.

    C. The process should be changed so that the internal audit department approves risk treatment decisions.

    D. The process should be changed so that external regulators approve risk treatment decisions.

4. To what audience should communication about new information risks be sent?

    A. Customers

    B. Security steering committee and executive management

    C. All personnel

    D. Board of directors

5. An internal audit team has completed a comprehensive internal audit and has determined that several controls are ineffective. What is the next step that should be performed?

    A. Correlate these results with an appropriately scoped penetration test.

    B. Develop compensating controls to reduce risk to acceptable levels.

    C. Perform a risk assessment.

    D. Develop a risk-based action plan to remediate ineffective controls.

6. A risk manager recently completed a risk assessment in an organization. Executive management asked the risk manager to remove one of the findings from the final report. This removal is an example of what?

   A. Gerrymandering

   B. Internal politics

   C. Risk avoidance

   D. Risk acceptance

7. Ravila, a CISO, reports security-related metrics to executive management. The trend for the past several months for the metric "Percent of patches applied within SLA for servers supporting manufacturing" is 100 percent, 99.5 percent, 100 percent, 100 percent, 99.2 percent, and 74.5 percent. What action should Ravila take with regard to these metrics?

   A. Explain that risk levels have dropped correspondingly.

   B. No action is required because this is normal for patch management processes.

   C. Investigate the cause of the reduction in patching and report to management.

   D. Wait until the next month to see if the metric returns to normal.

8. Duncan is the CISO in a large electric utility. Duncan received an advisory that describes a serious flaw in Intel CPUs that permits an attacker to take control of an affected system. Knowing that much of the utility's industrial control system (ICS) is Intel-based, what should Duncan do next?

   A. Report the situation to executive management.

   B. Create a new entry in the risk register.

   C. Analyze the situation to understand business impact.

   D. Declare a security incident.

9. Duncan is the CISO in a large electric utility. Duncan received an advisory that describes a serious flaw in Intel CPUs that permits an attacker to take control of an affected system. After analyzing the advisory and confirming that many of the ICS devices in the environment are Intel-based, what should Duncan do next?

   A. Create a new entry in the risk register.

   B. Report the situation to executive management.

   C. Create a new entry in the vulnerability register.

   D. Declare a security incident.

10. An internal audit of the employee termination process determined that in 20 percent of employee terminations, one or more terminated employee user accounts were not locked or removed. The internal audit department also found that formal monthly user access reviews identified 100 percent of missed account closures, resulting in those user accounts being closed no more than 60 days after users were terminated. What corrective actions, if any, are warranted?

   A. Increase user access review process frequency to twice per week.

   B. Increase user access review process frequency to weekly.

   C. No action is necessary since a monthly user access review process is effective.

   D. Improve the user termination process to reduce the number of missed account closures.

11. Russ, a security manager at a small online retailer, is completing a self-assessment questionnaire for PCI DSS compliance. In studying the questionnaire, Russ has noted that his organization is not in compliance with all requirements. No auditor will be verifying the accuracy of the questionnaire. What is Russ's best course of action?

   A. Complete the form truthfully and notify senior management of the exceptions.

   B. Complete the form truthfully and submit it to authorities.

   C. Mark each control as compliant and submit it to authorities.

   D. Mark each control as compliant and notify senior management that he must be truthful on the next such submission.

12. While deliberating an item in an organization's risk register, members of the cybersecurity steering committee have decided that the organization should discontinue a new feature in its online social media platform. This decision is an example of what?

   A. Risk transfer

   B. Risk acceptance

   C. Risk mitigation

   D. Risk avoidance

13. The internal audit department in an organization recently audited the control "User accounts for terminated workers shall be locked or removed within 48 hours of termination" and found that user accounts for terminated workers are not locked or removed 20 percent of the time. What recommendation should internal audit make?

   A. Change the timeframe in the control from 48 hours to 7 days.

   B. Add a new compensating control for monthly review of terminated user accounts.

   C. Add more staff to the team that manages user accounts.

   D. No changes are needed since 20 percent is an acceptable failure rate.

14. A software as a service (SaaS) provider performs penetration tests on its services once per year, and many findings are identified each time. The organization's CISO wants to make changes so that penetration test results will improve. The CISO should recommend all of the following changes *except* which one?

   A. Add a security review of all proposed software changes into the SDLC.

   B. Introduce safe coding training for all software developers.

   C. Increase the frequency of penetration tests from annually to quarterly.

   D. Include security and privacy requirements in the SDLC.

15. A SaaS provider performs penetration tests on its services once per year, and many findings are identified each time. What is the best way to report this matter to executive management?

   A. Develop a KRI that reports the trend of security defects over time.

   B. Penetration test reports should be distributed to executive management so that they can have a better understanding of the problem.

   C. The executive summary section of penetration test reports should be distributed to executive management.

   D. Report the number of defects found to executive management.

16. A SaaS provider performs penetration tests on its services once per year, and many findings are identified each time. What is the best KRI that would highlight risks to executives?

   A. Number of software vulnerabilities that exist on production SaaS applications

   B. Number of days that critical software vulnerabilities exist on production SaaS applications

   C. Number of vulnerability scans performed on production SaaS applications

   D. Names of developers who introduced the greatest number of security defects into production SaaS applications

17. The security leader at a SaaS provider has noticed that the number of security defects in the SaaS application is gradually climbing over time to unacceptable levels. What is the best first step the security leader should take?

   A. Contact the software development leader and report that more security defects are being created.

   B. Initiate the procurement process for a web application firewall.

   C. Initiate a low-severity security incident.

   D. Create a new risk register entry that describes the problem along with potential fixes.

18. Which is the best method for reporting risk matters to senior management?

   A. Sending after-action reviews of security incidents

   B. Sending the outcomes of risk treatment decisions

   C. Periodic briefing on the contents of the risk register

   D. Sending memos each time a new risk is identified

19. Janice has worked in the Telco Company for many years and is now the CISO. For several years, Janice has recognized that the engineering organization contacts information security just prior to the release of new products and features so that security can be added in at the end. Now that Janice is the CISO, what is the best long-range solution to this problem?

   A. Introduce security at the conceptual, requirements, and design steps in the product development process.

   B. Train engineering in the use of vulnerability scanning tools so that they can find and fix vulnerabilities on their own.

   C. Add security requirements to other requirements that are developed in product development projects.

   D. There is no problem to fix: it is appropriate for engineering to contact security prior to product release to add in necessary security controls.

20. Janice has worked in the Telco Company for many years and is now the CISO. For several years, Janice has recognized that the engineering organization contacts information security just prior to the release of new products and features so that security can be added in at the end. Now that Janice is the CISO, what is the best first step for Janice to take?

   A. Initiate a low-severity security incident.

   B. Create a new risk register entry that describes the problem along with potential fixes.

   C. Initiate a high-severity security incident.

   D. Write a memo to the leader of the engineering organization requesting that security be added to the product development life cycle.

21. An end user in an organization opened an attachment in e-mail, which resulted in ransomware running on the end user's workstation. This is an example of what?

   A. Incident

   B. Vulnerability

   C. Threat

   D. Insider threat

22. Joel, a CISO in a manufacturing company, has identified a new cybersecurity-related risk to the business and is discussing it privately with the chief risk officer (CRO). The CRO has asked Joel not to put this risk in the risk register. What form of risk treatment does this represent?

   A. This is not risk treatment, but the avoidance of managing the risk altogether.

   B. This is risk avoidance, where the organization elects to avoid the risk altogether.

   C. This is risk transfer, as the organization has implicitly transferred this risk to insurance.

   D. This is risk acceptance, as the organization is accepting the risk as-is.

23. Which is the best method for prioritizing risks and risk treatment?

    A. Threat event probability times asset value, from highest to lowest

    B. Threat event probability, followed by asset value

    C. Professional judgment

    D. A combination of threat event probability, asset value, and professional judgment

24. A security leader recently commissioned an outside company to assess the organization's performance against the NIST SP 800-53 control framework to see which controls the organization is operating properly and which controls require improvement. Who should decide which controls will be improved?

    A. CIO

    B. CISO

    C. Business unit leaders

    D. The outside company

25. An organization's information security department conducts quarterly user access reviews of the financial accounting system. Who is the best person to approve users' continued access to roles in the system?

    A. Security manager

    B. IT manager

    C. Corporate controller

    D. Users' respective managers

26. Which of the following is the best description of risk treatment?

    A. Adding a risk to the risk register

    B. Assigning a risk to a business unit leader or department head

    C. Reducing a risk through mitigation

    D. Deciding what to do about the risk

27. A risk analyst is studying a risk and its risk profile after a risk treatment decision of mitigation was made. The analyst has determined that mitigation does not eliminate all of the risk, but only a part of the risk. How should the risk analyst proceed?

    A. Reject the risk treatment plan.

    B. Record the leftover risk.

    C. Inform management that the risk treatment plan is incomplete.

    D. Do nothing.

28. Which of the following persons is most suitable for owning a control related to access to a business application?

    A. Head of the department that uses the application

    B. IT service desk

    C. Security manager

    D. IT leader

29. An organization recently commissioned an outside security company to perform a risk assessment. Each of the risks identified in the assessment report are to be added to the risk register. Who should be the owner of each of these new risks?

    A. The board of directors

    B. The security manager

    C. Department heads

    D. The outside security company

30. Which of the following categories of risk would be reported to a board of directors?

    A. All of the following

    B. Process-level risks

    C. Asset-level risks

    D. Risks in the ERM risk register

1. A
2. D
3. A
4. B
5. D
6. D
7. C
8. C
9. B
10. D
11. A
12. D
13. B
14. C
15. A

16. B
17. D
18. C
19. A
20. B
21. A
22. A
23. D
24. C
25. C
26. D
27. B
28. A
29. C
30. D

1. All of the following activities are typical inputs into a risk reporting process *except* which one?

   A. Code reviews

   B. Risk assessments

   C. Threat assessments

   D. Internal audits

   ☑ **A.** A code review is not a typical input to a risk reporting process, primarily because a code review represents a narrow, tactical examination of a program's source code. Output from a code review would likely be fed into a software defect tracking process or a vulnerability management process.

   ☒ **B, C,** and **D** are incorrect. They are incorrect because risk assessments, threat assessments, and internal audits *would* typically result in issues being the subject of a risk reporting process. The distinction is this: A standard risk management and reporting process is designed to tackle cyber risks that are systemic in an organization. Examples of such risks include weaknesses in business processes and overarching design problems in complex information systems. Issues such as missing patches, security configuration problems, and software vulnerabilities are instead handled by tactical vulnerability management and software defect management processes.

2. What are possible outcomes of a risk that has been identified and analyzed in a risk management process?

   A. Acceptance, avoidance, mitigation, transfer, residual

   B. Acceptance, elimination, reduction, transfer

   C. Acceptance, avoidance, elimination, mitigation, transfer

   D. Acceptance, avoidance, mitigation, transfer

   ☑ **D.** The four possible outcomes of a risk in a risk management process are acceptance, avoidance, mitigation, and transfer. These are known as *risk treatment* options.

   ☒ **A, B,** and **C** are incorrect because these are not the outcomes of risk treatment in a risk management process. Elimination is not a valid risk treatment option because risks cannot be eliminated altogether. Residual is not a valid risk treatment option; instead, residual risk is defined as the "leftover" risk after the original risk has been reduced through mitigation or transfer.

3. Dawn, a new CISO in a pharmaceutical company, is reviewing an existing risk management process. The process states that the CISO alone makes all risk treatment decisions. What should Dawn conclude from this observation?

   A. The process should be changed so that other business leaders may collaborate on risk treatment decisions.

   B. The process is appropriate, as it is the CISO's responsibility to make risk treatment decisions.

C. The process should be changed so that the internal audit department approves risk treatment decisions.

D. The process should be changed so that external regulators approve risk treatment decisions.

☑ **A.** Risk treatment decisions are business decisions that should be made by business leaders in collaboration with the CISO. The CISO should not be making unilateral decisions on behalf of the business.

☒ **B, C,** and **D** are incorrect. **B** is incorrect because the CISO should not be making unilateral decisions about risk on behalf of the business. Business leaders should *at least* participate in, and agree with, these decisions. **C** is incorrect because it is not appropriate for an internal audit department to make risk treatment decisions (except, possibly, for risk treatment decisions that are directly related to the internal audit function). **D** is incorrect because it is not appropriate for outside regulators to make an organization's risk treatment decisions; at most, regulators may be informed of such decisions.

4. To what audience should communication about new information risks be sent?

A. Customers

B. Security steering committee and executive management

C. All personnel

D. Board of directors

☑ **B.** New developments concerning information risk should be sent to the information security steering committee and executive management. This is a part of a typical risk management process that includes risk communication.

☒ **A, C,** and **D** are incorrect. **A** is incorrect because information risk matters are generally internal matters that are not shared with outside parties. Exceptions, of course, may include disclosures about risks and incidents as required by law, as well as through private legal obligations. **C** is incorrect because matters of information risk should not be shared to a wide audience such as all internal staff. **D** is incorrect because a board of directors does not necessarily need to know about all risks.

5. An internal audit team has completed a comprehensive internal audit and has determined that several controls are ineffective. What is the next step that should be performed?

A. Correlate these results with an appropriately scoped penetration test.

B. Develop compensating controls to reduce risk to acceptable levels.

C. Perform a risk assessment.

D. Develop a risk-based action plan to remediate ineffective controls.

☑ **D.** Typically, organizations are compelled to remediate most or all findings identified by an internal audit department. Taking a risk-based approach is sensible because this serves to remediate findings by addressing the highest-risk findings first.

☒ **A**, **B**, and **C** are incorrect. **A** is incorrect because correlation with a penetration test would rarely be a prudent next step (unless the internal audit was solely focused on security configuration of target systems). **B** is incorrect because compensating controls are not the "go-to" remedy for curing control ineffectiveness; in some cases, compensating controls may be used, but this is not a typical approach. **C** is incorrect because a risk assessment does nothing to remediate control effectiveness findings.

6. A risk manager recently completed a risk assessment in an organization. Executive management asked the risk manager to remove one of the findings from the final report. This removal is an example of what?

   A. Gerrymandering

   B. Internal politics

   C. Risk avoidance

   D. Risk acceptance

   ☑ **D**. Although this is a questionable approach, removal of a risk finding in a report is, implicitly, risk acceptance. It could, however, be even worse than that, and in some industries, this could be considered negligent and a failure of due care. A risk manager should normally object to such an action and may consider documenting the matter or even filing a formal protest.

   ☒ **A**, **B**, and **C** are incorrect. **A** is incorrect because the term "gerrymandering" is related to the formation of electoral districts in government. **B** is incorrect because, although the situation may be an example of internal politics, this is not the best answer. **C** is incorrect because risk avoidance is defined as a discontinuation of the activity related to the risk.

7. Ravila, a CISO, reports security-related metrics to executive management. The trend for the past several months for the metric "Percent of patches applied within SLA for servers supporting manufacturing" is 100 percent, 99.5 percent, 100 percent, 100 percent, 99.2 percent, and 74.5 percent. What action should Ravila take with regard to these metrics?

   A. Explain that risk levels have dropped correspondingly.

   B. No action is required because this is normal for patch management processes.

   C. Investigate the cause of the reduction in patching and report to management.

   D. Wait until the next month to see if the metric returns to normal.

   ☑ **C**. As patching is an important activity, and because the servers support critical business operations, this sudden drop in patch coverage needs to be investigated immediately and corrected as quickly as possible.

   ☒ **A**, **B**, and **D** are incorrect. **A** is incorrect because a reduction in risk levels would not result in a decrease in patching. **B** is incorrect because the reduction in patch coverage is *not* a normal event. **D** is incorrect because it would be unwise to "wait and see" regarding such an important activity as server patching.

8. Duncan is the CISO in a large electric utility. Duncan received an advisory that describes a serious flaw in Intel CPUs that permits an attacker to take control of an affected system. Knowing that much of the utility's industrial control system (ICS) is Intel-based, what should Duncan do next?

A. Report the situation to executive management.

B. Create a new entry in the risk register.

C. Analyze the situation to understand business impact.

D. Declare a security incident.

☑ **C.** Though it's tempting to notify executive management immediately, without first understanding any potential business impact, there's little to tell. For this reason, the best first step is to analyze the matter so that any business impact can be determined.

☒ **A, B,** and **D** are incorrect. **A** is incorrect because the impact is not yet known. **B** is incorrect because it is not the best answer. After understanding the matter, it may indeed be prudent to create a risk register entry, particularly if the matter is complicated and likely to persist for some time. **D** is incorrect because the impact of the advisory on the organization is not yet known. In some incident response plans, however, organizations may use advisories like this as a trigger for emergency analysis to take place.

9. Duncan is the CISO in a large electric utility. Duncan received an advisory that describes a serious flaw in Intel CPUs that permits an attacker to take control of an affected system. After analyzing the advisory and confirming that many of the ICS devices in the environment are Intel-based, what should Duncan do next?

A. Create a new entry in the risk register.

B. Report the situation to executive management.

C. Create a new entry in the vulnerability register.

D. Declare a security incident.

☑ **B.** Because the CISO has analyzed the advisory, the impact to the organization can be known. Duncan should report this matter to executive management and include an explanation of business impact and a remediation plan.

☒ **A, C,** and **D** are incorrect. **A** is incorrect because this matter has greater urgency than the risk management life cycle is likely to provide. If, however, it is determined that there is no easy or quick fix, a risk register entry might be warranted. **C** is incorrect because it may be necessary to create many entries instead of a single entry. There may be many different types of devices that are affected by the advisory, necessitating an entry for each time, or an entry for each device, depending upon how the organization manages its vulnerabilities. **D** is incorrect because most organizations' incident response plans do not address vulnerabilities, but actual threat realization events.

10. An internal audit of the employee termination process determined that in 20 percent of employee terminations, one or more terminated employee user accounts were not locked or removed. The internal audit department also found that formal monthly user access reviews identified 100 percent of missed account closures, resulting in those user accounts being closed no more than 60 days after users were terminated. What corrective actions, if any, are warranted?

A. Increase user access review process frequency to twice per week.

B. Increase user access review process frequency to weekly.

C. No action is necessary since a monthly user access review process is effective.

D. Improve the user termination process to reduce the number of missed account closures.

☑ **D.** The rate that user terminations are not performed properly is too high. Increasing the frequency of user access reviews will likely take too much time. The best remedy is to find ways of improving the user termination process. Since the "miss" rate is 20 percent, it is assumed that all processes are manual.

☒ **A, B,** and **C** are incorrect. **A** and **B** are incorrect because the user access review process likely takes too much effort. Since the "miss" rate is 20 percent, it is assumed that all processes are manual. **C** is incorrect because the "miss" rate of 20 percent would be considered too high in most organizations. An acceptable rate would be under 2 percent.

11. Russ, a security manager at a small online retailer, is completing a self-assessment questionnaire for PCI DSS compliance. In studying the questionnaire, Russ has noted that his organization is not in compliance with all requirements. No auditor will be verifying the accuracy of the questionnaire. What is Russ's best course of action?

A. Complete the form truthfully and notify senior management of the exceptions.

B. Complete the form truthfully and submit it to authorities.

C. Mark each control as compliant and submit it to authorities.

D. Mark each control as compliant and notify senior management that he must be truthful on the next such submission.

☑ **A.** Security professionals, particularly those who have industry certifications that have a code of conduct (including ISACA's CISM certification), must be truthful, even when there may be personal, professional, or organizational consequences. In this situation, the form must be completed accurately, even though this means that the organization may have some short-term compliance issues with authorities.

☒ **B, C,** and **D** are incorrect. **B** is incorrect because executive management should also be made aware of the compliance issue. **C** and **D** are incorrect because it would be unethical to falsify answers on the questionnaire.

12. While deliberating an item in an organization's risk register, members of the cybersecurity steering committee have decided that the organization should discontinue a new feature in its online social media platform. This decision is an example of what?

   A. Risk transfer

   B. Risk acceptance

   C. Risk mitigation

   D. Risk avoidance

   ☑ **D.** Risk avoidance is one of four risk treatment options. In risk avoidance, the activity associated with an identified risk is discontinued.

   ☒ **A**, **B**, and **C** are incorrect. Risk transfer, risk acceptance, and risk mitigation are not the correct terms associated with the organization's decision to discontinue the business activity discussed here.

13. The internal audit department in an organization recently audited the control "User accounts for terminated workers shall be locked or removed within 48 hours of termination" and found that user accounts for terminated workers are not locked or removed 20 percent of the time. What recommendation should internal audit make?

   A. Change the timeframe in the control from 48 hours to 7 days.

   B. Add a new compensating control for monthly review of terminated user accounts.

   C. Add more staff to the team that manages user accounts.

   D. No changes are needed since 20 percent is an acceptable failure rate.

   ☑ **B.** A compensating control in the form of a periodic access review is the best answer. Periodic access reviews are common and used for this purpose.

   ☒ **A**, **C**, and **D** are incorrect. **A** is incorrect because seven days is far too long for user accounts to be active after a worker is terminated. **C** is incorrect because staffing levels are not necessarily the cause of this control failure. **D** is incorrect because 20 percent is considered too high a failure rate for a terminated user account access control.

14. A software as a service (SaaS) provider performs penetration tests on its services once per year, and many findings are identified each time. The organization's CISO wants to make changes so that penetration test results will improve. The CISO should recommend all of the following changes *except* which one?

   A. Add a security review of all proposed software changes into the SDLC.

   B. Introduce safe coding training for all software developers.

   C. Increase the frequency of penetration tests from annually to quarterly.

   D. Include security and privacy requirements in the SDLC.

   ☑ **C.** Increasing the frequency of penetration tests is not likely to get to the root cause of the problem, which is the creation of too many security-related software defects.

☒ **A**, **B**, and **D** are incorrect. **A** is incorrect because the addition of a security review for proposed changes is likely to reveal issues that can be corrected prior to development. **B** is incorrect because safe coding training can help developers better understand coding practices that will result in fewer security defects. **D** is incorrect because the addition of security and privacy requirements will help better define the nature of new and changed features.

15. A SaaS provider performs penetration tests on its services once per year, and many findings are identified each time. What is the best way to report this matter to executive management?

   A. Develop a KRI that reports the trend of security defects over time.

   B. Penetration test reports should be distributed to executive management so that they can have a better understanding of the problem.

   C. The executive summary section of penetration test reports should be distributed to executive management.

   D. Report the number of defects found to executive management.

   ☑ **A.** A key risk indicator (KRI) should be developed that illustrates the risk that security defects pose to the organization. An example KRI for this situation could read, "Number of critical software defects introduced into SaaS Product."

   ☒ **B**, **C**, and **D** are incorrect. **B** is incorrect because penetration test reports are quite detailed and technical, and they provide little, if any, business insight to an executive. **C** is incorrect because even an executive summary section in a penetration test report is unlikely to express business risk in a meaningful way. **D** is incorrect because the number of defects alone is not a good risk indicator.

16. A SaaS provider performs penetration tests on its services once per year, and many findings are identified each time. What is the best KRI that would highlight risks to executives?

   A. Number of software vulnerabilities that exist on production SaaS applications

   B. Number of days that critical software vulnerabilities exist on production SaaS applications

   C. Number of vulnerability scans performed on production SaaS applications

   D. Names of developers who introduced the greatest number of security defects into production SaaS applications

   ☑ **B.** The total number of days that unmitigated software defects existed on production applications is the best key risk indicator, particularly when tracked over a period of time.

   ☒ **A**, **C**, and **D** are incorrect. **A** is incorrect because the number of vulnerabilities alone does not sufficiently convey risk; a better depiction of risk is the number of days that unpatched vulnerabilities were present on production systems. **C** is incorrect because the number of scans does not provide an indication of risk. **D** is incorrect because a list of offenders is not a key risk indicator.

17. The security leader at a SaaS provider has noticed that the number of security defects in the SaaS application is gradually climbing over time to unacceptable levels. What is the best first step the security leader should take?

   A. Contact the software development leader and report that more security defects are being created.

   B. Initiate the procurement process for a web application firewall.

   C. Initiate a low-severity security incident.

   D. Create a new risk register entry that describes the problem along with potential fixes.

   ☑ **D.** When there is a disturbing trend developing, such as an increase in the number of security vulnerabilities being identified, creating an entry in the risk register is the best first step. This will facilitate action in the organization's risk management process that will enable business and technology leaders to discuss the matter and make decisions to manage the risk.

   ☒ **A, B, and C** are incorrect. **A** is incorrect because this is not the best first choice. Contacting the development leader is, however, a prudent move so that the development leader will not feel blindsided by later proceedings. **B** is incorrect because a WAF may not be the best solution here; besides, this represents a unilateral decision on the part of the security leader, when a better approach would be a discussion with stakeholders. **C** is incorrect because a situation like this is not commonly regarded as a security incident.

18. Which is the best method for reporting risk matters to senior management?

   A. Sending after-action reviews of security incidents

   B. Sending the outcomes of risk treatment decisions

   C. Periodic briefing on the contents of the risk register

   D. Sending memos each time a new risk is identified

   ☑ **C.** The best method available here is to provide a summary briefing on the contents of the risk register. Providing a summary overview of the items of the risk register will enable the leadership team to focus on the key areas or emerging risks that need their attention. This will help senior management better understand the entire catalog of unmanaged risks in the organization.

   ☒ **A, B, and D** are incorrect. **A** is incorrect because risks often exist, apart from security incidents. **B** is incorrect because senior management should participate in risk treatment decisions, not merely be informed about them (implying that others are making those decisions). **D** is incorrect because sending memos is unstructured, and memos may not always be read. Further, a briefing from the risk register is much better, because this is an interactive event where senior management can ask questions about risks in the risk register.

19. Janice has worked in the Telco Company for many years and is now the CISO. For several years, Janice has recognized that the engineering organization contacts information security just prior to the release of new products and features so that security can be added in at the end. Now that Janice is the CISO, what is the best long-range solution to this problem?

A. Introduce security at the conceptual, requirements, and design steps in the product development process.

B. Train engineering in the use of vulnerability scanning tools so that they can find and fix vulnerabilities on their own.

C. Add security requirements to other requirements that are developed in product development projects.

D. There is no problem to fix: it is appropriate for engineering to contact security prior to product release to add in necessary security controls.

☑ **A.** The best long-term solution is the introduction of appropriate security activities throughout the product development life cycle, starting at the conceptual stage where new products and features are initially discussed. Security steps at the requirements and design stages will help ensure that products are secure by design.

☒ **B, C,** and **D** are incorrect. **B** is incorrect because vulnerability scanning will fail to identify many types of security problems. **C** is incorrect because adding security requirements alone, while helpful, is not the best choice. **D** is incorrect because responsible organizations ensure that their products are secure by design.

20. Janice has worked in the Telco Company for many years and is now the CISO. For several years, Janice has recognized that the engineering organization contacts information security just prior to the release of new products and features so that security can be added in at the end. Now that Janice is the CISO, what is the best first step for Janice to take?

A. Initiate a low-severity security incident.

B. Create a new risk register entry that describes the problem along with potential fixes.

C. Initiate a high-severity security incident.

D. Write a memo to the leader of the engineering organization requesting that security be added to the product development life cycle.

☑ **B.** Creation of a risk register entry is the best first step. Presuming that a cross-functional cybersecurity council exists, the next step will be discussion of the matter that will lead to an eventual decision.

☒ **A, C,** and **D** are incorrect. **A** and **C** are incorrect because initiation of a security incident is not an appropriate response. **D** is incorrect because a wider conversation should be conducted by cybersecurity steering committee members.

21. An end user in an organization opened an attachment in e-mail, which resulted in ransomware running on the end user's workstation. This is an example of what?

A. Incident

B. Vulnerability

C. Threat

D. Insider threat

☑ **A.** Ransomware executing on an end user's workstation is considered an incident. It may have been allowed to execute because of one or more vulnerabilities.

☒ **B**, **C**, and **D** are incorrect. **B** is incorrect because a vulnerability is a configuration setting or a software defect that can, if exploited, result in an incident. **C** is incorrect because ransomware, by itself, is considered a threat, but ransomware executing on a system is considered an incident. **D** is incorrect because this is not considered an insider threat. However, users having poor judgment (which may include clicking on phishing messages) is considered an insider threat.

22. Joel, a CISO in a manufacturing company, has identified a new cybersecurity-related risk to the business and is discussing it privately with the chief risk officer (CRO). The CRO has asked Joel not to put this risk in the risk register. What form of risk treatment does this represent?

    A. This is not risk treatment, but the avoidance of managing the risk altogether.

    B. This is risk avoidance, where the organization elects to avoid the risk altogether.

    C. This is risk transfer, as the organization has implicitly transferred this risk to insurance.

    D. This is risk acceptance, as the organization is accepting the risk as-is.

    ☑ **A.** The deliberate "burying" of a risk is not risk treatment, but the refusal to deal with the risk altogether. Although there may be legitimate reasons for this action, based on the information here, there is an appearance of negligence or a coverup on the part of the CRO.

    ☒ **B**, **C**, and **D** are incorrect. **B** is incorrect because risk avoidance is a formal decision wherein the organization will discontinue the activity that manifests the identified risk. **C** is incorrect because there is no indication in this question that cyber insurance will assume this risk. **D** is incorrect because formal risk acceptance involves the use of the risk management life cycle that includes the risk being recorded in the risk ledger, followed by analysis and a risk treatment decision.

23. Which is the best method for prioritizing risks and risk treatment?

    A. Threat event probability times asset value, from highest to lowest

    B. Threat event probability, followed by asset value

    C. Professional judgment

    D. A combination of threat event probability, asset value, and professional judgment

    ☑ **D.** The best method for prioritizing risks and risk treatment is to examine the probability of event occurrence (difficult though that may be), asset value, and impact to the organization. Professional judgment plays a big role as well because factors such as business reputation are difficult to quantify.

⊠ **A**, **B**, and **C** are incorrect. **A** is incorrect because this approach allows no room for professional judgment. **B** is incorrect because there is no logical sequence based on these two items that are measured differently. **C** is incorrect because professional judgment alone risks the failure to consider high-value assets, high impact, and high probability of occurrence.

24. A security leader recently commissioned an outside company to assess the organization's performance against the NIST SP 800-53 control framework to see which controls the organization is operating properly and which controls require improvement. Who should decide which controls will be improved?

    A. CIO

    B. CISO

    C. Business unit leaders

    D. The outside company

    ☑ **C.** Decisions to remediate risks are a risk treatment activity. Risk treatment decisions are typically made by risk owners, usually business unit leaders, with consultation from the security leader.

    ⊠ **A**, **B**, and **D** are incorrect. **A** and **B** are incorrect because the CIO and CISO are rarely the parties to make risk treatment decisions. **D** is incorrect because the outside company should not be making risk treatment decisions for the organization.

25. An organization's information security department conducts quarterly user access reviews of the financial accounting system. Who is the best person to approve users' continued access to roles in the system?

    A. Security manager

    B. IT manager

    C. Corporate controller

    D. Users' respective managers

    ☑ **C.** The best person to approve ongoing user access in an application is a business unit leader or department head or someone in the business responsible for the business process(es) supported by the information system.

    ⊠ **A**, **B**, and **D** are incorrect. **A** is incorrect because the security manager is not going to be as familiar with finance department operations to know which persons should continue to have access to roles. **B** is incorrect because the IT manager is not going to be as familiar with finance department operations to know which persons should continue to have access to roles. **D** is incorrect because users' managers are not going to be as familiar with finance department operations to know which persons should continue to have access to roles.

26. Which of the following is the best description of risk treatment?

   A. Adding a risk to the risk register

   B. Assigning a risk to a business unit leader or department head

   C. Reducing a risk through mitigation

   D. Deciding what to do about the risk

   ☑ **D.** Risk treatment is best described as a decision on what to do about a particular risk. The choices are to accept the risk, mitigate the risk, transfer the risk, or avoid the risk.

   ☒ **A**, **B**, and **C** are incorrect. **A** is incorrect because adding a risk to the risk register is not a description of risk treatment. **B** is incorrect because assigning a risk to someone is not a description of risk treatment. **C** is incorrect because risk reduction is not a description of risk treatment, but instead is one of the possible choices of a risk treatment decision.

27. A risk analyst is studying a risk and its risk profile after a risk treatment decision of mitigation was made. The analyst has determined that mitigation does not eliminate all of the risk, but only a part of the risk. How should the risk analyst proceed?

   A. Reject the risk treatment plan.

   B. Record the leftover risk.

   C. Inform management that the risk treatment plan is incomplete.

   D. Do nothing.

   ☑ **B.** After risk treatment, there is often leftover risk, known as residual risk, that is usually entered into the risk register as a new risk to be analyzed and treated.

   ☒ **A**, **C**, and **D** are incorrect. **A** is incorrect because risk treatment rarely eliminates all risk. **C** is incorrect because management is likely aware of the existence of residual risk. **D** is incorrect because doing nothing would amount to ignoring the residual risk, which should be recorded.

28. Which of the following persons is most suitable for owning a control related to access to a business application?

   A. Head of the department that uses the application

   B. IT service desk

   C. Security manager

   D. IT leader

   ☑ **A.** The most suitable choice for a control owner related to access to a business application is the head of the department that uses the application. This person will decide who should have access to the application and with what roles.

☒ **B, C,** and **D** are incorrect. **B** is incorrect because the IT service desk, even if they provision access to the system, should not be considered the control owner, because the IT service desk is ill-suited to make access decisions. **C** is incorrect because the security manager often will not know which persons should have access to the application. **D** is incorrect because the IT leader should not be making business decisions regarding who should have access to a business application.

29. An organization recently commissioned an outside security company to perform a risk assessment. Each of the risks identified in the assessment report are to be added to the risk register. Who should be the owner of each of these new risks?

    A. The board of directors

    B. The security manager

    C. Department heads

    D. The outside security company

    ☑ **C.** Risk ownership is best assigned to department heads and business unit owners associated with the business activity where the risk exists.

    ☒ **A, B,** and **D** are incorrect. **A** is incorrect because a board of directors is seldom assigned as a risk owner. **B** is incorrect because security managers and security leaders, including the CISO, are seldom assigned as a risk owner. **D** is incorrect because the company performing the risk assessment is not a part of the organization.

30. Which of the following categories of risk would be reported to a board of directors?

    A. All of the following

    B. Process-level risks

    C. Asset-level risks

    D. Risks in the ERM risk register

    ☑ **D.** Of the available choices, risks present in the ERM (enterprise risk management) risk register would be reported to a board of directors.

    ☒ **A, B,** and **C** are incorrect. **A** and **C** are incorrect because process-level risks and asset-level risks would not normally be reported to a board of directors, as this is an excessive amount of detail. **B** is incorrect because reporting ERM-level risks is a better choice than reporting process-level risks.

PART III

Information Security Program

CHAPTER 5

Information Security Program Development

This domain includes questions from the following topics:

- Resources and outcomes related to information security programs
- Asset, system, data, facilities, and personnel classification
- Control and security management framework development
- Policies, standards, guidelines, procedures, and requirements
- Metrics that tell the security management and operations story

This chapter covers Certified Information Security Manager (CISM) domain 3, "Information Security Program," part A, "Information Security Program Development." The entire Information Security Program domain represents 33 percent of the CISM examination.

Supporting Tasks in the CISM job practice that align with the Information Security Program / Information Security Program Development domain include:

5. Establish and maintain information security policies to guide the development of standards, procedures, and guidelines.

10. Evaluate and report information security metrics to key stakeholders.

11. Establish and/or maintain the information security program in alignment with the information security strategy.

12. Align the information security program with the operational objectives of other business functions.

13. Establish and maintain information security processes and resources to execute the information security program.

14. Establish, communicate, and maintain organizational information security policies, standards, guidelines, procedures, and other documentation.

20. Establish and/or maintain a process for information asset identification and classification.

Establishing and modernizing an organization's cybersecurity program is one of the most important and impactful activities with long-term benefits (and consequences) a security leader will undertake. Cybersecurity program improvements are implemented as a result of a strategic plan. Cybersecurity program development consists of creating policy, controls, standards, requirements, guidelines, and a formal structure for security functions. Security leaders can choose from one of several frameworks that describe the structure of a security program. Security leaders use metrics to measure events and activities, enabling senior management to see the results of their directives.

1. An organization's CISO is planning for the cybersecurity budget for the following year. One of the security analysts informed the CISO that she should add more licenses to the vulnerability scanning tool so that all of the organization's networks can be scanned; currently, there are only enough licenses to scan the primary on-premises data center, but not the secondary data center, office networks, or external-facing assets. How should the CISO respond to this request?

   A. Acquire licenses for all internal and external networks.

   B. No additional licenses are needed, since only the data center network needs to be scanned.

   C. No additional licenses are needed, because the scanner can scan all networks but will not maintain records for them because of license limitations.

   D. Acquire licenses for the secondary data center.

2. An organization has decided to improve its information security program by developing a full suite of policies, procedures, standards, and guidelines. Which of these must be developed first?

   A. Procedures

   B. Standards

   C. Processes

   D. Policies

3. What kind of statement is the following: "Passwords are to consist of upper- and lowercase letters, numbers, and symbols, and are to be at least 12 characters in length."

   A. Standard

   B. Policy

   C. Guideline

   D. Procedure

4. A CISO has developed and is publishing a new metric entitled, "Percentage of patches applied within SLAs to servers supporting manufacturing." What message does this metric convey to executives?

   A. The risk associated with SLAs and whether they are too long

   B. The amount of downtime in manufacturing while patches are being applied

   C. The amount of effort used to apply security patches to servers

   D. The risk of security incidents that could disrupt manufacturing operations

5. Which of the following reports is most appropriate to send to a board of directors?

    A. Quarterly high-level metrics and a list of security incidents

    B. Weekly detailed metrics

    C. Weekly detailed metrics and vulnerability scan reports

    D. Vulnerability scan reports and a list of security incidents

6. What is the best solution for protecting a software as a service (SaaS) application from a layer 7 attack?

    A. Advanced malware protection

    B. Cloud access security broker

    C. Web content filter

    D. Web application firewall

7. How does an acceptable use policy differ from an information security policy?

    A. They differ in name only; they are functionally the same.

    B. An acceptable use policy defines expected behavior from workers, while an information security policy details all of the business rules for cybersecurity.

    C. An information security policy defines expected behavior from workers, while an acceptable use policy details all of the business rules for cybersecurity.

    D. An acceptable use policy applies to nontechnical workers only, while an information security policy applies only to technical workers.

8. Which certification is recognized for knowledge and experience on the examination of information systems and on information system protection?

    A. CGEIT

    B. CRISC

    C. CISA

    D. CISSP

9. The CISO in a 1000-employee organization wants to implement a 24/7/365 security monitoring function. Currently no 24/7 IT operations exist in the organization. What is the best option for the CISO to implement a 24/7/365 security monitoring function?

    A. Outsource security monitoring to a managed security services provider (MSSP) that specializes in security event monitoring.

    B. Staff up a 24/7/365 IT operations and security event monitoring function with permanent full-time staff.

    C. Staff up a 24/7/365 security event monitoring function with permanent full-time staff.

    D. Implement a security event monitoring platform and have events sent to existing 5×8 staff (a staff that works five days a week for eight hours per day) after hours.

10. Which of the following is the best regimen for managing security policy content?

   A. Develop policy that aligns with ISO/IEC 27001, NIST SP 800-53, or CIS CSC, and review annually.

   B. Develop policy that aligns with known standards and the business; review annually and when the organization undergoes significant changes.

   C. Outsource policy development to a consulting firm; have the consulting firm review annually according to industry changes.

   D. Develop policy that aligns with known standards and the business.

11. A new CISO in a manufacturing company has developed statistics and metrics on the industrial control systems supporting automated manufacturing and has found that more than one-third of the operating systems are many years out of support because the ICS software does not support newer versions of operating systems and newer versions of ICS software are not available. What is the best response in this situation?

   A. Switch to software vendors that provide modern, supported operating systems.

   B. Upgrade operating systems and install backward-compatible libraries.

   C. Virtualize outdated operating systems.

   D. Isolate ICS systems in hardened networks.

12. A new CISO in a manufacturing company has developed statistics and metrics on the industrial control systems supporting automated manufacturing and has found that more than one-third of the operating systems are many years out of support because the ICS software does not support newer versions of operating systems and newer versions of ICS software are not available. How should this situation be described to senior management?

   A. The organization needs to step up and modernize its industrial control systems.

   B. The organization needs to isolate and protect its industrial control systems.

   C. The organization needs to require its ICS vendors to support modern operating systems.

   D. The organization needs to outsource its ICS to an ICS cloud provider.

13. Which of the following is the best language for a security policy in a multinational software organization regarding background checks?

   A. Prior to hire, all employees must undergo background investigations where permitted by law.

   B. Prior to hire, all workers, whether they are employees, contractors, or consultants, must undergo background investigations.

   C. Prior to hire, all workers, whether they are employees, contractors, temps, or consultants, must undergo background investigations where permitted by law.

   D. Prior to hire and annually thereafter, all employees must undergo background investigations.

14. An organization recently experienced a security incident in which an employee leaked vital information via an unapproved cloud-based storage provider. The employee stated that she "did not know" that it was against policy to store company data in unapproved cloud-based services. What is the best administrative control to prevent this type of event in the future?

    A. Require employees to acknowledge compliance to security policy annually in writing.

    B. Implement a CASB system.

    C. Implement endpoint-based DLP.

    D. Implement a GPO to block the use of USB mass storage devices.

15. What control can best improve software security in a software as a service organization that currently undergoes quarterly penetration tests of its SaaS software?

    A. SAST scans as a part of the software build process

    B. Monthly penetration tests

    C. Mandatory secure development training for all developers

    D. Daily web application scans of the production environment

16. Which of the following is the best source for system and component hardening standards?

    A. Microsoft

    B. NIST

    C. SANS

    D. The Center for Internet Security

17. An existing healthcare organization is developing a first-ever system and device hardening program and has chosen CIS Benchmarks as its industry standard. What is the best method for implementing CIS Benchmarks in server operating systems in production environments?

    A. Implement CIS Benchmark configurations all at once in test environments and then in production environments.

    B. Implement CIS Benchmark configurations slowly in test environments and then in production environments.

    C. Implement CIS Benchmark configurations all at once in production environments.

    D. Implement CIS Benchmark configurations slowly in production environments.

18. What is the best use for requiring security certifications when screening candidates for a security director position in a midsized financial services organization?

    A. Require CISSP or CISM or similar certifications.

    B. Desire CISSP or CISM and relevant experience.

    C. Require CISSP and CISM.

    D. Require CISSP or CISM, as well as an advanced degree.

19. How could a statistic about security scanning be transformed into a metric meaningful to senior management?

    A. Avoid the use of technical jargon.

    B. Express the metric in business terms and potential business outcomes.

    C. Show the metric on an easily viewed dashboard.

    D. Describe the statistic in an executive summary narrative.

20. What does the following vulnerability management dashboard indicate to management?

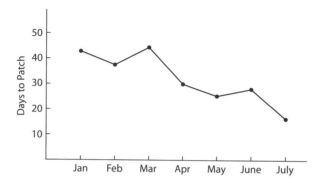

    A. It takes more days to patch systems.

    B. It takes fewer days to patch systems.

    C. Risk is increasing over time.

    D. Risk is decreasing over time.

21. All of the following are advantages to outsourcing an IS audit function, *except* which one?

    A. Avoidance of hiring and retaining talent

    B. Cost savings of contractors versus full-time employees

    C. No need to find onsite workspace

    D. Cost savings for training and professional development

22. Which of the following statements about guidelines is correct?

    A. Guidelines are mandatory.

    B. Guidelines are optional and not required.

    C. Security policies are derived from guidelines.

    D. Security controls are derived from guidelines.

23. An online retail organization accepts credit card payments and is therefore required to comply with PCI DSS. Which of the following statements is correct regarding the organization's service providers that have access to the organization's credit card payment information?

    A. The organization is required to verify each service provider's PCI DSS compliance annually.

    B. The organization is required to verify each service provider's PCI DSS compliance status annually.

    C. The organization is required to assess each service provider's PCI DSS compliance annually.

    D. The organization is required to verify each service provider's PCI DSS compliance quarterly.

24. Which of the following is the best approach for a "state of the security program" report for the board of directors?

    A. Executive summary and details from an enterprise risk assessment

    B. Executive summary portion of an enterprise risk assessment

    C. Detailed workbook containing statistics and metrics for the past 12 months

    D. Short slide deck showing key risk indicators, accomplishments, and incidents

25. An organization has hired a new CISO to make strategic improvements to the information security program. As one of her first important tasks, the new CISO is going to write a program charter document that describes the organization's security program, key roles and responsibilities, primary business processes, and relationships with key business stakeholders and external parties. What is the best approach to producing this charter document?

    A. Develop the charter document based upon ISO/IEC 27001.

    B. First identify and interview key business stakeholders to understand their cyber-risk needs and concerns.

    C. Develop the charter document based upon information security best practices.

    D. Develop the charter document based upon industry-sector best practices.

26. Approximately how many personnel would need to be identified to fully staff a 24/7/365 SOC, which can ensure shift coverage even during vacation and sick time?

    A. 12

    B. 3

    C. 9

    D. 24

27. The statement, "Passwords can be constructed from words, phrases, numbers, and special characters in a variety of ways that are easily remembered but not easily guessed," is an example of what?

    A. A guideline

    B. A standard

    C. A policy

    D. A procedure

28. Which of the following statements is correct about PCI DSS audits?

    A. An organization with a PCI ISA (Internal Security Assessor) does not have to undergo external PCI DSS audits.

    B. An organization can be compliant with PCI DSS if it completes the audit and has project plans for noncompliant controls.

    C. An organization must have all applicable PCI DSS requirements in place to be compliant with PCI DSS.

    D. An organization must complete a PCI DSS audit to be compliant with PCI DSS.

29. Which of the following is the most effective means for making information security policies, standards, and guidelines available to an organization's workforce?

    A. Policies, standards, and guidelines should be on a "need to know" basis and not published or sent to personnel.

    B. Publish policies, standards, and guidelines on an intranet site where they can be easily found.

    C. E-mail policies, standards, and guidelines to the workforce once per year.

    D. Publish policies, standards, and guidelines in hard copy and have copies available at the security office.

30. What is the best approach in most organizations for ensuring that cybersecurity personnel remain current in their knowledge and skills?

    A. Security personnel can study on their own and do not require support from the organization.

    B. Build a library of books on various security topics that security personnel can check out and read.

    C. Provide at least one month of formal training per year.

    D. Provide at least one week of formal training per year.

31. Of what value are metrics about dropped packets on firewalls?

    A. These metrics are a measure of security breaches that have been avoided.

    B. These metrics are of operational value only.

    C. These metrics are a measure of DDoS attacks that have been blocked.

    D. These metrics are of no value.

32. James, a CISO in a software company, is preparing a report for the board of directors prior to an upcoming board meeting. What is the best method for James to deliver this report to board members?

   A. E-mail the report to board members.

   B. Orally deliver the report to the board members during the board meeting.

   C. Provide hard copies of the report to board members during the board meeting discussion.

   D. Securely send the report to board members in advance of the board meeting, and then review and discuss the report at the board meeting.

33. What is the purpose of KRIs in an information security program?

   A. To provide an indicator of potential cyber-risk hot spots

   B. To measure the likelihood of an attack on the organization

   C. To predict the likelihood of an attack on an organization

   D. To predict the method of an attack on an organization

34. Which security metric is best considered a leading indicator of an attack?

   A. Number of firewall rules triggered

   B. Number of security awareness training sessions completed

   C. Percentage of systems scanned

   D. Mean time to apply security patches

35. Steve, a CISO, has vulnerability management metrics and needs to build business-level metrics. Which of the following is the best leading indicator metric suitable for his organization's board of directors?

   A. Average time to patch servers supporting manufacturing processes

   B. Frequency of security scans of servers supporting manufacturing processes

   C. Percentage of servers supporting manufacturing processes that are scanned by vulnerability scanning tools

   D. Number of vulnerabilities remediated on servers supporting manufacturing processes

36. The metric "percentage of systems with completed installation of advanced antimalware" is best described as what?

   A. Key operational indicator (KOI)

   B. Key performance indicator (KPI)

   C. Key goal indicator (KGI)

   D. Key risk indicator (KRI)

37. A member of the board of directors has asked Ravila, a CIRO, to produce a metric showing the reduction of risk as a result of the organization making key improvements to its security information and event management system. Which type of metric is most suitable for this purpose?

    A. KGI

    B. RACI

    C. KRI

    D. ROSI

38. A common way to determine the effectiveness of security and risk metrics is the SMART method. What does SMART stand for?

    A. Security Metrics Are Risk Treatment

    B. Specific, measurable, achievable, relevant, time-related

    C. Specific, measurable, actionable, relevant, time-related

    D. Specific, manageable, actionable, relevant, time-related

39. Key metrics showing effectiveness of a risk management program would *not* include which of the following?

    A. Reduction in the number of security events

    B. Reduction in the impact of security events

    C. Reduction in the time to remediate vulnerabilities

    D. Reduction in the number of patches applied

40. Examples of security program performance metrics include all of the following *except*:

    A. Time to detect security incidents

    B. Time to remediate security incidents

    C. Time to perform security scans

    D. Time to discover vulnerabilities

41. What is the purpose of value delivery metrics?

    A. Long-term reduction in costs

    B. Reduction in ROSI

    C. Increase in ROSI

    D. Increase in net profit

42. Joseph, a CISO, is collecting statistics on several operational areas and needs to find a standard way of measuring and publishing information about the effectiveness of his program. Which of the following is the best approach to follow?

   A. Scaled score

   B. NIST Cybersecurity Framework (CSF)

   C. Business Model for Information Security (BMIS)

   D. Balanced scorecard (BSC)

43. Which of the following is the best description of the COBIT framework?

   A. A security process and controls framework that can be integrated with ITIL or ISO/IEC 20000

   B. An IT controls and process framework on which IT controls and processes can be added at an organization's discretion

   C. An IT process framework with optional security processes when Extended COBIT is implemented

   D. An IT process framework that includes security processes that are interspersed throughout the framework

44. An organization is required by PCI to include several policies that are highly technical and not applicable to the majority of its employees. What is the best course of action for implementing these policies?

   A. Implement a technical security policy containing these required items, with a separate acceptable use policy for all workers.

   B. Incorporate all PCI-required policies in the organization's information policy and let users figure out what is relevant to them.

   C. Include all PCI-related policies and indicate which are applicable to end users.

   D. Keep the PCI-related policies out of the overall security policy because it will confuse nontechnical end users.

45. Which of the following is the best management-level metric for a vulnerability management process?

   A. Average time from availability of a patch to the successful application of a patch

   B. Average time from a vulnerability scan to the successful application of a patch

   C. Average time to apply a security patch successfully

   D. Number of security patches applied

46. An organization's security leader, together with members of its information security steering committee, has decided to require that all encryption of data at rest must use AES-256 or better encryption. The organization needs to update what document?

   A. Policies

   B. Standards

   C. Guidelines

   D. Systems

47. Why might the first control objective of CIS CSC be "Inventory and Control of Enterprise Assets"?

   A. Most organizations are required to have effective asset inventory processes.

   B. The CIS controls framework is hardware asset–centric.

   C. Several IT and security processes depend upon an effective hardware inventory.

   D. The CIS controls framework is an antiquated controls framework.

48. Which of the following security-based metrics is most likely to provide value when reported to management?

   A. Number of firewall packets dropped per server per day

   B. Number of persons who have completed security awareness training

   C. Number of phishing messages blocked per month

   D. Percent of production servers that have been patched within SLA

49. To optimize security operations processes, the CISO in an organization wants to establish an asset classification scheme. The organization has no data classification program. How should the CISO proceed?

   A. Establish an asset classification scheme based upon operational criticality.

   B. Establish an asset classification scheme based upon operational criticality and data classification.

   C. First establish a data classification scheme and then an asset classification scheme based on data classification.

   D. Treat all assets equally until a data classification program has been established.

1. A	18. B	35. A
2. D	19. B	36. C
3. A	20. D	37. C
4. D	21. B	38. B
5. A	22. B	39. D
6. D	23. B	40. C
7. B	24. D	41. A
8. C	25. B	42. D
9. A	26. A	43. D
10. B	27. A	44. A
11. D	28. C	45. A
12. B	29. B	46. B
13. C	30. D	47. C
14. A	31. B	48. D
15. A	32. D	49. A
16. D	33. A	
17. B	34. D	

1. An organization's CISO is planning for the cybersecurity budget for the following year. One of the security analysts informed the CISO that she should add more licenses to the vulnerability scanning tool so that all of the organization's networks can be scanned; currently, there are only enough licenses to scan the primary on-premises data center, but not the secondary data center, office networks, or external-facing assets. How should the CISO respond to this request?

   A. Acquire licenses for all internal and external networks.

   B. No additional licenses are needed, since only the data center network needs to be scanned.

   C. No additional licenses are needed, because the scanner can scan all networks but will not maintain records for them because of license limitations.

   D. Acquire licenses for the secondary data center.

   ☑ **A.** The CISO should expand licensing for the vulnerability scanning tool to include all internal and external networks. Many vulnerability scanning tools maintain databases that track the history of vulnerabilities for each asset; expanding licensing to include all networks will enable this feature to be used.

   ☒ **B, C,** and **D** are incorrect. **B** is incorrect because licenses should be increased to include all internal and external networks and not just the primary data center. **C** is incorrect because the licensing limitation will mean that reconfiguring the scanning tool to scan various internal networks will destroy valuable scanning and remediation history, depriving the security team of the history of scans, vulnerabilities, and remediation for every asset. **D** is incorrect because the addition of the secondary data center, though a move in the right direction, is insufficient; the scanning tool should be licensed to scan all assets in all internal and external networks.

2. An organization has decided to improve its information security program by developing a full suite of policies, procedures, standards, and guidelines. Which of these must be developed first?

   A. Procedures

   B. Standards

   C. Processes

   D. Policies

   ☑ **D.** Policies, which are business rules governing behavior in an organization, should be developed first. Then, processes and procedures that align with policy can be developed next. Standards, which specify how policies are to be implemented, can be developed alongside processes and procedures. Next, guidelines, which offer suggestions on the implementation of policies and standards, can be developed.

☒ **A**, **B**, and **C** are incorrect. **A** is incorrect because procedures should not be created until policies are first developed, followed by processes. **B** is incorrect because standards should not be created until policies are first developed. **C** is incorrect because processes should not be developed until policies are in place.

3. What kind of statement is the following: "Passwords are to consist of upper- and lowercase letters, numbers, and symbols, and are to be at least 12 characters in length."

   A. Standard

   B. Policy

   C. Guideline

   D. Procedure

   ☑ **A.** The statement is a standard. Detailed specifications on any topic should appear in a standard, not in a policy.

   ☒ **B**, **C**, and **D** are incorrect. **B** is incorrect because the statement is too detailed to be a policy. **C** is incorrect because a guideline on passwords would offer suggestions and ideas on the topic of "good" passwords. **D** is incorrect because the statement is not a step-by-step procedure, but instead a list of configuration specifications.

4. A CISO has developed and is publishing a new metric entitled, "Percentage of patches applied within SLAs to servers supporting manufacturing." What message does this metric convey to executives?

   A. The risk associated with SLAs and whether they are too long

   B. The amount of downtime in manufacturing while patches are being applied

   C. The amount of effort used to apply security patches to servers

   D. The risk of security incidents that could disrupt manufacturing operations

   ☑ **D.** The metric in this case helps management understand the risk of a security incident or breach. If the percentage trends down, it's taking longer for servers to get patched, which means an intrusion and potential disruptions to manufacturing would be more likely to occur.

   ☒ **A**, **B**, and **C** are incorrect. **A** is incorrect because this metric does not address the risk with the SLA itself, but with the organization's performance to the SLA. **B** is incorrect because the metric does not directly reveal any downtime information. **C** is incorrect because the amount of effort to patch servers is not revealed by this metric.

5. Which of the following reports is most appropriate to send to a board of directors?

   A. Quarterly high-level metrics and a list of security incidents

   B. Weekly detailed metrics

   C. Weekly detailed metrics and vulnerability scan reports

   D. Vulnerability scan reports and a list of security incidents

☑ **A.** A board of directors is going to be interested in high-level information about a security program, usually in summary form.

☒ **B, C,** and **D** are incorrect. **B** and **C** are incorrect because weekly detailed metrics and vulnerability scan reports are far too detailed and voluminous for consumption by a board of directors. **D** is incorrect because a board of directors is not going to be interested in vulnerability scan reports.

6. What is the best solution for protecting a software as a service (SaaS) application from a layer 7 attack?

   A. Advanced malware protection

   B. Cloud access security broker

   C. Web content filter

   D. Web application firewall

   ☑ **D.** A web application firewall is the best solution for protecting a SaaS application from layer 7 attacks such as script injection, buffer overflow, and reflected cross-site scripting.

   ☒ **A, B,** and **C** are incorrect. **A** is incorrect because advanced malware protection is a solution used on endpoints to detect and block exploits from malware. **B** is incorrect because a cloud access security broker (CASB) does not protect web applications from threats. Instead, a CASB is used to control end users' access to Internet websites in order to manage the use of external service providers and control sensitive content. **C** is incorrect because a web content filter is a solution used to protect endpoints from malicious websites and to control the categories of websites that users are permitted to visit.

7. How does an acceptable use policy differ from an information security policy?

   A. They differ in name only; they are functionally the same.

   B. An acceptable use policy defines expected behavior from workers, while an information security policy details all of the business rules for cybersecurity.

   C. An information security policy defines expected behavior from workers, while an acceptable use policy details all of the business rules for cybersecurity.

   D. An acceptable use policy applies to nontechnical workers only, while an information security policy applies only to technical workers.

   ☑ **B.** An acceptable use policy (AUP) defines expected behavior for all workers in an organization. An information security policy, which also applies to everyone, defines cybersecurity-related business rules on many topics, including some that are not relevant to nontechnical workers (for example, policy on secure software development).

   ☒ **A, C,** and **D** are incorrect. **A** is incorrect because an acceptable use policy and an information security policy are distinctly different from one another. **C** is incorrect because the definitions are reversed. **D** is incorrect because an AUP applies to all workers, while an information security policy generally applies only to technical workers.

8. Which certification is recognized for knowledge and experience on the examination of information systems and on information system protection?

    A. CGEIT

    B. CRISC

    C. CISA

    D. CISSP

    ☑ **C.** CISA, or Certified Information Systems Auditor, is recognized for its requirement for experience in information systems audit and information systems protection.

    ☒ **A, B**, and **D** are incorrect. **A** is incorrect because CGEIT (Certified in the Governance of Enterprise IT) is not related to information systems audit or protection. **B** is incorrect because CRISC (Certified in Risk and Information Systems Control) is related to risk management. **D** is incorrect because CISSP (Certified Information Systems Security Professional) is a general-purpose security certification.

9. The CISO in a 1000-employee organization wants to implement a 24/7/365 security monitoring function. Currently no 24/7 IT operations exist in the organization. What is the best option for the CISO to implement a 24/7/365 security monitoring function?

    A. Outsource security monitoring to a managed security services provider (MSSP) that specializes in security event monitoring.

    B. Staff up a 24/7/365 IT operations and security event monitoring function with permanent full-time staff.

    C. Staff up a 24/7/365 security event monitoring function with permanent full-time staff.

    D. Implement a security event monitoring platform and have events sent to existing 5×8 staff (a staff that works five days a week for eight hours per day) after hours.

    ☑ **A.** The CISO's best option is to outsource security event monitoring to an MSSP. The main advantage of an MSSP is cost: an MSSP's fees for 24/7/365 monitoring will be a fraction of the cost of hiring and equipping a full-time staff capable of fully covering 21 shifts per week with coverage for vacation, sick days, and training.

    ☒ **B, C**, and **D** are incorrect. **B** is incorrect because staffing an IT and security monitoring function is cost-prohibitive compared to outsourcing IT and security ops to an MSSP. **C** is incorrect because staffing and equipping a 24/7/365 security event monitoring function is cost-prohibitive. **D** is incorrect because alerts reaching 5×8 staff at night and on weekends will bring on fatigue, burnout, and turnover.

10. Which of the following is the best regimen for managing security policy content?

    A. Develop policy that aligns with ISO/IEC 27001, NIST SP 800-53, or CIS CSC, and review annually.

    B. Develop policy that aligns with known standards and the business; review annually and when the organization undergoes significant changes.

C. Outsource policy development to a consulting firm; have the consulting firm review annually according to industry changes.

D. Develop policy that aligns with known standards and the business.

☑ **B.** The best initial security policy is one that harmonizes with the organization and is structured on an appropriate standard such as ISO/IEC 27001, NIST SP 800-53, CSC 20, or another relevant standard. Policy should be reviewed at least annually and approved by management. If the organization undergoes significant changes, policy should be reviewed and altered at that time if needed.

☒ **A, C,** and **D** are incorrect. **A** is incorrect because this choice does not state that policy needs to align with the business, nor does it state the need for policy to be reviewed when the organization undergoes significant changes. **C** is incorrect because, although outsourcing policy development can be a good move if the organization doesn't have that expertise in house, this choice states that the outsourced firm should perform the review; even if an organization outsources the initial creation of its security policy, the organization itself should perform the annual review. If the firm lacks someone with sufficient experience to conduct the review, the outsourced firm can facilitate a review with representatives from the organization. **D** is incorrect because this choice lacks an annual review as well as a review when significant changes occur in the business.

11. A new CISO in a manufacturing company has developed statistics and metrics on the industrial control systems supporting automated manufacturing and has found that more than one-third of the operating systems are many years out of support because the ICS software does not support newer versions of operating systems and newer versions of ICS software are not available. What is the best response in this situation?

A. Switch to software vendors that provide modern, supported operating systems.

B. Upgrade operating systems and install backward-compatible libraries.

C. Virtualize outdated operating systems.

D. Isolate ICS systems in hardened networks.

☑ **D.** Many organizations face the problem of being "marooned" on old versions of ICS software, subsystems, and computer operating systems, because the old versions of ICS software are not supported on newer operating systems. Often, newer versions of ICS software are prohibitively expensive or simply not available. The best response is to isolate ICS environments in separate, hardened networks with very tight access controls so that common threats are greatly reduced in both probability and impact.

☒ **A, B,** and **C** are incorrect. **A** is incorrect because switching software vendors is often prohibitively expensive—and sometimes not available at all. **B** is incorrect because of the scarcity of libraries in newer operating systems to mimic older operating systems. **C** is incorrect because virtualizing older OSs does not alter the fact that an older and potentially vulnerable OS is still present.

12. A new CISO in a manufacturing company has developed statistics and metrics on the industrial control systems supporting automated manufacturing and has found that more than one-third of the operating systems are many years out of support because the ICS software does not support newer versions of operating systems and newer versions of ICS software are not available. How should this situation be described to senior management?

A. The organization needs to step up and modernize its industrial control systems.

B. The organization needs to isolate and protect its industrial control systems.

C. The organization needs to require its ICS vendors to support modern operating systems.

D. The organization needs to outsource its ICS to an ICS cloud provider.

☑ B. The best message to senior management is one of mitigation through protective isolation of its industrial control systems. Even ICS environments with modern, supported operating systems should be isolated from the rest of the organization's networks.

☒ A, C, and D are incorrect. A is incorrect because modernization of its ICS environment will probably be prohibitively expensive—in fact, this is probably the highest-cost option. C is incorrect because simply requiring ICS vendors to support newer operating systems is probably a nonstarter: in some cases, the ICS vendors are no longer in business; in other cases, upgrades to newer ICSs are possible but include a costly upgrade of ICS equipment in addition to ICS software. D is incorrect because the prospect of outsourcing ICS may not effectively address the overall situation.

13. Which of the following is the best language for a security policy in a multinational software organization regarding background checks?

A. Prior to hire, all employees must undergo background investigations where permitted by law.

B. Prior to hire, all workers, whether they are employees, contractors, or consultants, must undergo background investigations.

C. Prior to hire, all workers, whether they are employees, contractors, temps, or consultants, must undergo background investigations where permitted by law.

D. Prior to hire and annually thereafter, all employees must undergo background investigations.

☑ C. Background investigations, sometimes called background checks, are an essential safeguard in organizations. However, background checks, such as those performed in the United States, are not permitted in many countries. The best language here, "as permitted by law," requires background investigations to be performed where they are permitted. Also, it is essential that not only full-time employees but also part-time employees, contractors, temporary workers, and consultants undergo background investigations—where permitted by law.

☒ **A**, **B**, and **D** are incorrect. **A** is incorrect because this language excludes background investigations for part-time workers, temporary workers, contractors, and consultants. All of them should also have background investigations done prior to their having access to information systems and data. **B** is incorrect because background investigations are not permitted in many countries. The language here is inflexible and would result in the need for policy exceptions. **D** is incorrect because this language excludes all other types of workers: part-time, temporary, contractor, and consultant. Also, this language excludes "as permitted by law" that recognizes that background investigations are not permitted in every country.

14. An organization recently experienced a security incident in which an employee leaked vital information via an unapproved cloud-based storage provider. The employee stated that she "did not know" that it was against policy to store company data in unapproved cloud-based services. What is the best administrative control to prevent this type of event in the future?

    A. Require employees to acknowledge compliance to security policy annually in writing.

    B. Implement a CASB system.

    C. Implement endpoint-based DLP.

    D. Implement a GPO to block the use of USB mass storage devices.

    ☑ **A.** Requiring employees to acknowledge compliance to security policy is the best option. This answer is the only administrative control of the four answers available.

    ☒ **B**, **C**, and **D** are incorrect. Although these may be effective automatic controls, they are not administrative controls, as the question stated, but rather technical controls.

15. What control can best improve software security in a software as a service organization that currently undergoes quarterly penetration tests of its SaaS software?

    A. SAST scans as a part of the software build process

    B. Monthly penetration tests

    C. Mandatory secure development training for all developers

    D. Daily web application scans of the production environment

    ☑ **A.** SAST (static application security testing) integration into the SaaS product build environment is the best solution. Modern organizations, particularly SaaS providers, are moving toward DevOps and away from waterfall development cycles. To improve security, DevOps is giving way to DevSecOps, where security such as SAST and DAST (dynamic application security testing) tools are integrated into software automation.

    ☒ **B**, **C**, and **D** are incorrect. **B** is incorrect because an increase in the frequency of penetration tests is not the best available option. **C** is incorrect because security development training, while important, produces only gradual improvement in software security, and it rarely, if ever, results in the complete absence of exploitable security defects. **D** is incorrect because daily scans, while effective in detecting many (but not all) security defects, is not as effective as a SAST solution. It is important that organizations move security controls "to the left" (earlier in the development cycle).

16. Which of the following is the best source for system and component hardening standards?

    A. Microsoft

    B. NIST

    C. SANS

    D. The Center for Internet Security

    ☑ **D.** The Center for Internet Security, commonly known as CIS, has a comprehensive library of hardening standards for server operating systems, endpoint operating systems, mobile device operating systems, network devices, and numerous software subsystems including database management systems and application platforms. CIS controls are highly respected and kept up to date.

    ☒ **A**, **B**, and **C** are incorrect. **A** is incorrect because Microsoft, while a reliable source for hardening techniques for its own products, is not a source for hardening for leading operating systems, subsystems, and network devices. **B** is incorrect because NIST is not the best source for hardening information for a wide variety of hardware and software products. **C** is incorrect because SANS is not the best source for hardening standards.

17. An existing healthcare organization is developing a first-ever system and device hardening program and has chosen CIS Benchmarks as its industry standard. What is the best method for implementing CIS Benchmarks in server operating systems in production environments?

    A. Implement CIS Benchmark configurations all at once in test environments and then in production environments.

    B. Implement CIS Benchmark configurations slowly in test environments and then in production environments.

    C. Implement CIS Benchmark configurations all at once in production environments.

    D. Implement CIS Benchmark configurations slowly in production environments.

    ☑ **B.** The CIS Benchmarks are highly detailed and voluminous, particularly for server operating systems. There are dozens of configuration settings, which should be applied gradually rather than all at once. Implementing these changes of configuration in test environments first ensures that configuration changes do not adversely affect production systems.

    ☒ **A**, **C**, and **D** are incorrect. **A** is incorrect because implementing all of the configuration changes in CIS Benchmarks all at once is likely to result in server or application malfunctions that may be difficult to troubleshoot, since so many changes will have been made at one time. **C** and **D** are incorrect because it is not a good practice to implement server configuration changes in production environments without first testing those changes in test environments.

18. What is the best use for requiring security certifications when screening candidates for a security director position in a midsized financial services organization?

    A. Require CISSP or CISM or similar certifications.

    B. Desire CISSP or CISM and relevant experience.

C. Require CISSP and CISM.

D. Require CISSP or CISM, as well as an advanced degree.

☑ **B.** Relevant experience is the most important characteristic in a security director candidate. Certifications such as CISSP and CISM are great additions. Today, many organizations are excessively requiring advanced certifications such as CISSP and CISM not only for leadership positions but also for individual contributor positions. This in part is a cause of the perceived shortage of qualified personnel.

☒ **A, C,** and **D** are incorrect. **A** and **C** are incorrect because requiring advanced security certifications alone is vastly insufficient for a security leader candidate. **D** is incorrect because requiring an advanced security certification such as CISSP and CISM, as well as requiring an advanced degree, will result in many candidates—including potentially the most qualified candidates—not being considered.

19. How could a statistic about security scanning be transformed into a metric meaningful to senior management?

A. Avoid the use of technical jargon.

B. Express the metric in business terms and potential business outcomes.

C. Show the metric on an easily viewed dashboard.

D. Describe the statistic in an executive summary narrative.

☑ **B.** A statistic or metric that is operational in nature can be transformed into a meaningful business metric by using business terms and language and describing business outcomes. For example, a statistic related to the time required to install security patches can be described in terms of IT equipment that supports key business functions together with their compliance to a security process designed to reduce the probability or impact of a breach that could disrupt business operations.

☒ **A, C,** and **D** are incorrect. **A** is incorrect because the removal of technical jargon alone may not be enough to provide business context. **C** is incorrect because an attractive visual display may simply provide little-understood information in visual form. **D** is incorrect because the statistic should first be portrayed in some kind of a quantitative format that can reveal trends over time. Still, a narrative may be helpful at times.

20. What does the following vulnerability management dashboard indicate to management?

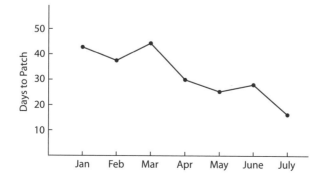

A. It takes more days to patch systems.

B. It takes fewer days to patch systems.

C. Risk is increasing over time.

D. Risk is decreasing over time.

   ☑ **D.** Patches are being applied more quickly. Thus, risk is decreasing over time because corresponding threats have a lower probability of occurrence, thereby reducing risk.

   ☒ **A, B,** and **C** are incorrect. **A** is incorrect because it is taking fewer days to patch systems, according to the chart. **B** is incorrect because the story here is that risk is decreasing as a result of patches being applied more quickly. **C** is incorrect because patches are being applied more quickly, which means risk is decreasing.

21. All of the following are advantages to outsourcing an IS audit function, *except* which one?

A. Avoidance of hiring and retaining talent

B. Cost savings of contractors versus full-time employees

C. No need to find onsite workspace

D. Cost savings for training and professional development

   ☑ **B.** There is usually no cost savings for outsourcing IS audits, because these personnel generally perform their work onsite. Consulting and contracting costs are almost always significantly higher than salaries of equivalent full-time personnel.

   ☒ **A, C,** and **D** are incorrect. **A** is incorrect because an organization that outsources IS auditors does not need to worry about hiring and retaining talent; instead, this is a problem for the consulting firm or contracting agency. **C** is incorrect because IS auditors still need workspace because much of their work is performed onsite. **D** is incorrect because organizations do not need to manage training and professional development for contractors and consultants.

22. Which of the following statements about guidelines is correct?

A. Guidelines are mandatory.

B. Guidelines are optional and not required.

C. Security policies are derived from guidelines.

D. Security controls are derived from guidelines.

   ☑ **B.** Guidelines describe various ways that security policies can be implemented. They are not required, but they provide guidance to personnel who are looking for ways of implementing policies.

   ☒ **A, C,** and **D** are incorrect. **A** is incorrect because guidelines are not mandatory, but instead offer guidance on the implementation of policy. **C** is incorrect because policies are not derived from guidelines; instead, guidelines are derived from policies. **D** is incorrect because controls are not derived from guidelines.

23. An online retail organization accepts credit card payments and is therefore required to comply with PCI DSS. Which of the following statements is correct regarding the organization's service providers that have access to the organization's credit card payment information?

A. The organization is required to verify each service provider's PCI DSS compliance annually.

B. The organization is required to verify each service provider's PCI DSS compliance status annually.

C. The organization is required to assess each service provider's PCI DSS compliance annually.

D. The organization is required to verify each service provider's PCI DSS compliance quarterly.

☑ **B.** According to PCI DSS requirement 12.8.4 (in PCI DSS version 3.2), each organization is required to "maintain a program to monitor its service providers' PCI DSS compliance status at least annually." This can be as simple as requesting each service provider to send a copy of its most recent Attestation of Compliance (AOC) to the organization.

☒ **A, C,** and **D** are incorrect. **A** is incorrect because organizations are not required to verify each service provider's compliance (implying some kind of an audit). **C** is incorrect because organizations are not required to assess its service providers for PCI DSS compliance. **D** is incorrect because organizations are not required to verify its service providers' PCI DSS compliance quarterly, but rather annually.

24. Which of the following is the best approach for a "state of the security program" report for the board of directors?

A. Executive summary and details from an enterprise risk assessment

B. Executive summary portion of an enterprise risk assessment

C. Detailed workbook containing statistics and metrics for the past 12 months

D. Short slide deck showing key risk indicators, accomplishments, and incidents

☑ **D.** A typical board of directors is going to be most interested in summary information and trends. A list of security incidents is valuable information as well.

☒ **A, B,** and **C** are incorrect. **A** and **B** are incorrect because a risk assessment paints a picture of risk at a point in time, but it does not provide trends that tell the audience whether the security program is improving or whether it is reducing risk. **C** is incorrect because most boards are not going to want detailed information, but instead will want summary information that describes what the detailed information means. In some cases, some board members may want to reference detailed information as supporting evidence.

25. An organization has hired a new CISO to make strategic improvements to the information security program. As one of her first important tasks, the new CISO is going to write a program charter document that describes the organization's security program, key roles and responsibilities, primary business processes, and relationships with key business stakeholders and external parties. What is the best approach to producing this charter document?

   A. Develop the charter document based upon ISO/IEC 27001.

   B. First identify and interview key business stakeholders to understand their cyber-risk needs and concerns.

   C. Develop the charter document based upon information security best practices.

   D. Develop the charter document based upon industry-sector best practices.

   ☑ B. To align a security program to the business, it is first necessary to become familiar with key attributes of the organization, which is best obtained through discussions with key business stakeholders, business unit leaders, and department heads. Only then can a security leader hope to develop an information security program that is aligned to the business.

   ☒ A, C, and D are incorrect. A is incorrect because the alignment of an information security program charter is a secondary concern, once a security leader has determined how to align a program to the business. C and D are incorrect because alignment to general and industry-sector best practices runs the risk of misalignment with the organization.

26. Approximately how many personnel would need to be identified to fully staff a 24/7/365 SOC, which can ensure shift coverage even during vacation and sick time?

   A. 12

   B. 3

   C. 9

   D. 24

   ☑ A. At least 12 persons are needed to cover all working shifts each week in a security operations center (SOC), assuming eight-hour shifts.

   ☒ B, C, and D are incorrect. B and C are incorrect because even nine workers cannot fully cover all of the shifts during a week, as well as cover staff absences due to vacation, sick leave, and training. D is incorrect because it indicates more workers than are necessary.

27. The statement, "Passwords can be constructed from words, phrases, numbers, and special characters in a variety of ways that are easily remembered but not easily guessed," is an example of what?

   A. A guideline

   B. A standard

   C. A policy

   D. A procedure

☑ **A.** The phrase, "Passwords can be constructed from words, phrases, numbers, and special characters in a variety of ways that are easily remembered but not easily guessed," is a guideline, as it is guidance to users to help them determine how to comply with a policy or standard. One hint that this is a guideline is the lack of minimum length of a password.

☒ **B, C,** and **D** are incorrect. **B** is incorrect because a standard would specify minimum password length, which is not included in the example. **C** is incorrect because this statement is not a policy statement. **D** is incorrect because the statement is not a procedure for setting a password, but rather offers guidance on its composition.

28. Which of the following statements is correct about PCI DSS audits?

    A. An organization with a PCI ISA (Internal Security Assessor) does not have to undergo external PCI DSS audits.

    B. An organization can be compliant with PCI DSS if it completes the audit and has project plans for noncompliant controls.

    C. An organization must have all applicable PCI DSS requirements in place to be compliant with PCI DSS.

    D. An organization must complete a PCI DSS audit to be compliant with PCI DSS.

    ☑ **C.** For an organization to be compliant with PCI DSS, all applicable PCI DSS requirements must be in place. This includes any compensating requirements that may be mandated.

    ☒ **A, B,** and **D** are incorrect. **A** is incorrect because organizations that meet specific criteria (including but not limited to credit card transaction volume thresholds) are required to undergo PCI DSS external audits, regardless of whether they have an ISA on staff or not. **B** is incorrect because the rules of PCI DSS compliance state that all requirements must be in place; plans for implementing requirements later are not valid substitutes for ineffective controls. **D** is incorrect because completing an audit does not necessarily mean the audit was completed successfully.

29. Which of the following is the most effective means for making information security policies, standards, and guidelines available to an organization's workforce?

    A. Policies, standards, and guidelines should be on a "need to know" basis and not published or sent to personnel.

    B. Publish policies, standards, and guidelines on an intranet site where they can be easily found.

    C. E-mail policies, standards, and guidelines to the workforce once per year.

    D. Publish policies, standards, and guidelines in hard copy and have copies available at the security office.

    ☑ **B.** For most organizations, the most effective way to make security-related content available, including policies, standards, guidelines, and other materials, is to publish them on an internal user website (an intranet) where they can be easily accessed.

☒ **A**, **C**, and **D** are incorrect. **A** is incorrect because security-related content, including policies, standards, and guidelines, should be made available to all personnel. **C** is incorrect because e-mailing security policies, standards, and guidelines is not an effective way of communicating this kind of content in most organizations. Often, people will read and then discard such messages and then will not have that content at hand later on if needed. **D** is incorrect because it is impractical in most organizations to publish security-related content such as policies, standards, and guidelines in hard copy format, because workers at other locations would not have ready access to them.

30. What is the best approach in most organizations for ensuring that cybersecurity personnel remain current in their knowledge and skills?

   A. Security personnel can study on their own and do not require support from the organization.

   B. Build a library of books on various security topics that security personnel can check out and read.

   C. Provide at least one month of formal training per year.

   D. Provide at least one week of formal training per year.

   ☑ **D**. The best approach to help keep security personnel current on knowledge and skills is to make at least one week of training available to them once per year. Different personnel will opt for various approaches, including attending a conference with training sessions, taking a long web-based study course, studying for certifications, or a number of half-day or one-day training events. Organizations that fail to provide this type of training support to its cybersecurity personnel often experience excessive staff turnover: the threats, practices, and tools in cybersecurity are changing rapidly, and a week of training helps security personnel keep up, at best.

   ☒ **A**, **B**, and **C** are incorrect. **A** is incorrect because it is unwise to require security personnel to fend for themselves, as they will be more likely to seek employment elsewhere. **B** is incorrect because a library is practical more for reference than for building new skills; further, in distributed organizations, a library would benefit only workers near the library (or there would be the trouble of shipping books to them). **C** is incorrect because a full month of training is impractical because of the costs involved.

31. Of what value are metrics about dropped packets on firewalls?

   A. These metrics are a measure of security breaches that have been avoided.

   B. These metrics are of operational value only.

   C. These metrics are a measure of DDoS attacks that have been blocked.

   D. These metrics are of no value.

   ☑ **B**. Metrics about firewall-dropped packets generally are of operational value only, related to firewall workload and whether they are of sufficient capacity to protect networks properly from intrusion.

☒ **A**, **C**, and **D** are incorrect. **A** is incorrect because dropped packets are rarely about security breaches. **C** is incorrect because dropped packets are rarely about DDoS attacks. **D** is incorrect because the volume of dropped packets has some operational value related to firewall performance.

32. James, a CISO in a software company, is preparing a report for the board of directors prior to an upcoming board meeting. What is the best method for James to deliver this report to board members?

    A. E-mail the report to board members.

    B. Orally deliver the report to the board members during the board meeting.

    C. Provide hard copies of the report to board members during the board meeting discussion.

    D. Securely send the report to board members in advance of the board meeting, and then review and discuss the report at the board meeting.

☑ **D.** The best approach is to provide a "preread" copy (a full copy) to board members a week or more before the board meeting and then to discuss the contents of the report at the board meeting. By providing the report in advance, board members can read the report at their leisure and prepare comments and questions for the CISO.

☒ **A**, **B**, and **C** are incorrect. **A** is incorrect because simply e-mailing the report to board members is insufficient; it is likely that they will want to engage in a live discussion about the contents of the report. **B** is incorrect because simply delivering the report orally deprives board members of the report itself, which probably contains considerably more detail. **C** is incorrect because it is better that hard copies be provided in advance of the meeting so that board members can read the report in advance and formulate questions for the CISO.

33. What is the purpose of KRIs in an information security program?

    A. To provide an indicator of potential cyber-risk hot spots

    B. To measure the likelihood of an attack on the organization

    C. To predict the likelihood of an attack on an organization

    D. To predict the method of an attack on an organization

☑ **A.** The purpose of KRIs (key risk indicators) is to provide a way of indicating areas of potential risk that may be higher than management is willing to accept.

☒ **B**, **C**, and **D** are incorrect. All are incorrect because KRIs cover a broader subject area than simply cyberattacks, encompassing other types of cyber risks as well.

34. Which security metric is best considered a leading indicator of an attack?

    A. Number of firewall rules triggered

    B. Number of security awareness training sessions completed

    C. Percentage of systems scanned

    D. Mean time to apply security patches

   ☑ **D**. There is a strong correlation between the absence of security patches and the likelihood and success of attacks on systems. Information systems patched soon after patches are available are far less likely to be successfully attacked, whereas systems without security patches (and those in which the organization takes many months to apply patches) are easy targets for intruders.

   ☒ **A**, **B**, and **C** are incorrect. **A** is incorrect because this is not the best answer. Although the number of firewall rules triggered may signal the level of unwanted network activity, there is not necessarily a strong correlation between this and the likelihood of an attack. This is because the likelihood of a successful attack is more dependent on other conditions such as patch levels and login credentials. **B** is incorrect because this is not the best answer. Although a higher percentage of completion of security awareness training may indicate a workforce that is more aware of social engineering techniques, other factors such as patch levels are usually more accurate indicators. **C** is incorrect because the percentage of systems scanned is not a reliable attack indicator. This is still a valuable metric, however, because it contributes to an overall picture of vulnerability management process effectiveness.

35. Steve, a CISO, has vulnerability management metrics and needs to build business-level metrics. Which of the following is the best leading indicator metric suitable for his organization's board of directors?

   A. Average time to patch servers supporting manufacturing processes

   B. Frequency of security scans of servers supporting manufacturing processes

   C. Percentage of servers supporting manufacturing processes that are scanned by vulnerability scanning tools

   D. Number of vulnerabilities remediated on servers supporting manufacturing processes

   ☑ **A**. This is the best metric that serves as a leading indicator. This metric portrays the average time that critical servers are potentially exposed to new security threats. A metric is considered a leading indicator if it foretells future events.

   ☒ **B**, **C**, and **D** are incorrect. **B** is incorrect because the number of scans provides no information about vulnerabilities and, therefore, risk of successful attack. Frequency of security scans is a good operational metric, although a better one would be percentage of critical servers scanned. **C** is incorrect because the percentage of critical systems scanned reveals little about vulnerabilities and their remediation. This is, however, a good operational metric that helps the CISO understand the effectiveness of the vulnerability management process. **D** is incorrect because a raw number, such as number of vulnerabilities remediated, tells board members little or nothing useful to them.

36. The metric "percentage of systems with completed installation of advanced antimalware" is best described as what?

   A. Key operational indicator (KOI)

   B. Key performance indicator (KPI)

C. Key goal indicator (KGI)

D. Key risk indicator (KRI)

☑ **C.** An installation completion metric is most likely associated with a strategic goal, in this case, the installation of advanced antimalware on systems. This metric could arguably be a KRI as well, because this may also indicate risk reduction on account of an improved capability.

☒ **A**, **B**, and **D** are incorrect. **A** is incorrect because key operational indicator is not an industry standard term. Still, this type of metric is not operational in nature, but more associated with the completion of a strategic objective. **B** is incorrect because KPI is not the best description of this type of metric, and this activity of completion of software installations is not typically associated with performance (except, possibly, the performance of the team performing the installations). **D** is incorrect because this metric is a better KGI than it is a KRI. However, this metric could also be considered a KRI if the installation of advanced antimalware can be shown to help reduce risk.

37. A member of the board of directors has asked Ravila, a CIRO, to produce a metric showing the reduction of risk as a result of the organization making key improvements to its security information and event management system. Which type of metric is most suitable for this purpose?

A. KGI

B. RACI

C. KRI

D. ROSI

☑ **C.** The most suitable metric is a key risk indicator (KRI). Still, this will be a challenge because high-impact events usually occur rarely.

☒ **A**, **B**, and **D** are incorrect. **A** is incorrect because a key goal indicator is not the best indicator of risk. **B** is incorrect because the answer is a distractor. RACI stands for Responsible, Accountable, Consulted, and Informed and is used to assign roles and responsibilities. **D** is incorrect, as return on security investment (ROSI) is not a suitable metric because significant events generally occur rarely.

38. A common way to determine the effectiveness of security and risk metrics is the SMART method. What does SMART stand for?

A. Security Metrics Are Risk Treatment

B. Specific, measurable, achievable, relevant, time-related

C. Specific, measurable, actionable, relevant, time-related

D. Specific, manageable, actionable, relevant, time-related

☑ **B.** SMART, in the context of metrics, stands for specific, measurable, achievable, relevant, and time-related.

☒ **A**, **C**, and **D** are incorrect. **A** is incorrect because the answer Security Metrics Are Risk Treatment is a distractor. **C** and **D** are incorrect because these are not definitions of SMART in the context of metrics.

39. Key metrics showing effectiveness of a risk management program would *not* include which of the following?

    A. Reduction in the number of security events

    B. Reduction in the impact of security events

    C. Reduction in the time to remediate vulnerabilities

    D. Reduction in the number of patches applied

    ☑ **D**. The number of patches applied is not a metric that indicates a risk management program's effectiveness, nor the effectiveness of a vulnerability management program.

    ☒ **A**, **B**, and **C** are incorrect. They are all incorrect because each of them *is* potentially a useful risk management program metric.

40. Examples of security program performance metrics include all of the following *except*:

    A. Time to detect security incidents

    B. Time to remediate security incidents

    C. Time to perform security scans

    D. Time to discover vulnerabilities

    ☑ **C**. The time required to perform security scans is *not* a good example of a security program performance metric.

    ☒ **A**, **B**, and **D** are incorrect. **A** is incorrect because time to detect security incidents *is* a good example of a security program performance metric. **B** is incorrect because time to remediate security incidents *is* a good example of a security program performance metric. **D** is incorrect because time to discover vulnerabilities *is* a good example of a security program performance metric.

41. What is the purpose of value delivery metrics?

    A. Long-term reduction in costs

    B. Reduction in ROSI

    C. Increase in ROSI

    D. Increase in net profit

    ☑ **A**. Value delivery metrics are most often associated with the long-term reduction in costs in proportion to other measures such as the number of employees and assets.

    ☒ **B**, **C**, and **D** are incorrect. **B** and **C** are incorrect because value delivery metrics are not usually associated with return on security investment (ROSI). **D** is incorrect because value delivery metrics are not associated with profit.

42. Joseph, a CISO, is collecting statistics on several operational areas and needs to find a standard way of measuring and publishing information about the effectiveness of his program. Which of the following is the best approach to follow?

    A. Scaled score

    B. NIST Cybersecurity Framework (CSF)

    C. Business Model for Information Security (BMIS)

    D. Balanced scorecard (BSC)

    ☑ **D.** The balanced scorecard is a well-known framework that is used to measure the performance and effectiveness of an organization. The balanced scorecard framework is used to determine how well an organization can fulfill its mission and strategic objectives and how well it is aligned with overall organizational objectives.

    ☒ **A**, **B**, and **C** are incorrect. **A** is incorrect because a scaled score is not a method used to publish metrics. **B** is incorrect because the NIST CSF is not typically used as a framework for publishing security program metrics. **C** is incorrect, as the Business Model for Information Security (BMIS), while valuable for understanding the relationships between people, process, technology, and the organization, is not used for publishing metrics.

43. Which of the following is the best description of the COBIT framework?

    A. A security process and controls framework that can be integrated with ITIL or ISO/IEC 20000

    B. An IT controls and process framework on which IT controls and processes can be added at an organization's discretion

    C. An IT process framework with optional security processes when Extended COBIT is implemented

    D. An IT process framework that includes security processes that are interspersed throughout the framework

    ☑ **D.** COBIT is an IT process framework with security processes that appear throughout the framework. Developed by ISACA, COBIT's four domains are plan and organize, acquire and implement, deliver and support, and monitor and evaluate. IT and security processes are contained in each of these domains.

    ☒ **A**, **B**, and **C** are incorrect. **A** is incorrect because COBIT is not strictly a security controls framework. **B** is incorrect because the security processes are not considered optional in COBIT. **C** is incorrect because there is no such thing as Extended COBIT.

44. An organization is required by PCI to include several policies that are highly technical and not applicable to the majority of its employees. What is the best course of action for implementing these policies?

    A. Implement a technical security policy containing these required items, with a separate acceptable use policy for all workers.

    B. Incorporate all PCI-required policies in the organization's information policy and let users figure out what is relevant to them.

C. Include all PCI-related policies and indicate which are applicable to end users.

D. Keep the PCI-related policies out of the overall security policy because it will confuse nontechnical end users.

☑ **A.** The best approach in an organization in scope for PCI is to segregate its policy content into separate documents: a technical or mandate-specific security policy document for technical workers that includes all PCI-related policies and a separate acceptable use policy (AUP) that contains security policy content for all end users.

☒ **B, C,** and **D** are incorrect. **B** is incorrect because a bulky information security policy that contains numerous technical policies and technical jargon is not likely to be effective for end users, who would have trouble understanding much of it and who would fail to comply with the other policy statements applicable to them. **C** is incorrect because this is not the best answer. This approach, however, may be viable in organizations that desire to have all security policy content in a single document. It would be more complicated for end users to consume than a lightweight AUP written expressly for end users. **D** is incorrect because this approach is likely to cause the organization to fail to comply with PCI, which is explicit in its requirements for specific policies in an organization.

45. Which of the following is the best management-level metric for a vulnerability management process?

A. Average time from availability of a patch to the successful application of a patch

B. Average time from a vulnerability scan to the successful application of a patch

C. Average time to apply a security patch successfully

D. Number of security patches applied

☑ **A.** This is the most meaningful metric for management. This tells the story about how long servers are unprotected by security patches, which equates to exposure and risk of an intrusion and breach that pose potentially damaging impacts to the organization.

☒ **B, C,** and **D** are incorrect. **B** is incorrect because this measures time from the vulnerability scan instead of from the time that the patch is available. **C** is incorrect because the time required to apply a patch has little relevance to the business. **D** is incorrect because the number of patches applied tells management little about the effectiveness of the process. This is, however, a potentially useful metric for measuring personnel workload.

46. An organization's security leader, together with members of its information security steering committee, has decided to require that all encryption of data at rest must use AES-256 or better encryption. The organization needs to update what document?

A. Policies

B. Standards

C. Guidelines

D. Systems

☑ **B.** A standards document is the correct type of document for identifying specific protocols, configurations, and algorithms for use in an organization.

☒ **A, C,** and **D** are incorrect. **A** is incorrect because a policy should not include details such as protocols, configurations, and algorithms for use in an organization. Instead, a standard should be used. **C** is incorrect because a guideline is generally considered a suggestion for implementation of a policy or standard, but it does not carry the rule of law that is needed in this case. **D** is incorrect because, although it may be true that the organization needs to update some information systems to align with this recent decision, the best answer here is that the organization must first update its standards.

47. Why might the first control objective of CIS CSC be "Inventory and Control of Enterprise Assets"?

   A. Most organizations are required to have effective asset inventory processes.

   B. The CIS controls framework is hardware asset–centric.

   C. Several IT and security processes depend upon an effective hardware inventory.

   D. The CIS controls framework is an antiquated controls framework.

☑ **C.** It is postulated that CIS places hardware asset inventory as its first control because hardware inventory is central to critical processes such as vulnerability management, security event monitoring, malware prevention and response, and other essential security-related activities.

☒ **A, B,** and **D** are incorrect. **A** is incorrect because this answer is a distractor. **B** and **D** are incorrect because these statements about CIS are untrue.

48. Which of the following security-based metrics is most likely to provide value when reported to management?

   A. Number of firewall packets dropped per server per day

   B. Number of persons who have completed security awareness training

   C. Number of phishing messages blocked per month

   D. Percent of production servers that have been patched within SLA

☑ **D.** Of the choices listed, this metric will provide the most value and meaning to management, because this helps to reveal the security posture of production servers that support the business.

☒ **A, B,** and **C** are incorrect. **A** is incorrect because the number of packets dropped by the firewall does not provide any business value to management. **B** is incorrect because, although it does provide some value to management, this is not as good an answer as **D**. **C** is incorrect because the number of phishing messages blocked does not provide much business value to management.

49. To optimize security operations processes, the CISO in an organization wants to establish an asset classification scheme. The organization has no data classification program. How should the CISO proceed?

A. Establish an asset classification scheme based upon operational criticality.

B. Establish an asset classification scheme based upon operational criticality and data classification.

C. First establish a data classification scheme and then an asset classification scheme based on data classification.

D. Treat all assets equally until a data classification program has been established.

☑ **A.** Even in the absence of a data classification program, an asset classification program can be developed. In such a case, asset classification cannot be based on data classification, but assets can be classified according to business operational criticality. For example, assets can be mapped to a business impact analysis (BIA) to determine which assets are the most critical to the business.

☒ **B, C,** and **D** are incorrect. **B** is incorrect because there is no data classification scheme upon which to base an asset classification scheme. **C** is incorrect because it can take a great deal of time to develop a data classification scheme and map data to assets. It is assumed that the CISO wants to establish the asset classification scheme quickly. **D** is incorrect because there should be an opportunity to classify assets according to operational criticality. If, however, there is little or no sense of business process priority and criticality, then, yes, it might be premature to develop an asset classification scheme.

CHAPTER 6

Information Security Program Management

This domain includes questions from the following topics:
- Controls and control design
- Managing controls throughout their life cycle
- Assessing controls to determine effectiveness
- Reducing risk by conducting security awareness training
- Identifying and managing third-party service providers
- Communicating and reporting the state of the security program

This chapter covers Certified Information Security Manager (CISM) Domain 3, "Information Security Program," part B, "Information Security Program Management." The entire Information Security Program domain represents 33 percent of the CISM examination.

Supporting Tasks in the CISM job practice that align with the Information Security Program / Information Security Program Development domain include:

15. Establish, promote, and maintain a program for information security awareness and training.

16. Integrate information security requirements into organizational processes to maintain the organization's security strategy.

17. Integrate information security requirements into contracts and activities of external parties.

18. Monitor external parties' adherence to established security requirements.

19. Define and monitor management and operational metrics for the information security program.

Information security program management includes several types of activities intended to ensure that organizational objectives are met. These activities include resource management (staff, professional services, budget, and equipment), decision-making at every level, and coordination of activities through projects, tasks, and routine operations. In this domain, information security program management includes the design, selection, implementation, and testing of controls, as well as security awareness training, third-party risk management, and security program communications and reporting.

1. Ravila is a new CISO in a healthcare organization. During strategy development, Ravila found that IT system administrators apply security patches when the security team sends them quarterly vulnerability scan reports. What is the most effective change that can be made in the vulnerability management process to make it more proactive versus reactive?

   A. Have IT system administrators run vulnerability scans on their own systems.

   B. No change is needed because this process is already working properly.

   C. Revise the patching process to ensure patches are applied on a defined process schedule based on the risk of the vulnerability. Leverage the quarterly scanning process as a QA.

   D. Run vulnerability scan reports monthly instead of quarterly.

2. An organization has outsourced most of its business applications and IT operations to software as a service (SaaS) providers and other service providers. Currently, the organization has no master list of service providers. Instead, IT, legal, procurement, and security have separate lists that are not in alignment. What is the first step that should take place?

   A. Implement a cloud access security broker (CASB) system to discover what other service providers are in use.

   B. Create a master list of service providers from the lists from IT, legal, procurement, and security.

   C. Develop a policy that requires that the security team assess all new service providers.

   D. Develop a policy that requires the legal team to review all contracts with all new service providers.

3. A global manufacturing organization has decided to develop a SaaS solution in support of one of its products. What security-related resources will need to be acquired in support of this new endeavor?

   A. Functional requirements, source code control system, and IDEs

   B. Secure coding training, web content scanning tools, and a web application firewall

   C. Secure coding training, DAST and SAST tools, and a web application firewall

   D. Secure coding training, web application scanning tools, and a web application firewall

4. What is the purpose of developing security awareness content in various forms?

   A. To provide unexpected messages that users are less likely to notice

   B. To maximize the value of security awareness training content licensing

   C. To relieve personnel of boredom from only one form of messaging

   D. To address the issue that different people have different learning and cognition styles

5. The CISO in a venture capital firm wants the firm's acquisition process to include a cybersecurity risk assessment prior to the acquisition of a new company, not after the acquisition, as has been done in the past. What is the best reason for this change?

   A. To discover compliance risks prior to the acquisition

   B. To discover cybersecurity-related risks that may impact the valuation of the company

   C. To get a head start on understanding risks that should be remediated

   D. To understand cybersecurity-related risks prior to connecting networks together

6. What is the purpose of sending security questionnaires to third parties at the start of the due diligence process?

   A. To determine the firewall rules required to connect to a third party

   B. To determine which controls need to be added or changed

   C. To address risks during contract negotiations

   D. To register the third party with regulatory authorities

7. An organization's CISO has examined statistics and metrics and has determined that the organization's software development organization is introducing a growing number of serious security vulnerabilities. What new control would be most effective at ensuring that production systems are free of these vulnerabilities?

   A. Implement an intrusion prevention system.

   B. Implement a web application firewall.

   C. Perform a security scan during the software build process and require that no critical or high-level vulnerabilities exist in software released to production.

   D. Administer secure code training to all developers once per year.

8. What is the most effective way of ensuring that personnel are aware of an organization's security policies?

   A. Require personnel to acknowledge compliance to security policies in writing annually.

   B. Require personnel to acknowledge compliance to security policies at the time of hire.

   C. Post information security policies on the organization's intranet.

   D. Distribute hard copies of information security policies to all personnel.

9. What is the best method for determining whether employees understand an organization's information security policy?

   A. Require employees to acknowledge the information security policy in writing.

   B. Incorporate quizzes into security awareness training.

   C. Require employees to read the information security policy.

   D. Distribute copies of the information security policy to employees.

10. An access management process includes an access request procedure, an access review procedure, and an access termination procedure. In the access request procedure, an employee submits an access request; it is approved by the application owner, and it is provisioned by the IT service desk. Which party should periodically review access requests to ensure that records are complete and that accesses were properly provisioned?

    A. IT service desk

    B. Internal audit

    C. Application owner

    D. Employee's manager

11. When is the best time for the legal department to review a contract with a third-party service provider?

    A. After a security questionnaire has been completed by the service provider

    B. At the start of the procurement process

    C. At the vendor selection stage

    D. Before a security questionnaire has been sent to the service provider

12. What aspects of security access reviews would best be reported to senior management?

    A. Number of accounts reviewed in security access reviews

    B. Number of security access reviews completed

    C. Number of security access reviews performed

    D. Number of exceptions identified during security access reviews

13. In an audit of the user account deprovisioning process for a financial application, three out of ten randomly selected samples indicated that user accounts were not terminated within the 24-hour control limit. How should the audit proceed from this point?

    A. Publish audit findings and declare the control as ineffective.

    B. Select another sample of ten records and publish audit findings based on the twenty samples.

    C. Test all remaining termination requests to see if more were missed.

    D. Publish audit findings and declare the control as effective.

14. The board of directors in a manufacturing company has asked for a report from the CISO that describes the state of the organization's cybersecurity program. Which of the following is the best way for the CISO to fulfill this request?

    A. Meet with the board at its next scheduled meeting, provide a state of the state for the cybersecurity program, and answer questions by board members.

    B. Send the most recent penetration test to the board members.

    C. Send the most recent risk assessment to the board members.

    D. Send the risk register to the board members.

15. One of the objectives in the long-term strategy for an organization's information security program states that a concerted effort at improving software development will be undertaken. Which of the following approaches will be *least* effective at reaching this objective?

   A. Enact financial compensation incentives for developers based on reductions in security defects.

   B. Implement web application firewalls (WAFs) and intrusion prevention systems (IPSs) to protect applications from attack.

   C. Enact a policy stating that new software release packages cannot be released until critical and high-level vulnerabilities are remediated.

   D. Provide mandatory secure development training for all software developers.

16. The human resources arm of a large multinational company is planning to consolidate its HR information systems (HRIS) onto a single platform. How can the information security function align its strategy to this initiative?

   A. Contractors and temporary workers can be managed in the new global HRIS.

   B. Workers in all countries can acknowledge compliance with the information security policy.

   C. Workers in all countries can be enrolled in security awareness training.

   D. The identity and access management function can be integrated with the new global HRIS.

17. What is the most effective way to confirm overall compliance with security policy?

   A. Perform penetration tests of key systems and applications, and scan source code if applicable.

   B. Review test scores from security awareness training quizzes.

   C. Circulate questionnaires to process owners and ask them to attach evidence.

   D. Interview process owners and examine business records.

18. What is the purpose of a phishing exercise?

   A. Determine whether phishing messages can bypass phishing controls

   B. Determine whether the links in phishing messages can be confirmed

   C. Determine how many personnel can be tricked by phishing messages

   D. Determine how many actual phishing messages bypass antiphishing defenses

19. A security team has performed a risk assessment of a third-party service provider that hosts the organization's financial accounting system. The risk assessment has identified some critical risks. How should the security team and its leader respond?

   A. Discuss the matter with the service provider to see what mitigations can be implemented.

   B. Enact controls to mitigate the critical risks.

   C. Negotiate a new agreement with the service provider.

   D. Select a different service provider based on the absence of these risks.

20. What is the best time to identify security and privacy requirements in a project to identify and evaluate a software service provider?

    A. Just prior to implementation

    B. At the same time that business functional requirements are identified

    C. Post-implementation after the first penetration test

    D. Post-implementation before the first penetration test

21. What is the primary reason for discontinuing the use of SMS for two-factor authentication?

    A. SMS messages can be easily spoofed.

    B. SIM switching attacks can cause SMS messages to be sent elsewhere.

    C. SMS messages are not encrypted in transit.

    D. One-time passwords sent via SMS do not prove physical possession of a trusted device.

22. An organization recently experienced a security incident in which an employee leaked vital information via an unapproved cloud-based storage provider. The employee stated that she "did not know" that it was against policy to store company data in unapproved cloud-based services. What is the best automatic control to prevent this type of event in the future?

    A. Require employees to acknowledge compliance to security policy annually in writing.

    B. Implement a CASB system.

    C. Implement endpoint-based DLP.

    D. Implement a GPO to block the use of USB mass storage devices.

23. Which of the following is the best vulnerability management process?

    A. Proactive patching and hardening according to SLAs and security scanning as a QA activity

    B. Security scanning reports initiate patching and hardening according to SLAs

    C. Proactive patching according to SLAs and security scanning as a QA activity

    D. Security scanning reports initiate patching according to SLAs

24. What is the greatest advantage of implementing smaller units of security awareness training quarterly as opposed to all-at-once training annually?

    A. More straightforward recordkeeping for compliance purposes

    B. Less disruption to workers in an organization

    C. Decreased license costs from security awareness training content providers

    D. Keeping the topic of information security current through more frequent training

25. What is the purpose of periodically assessing risks at a third-party service provider?

   A. Periodic assessment of third parties is required by PCI DSS.

   B. Assessing a third party is wise when the business relationship changes or increases.

   C. Assessing periodically helps with detection of changes in risk that may not have existed at the start of the third-party relationship.

   D. Periodic assessments determine the need to perform penetration tests of specific third-party service providers.

26. In large organizations, what is the best technique for incorporating cybersecurity-related language into contracts with third-party service providers?

   A. Develop custom legal terms for each service provider based on questionnaires.

   B. Develop custom legal terms for each service provider based on risk.

   C. Develop templates of legal terms for various types of service providers.

   D. Develop templates of legal terms for various types of service providers, and tailor them as needed.

27. The security leader in an organization learned about a security breach at a strategic service provider that provides data storage services. What first step should the security leader take regarding the relationship with the service provider?

   A. Examine the agreement to see what the service provider's obligations are.

   B. Terminate the contract if there is a breach exit clause.

   C. Request a copy of the security incident from the service provider.

   D. Perform a penetration test of the service provider's service endpoints.

28. Which of the following is the best method for testing the following control: "Only authorized persons may approve user access requests"?

   A. Make some dummy access requests and see who approves them.

   B. Interview at least two process SMEs and review business records.

   C. Interview process owners and ask who the approvers are.

   D. Review business records and see who approved access requests.

29. In an organization's information security program, one of the strategy statements reads, "Improve security awareness outreach to company workers." Which activities would best support this objective?

   A. Scan end-user workstations more frequently.

   B. Raise the minimum score required to complete security awareness training successfully.

   C. Publish a quarterly newsletter with security tips and articles.

   D. All of these are correct.

30. A company's IT organization has decided to implement a single sign-on (SSO) portal in the coming year. What are the most important security-related considerations that should be included in advance planning for the SSO portal?

    A. SAML integration with applications

    B. Password quality and password reset

    C. Multifactor authentication

    D. HMAC integration

31. What is the purpose of a security awareness program?

    A. Helps personnel understand proper computer usage

    B. Informs personnel about security policy

    C. Helps personnel develop better judgment when handling company information

    D. Meets compliance requirements for PCI DSS and SOX

32. What is meant by the term "move to the left" in the context of information security and systems development?

    A. Introduce security earlier in the development life cycle.

    B. Introduce security later in the development life cycle.

    C. Remediate security flaws more slowly.

    D. Remediate security flaws more quickly.

33. An organization performs phishing testing on a monthly basis. Over the past year, the average of click-through rates has changed from 42 percent to 14 percent. What conclusion can be drawn from this trend?

    A. End users are more likely to click actual phishing messages.

    B. Phishing messages are more likely to reach end users' inboxes.

    C. End users are less likely to click actual phishing messages.

    D. Phishing messages are less likely to reach end users' inboxes.

34. What is the best approach for initial implementation of a DLP system in an organization's e-mail environment?

    A. Develop a data classification policy, and implement active controls.

    B. Develop a data classification policy, train users, and perform scans of unstructured data stores.

    C. Develop a data classification policy, train users, and implement active controls.

    D. Develop a data classification policy, train users, and implement passive controls.

35. An organization has experienced numerous instances of unintended data exfiltration via its corporate e-mail system. All of the following approaches for solving this problem are valid *except* which one?

    A. Warn users who are sending e-mail to external recipients so they can double-check recipients.

    B. Automatically encrypt attachments in outgoing messages to external recipients.

    C. Disable e-mail recipient auto-complete.

    D. Warn users who are sending e-mail with attachments to external recipients so they can double-check recipients.

36. In an organization with an established security culture, some personnel complain about the time required to undergo the annual eight-hour security awareness training, claiming that they are already proficient in the subject matter and that the organization would benefit more from their continuing their work duties. What is the best approach to address this matter?

    A. Permit personnel to skip security awareness training topics if they first pass tests on those topics.

    B. Permit those personnel to skip security awareness training.

    C. Permit personnel to skip security awareness training if they achieved good test scores in previous years.

    D. Require all personnel to undergo training because it is required by policy.

37. An organization undergoes quarterly phishing testing to see how proficient its workforce is in detecting phishing messages. What is the best approach to take for individuals who fail to detect test phishing messages and instead click their contents?

    A. Post their names on a "wall of shame" as a way of ensuring that personnel work harder to detect phishing messages properly.

    B. Require that they undergo reinforcement training.

    C. Remove their access privileges for a period of time.

    D. Require that they write a short essay on the risk of phishing messages.

38. An organization is required, via a legal agreement, to perform account activity reviews. Which of the following best defines an account activity review?

    A. A review to see how many changes to users' accounts are performed during a time period

    B. A review to see how frequently users log in to their accounts

    C. A review to see how busy users are when they log in to their accounts

    D. A review to see whether users have logged in to their accounts during a specific time period

39. A particular organization is a financial software as a service (SaaS) provider in the financial services industry. Many of the organization's customers claim that they have a regulatory requirement to conduct audits of the SaaS provider. What remedy is available to the SaaS provider to minimize or eliminate these customer audits?

    A. Undertake an annual SOC 2 Type 2 audit.

    B. Undertake an annual SOC 2 Type 1 audit.

    C. Undertake an annual SOC 1 Type 2 audit of relevant controls.

    D. Undertake an annual SOC 1 Type 1 audit of relevant controls.

40. An organization provides training content to corporate customers via a SaaS platform. Because the organization's SaaS platform includes some sensitive information about its customers, some of the customers want to perform audits of the SaaS organization. What can the SaaS organization do to reduce the number of such audit requests?

    A. Undergo an annual penetration test of its SaaS application.

    B. Undergo an annual penetration test of its infrastructure.

    C. Undergo an annual SOC 2 Type 1 audit.

    D. Undergo an annual SOC 2 Type 2 audit.

41. A CISO is turning her attention to the organization's third-party risk management process, which has risk classification tiers into which each third party is classified. The CISO is concerned with "scope creep" among its third parties. In this context, what does this mean?

    A. Third parties that, over time, provide additional services that should elevate them into higher-risk tiers

    B. Third parties whose security programs degrade over time

    C. Third parties that outsource more and more of their operations to fourth parties

    D. Third parties that improve their security programs over time

42. When in an audit is it acceptable to use a sample instead of an entire population?

    A. When the entire population is too large to test

    B. When automation is in place to ensure consistency

    C. When logging is in place to measure results

    D. When alerting is in place to notify personnel of exceptions

43. An audit of a privileged user account has turned up a high number of exceptions from the sample. What is the appropriate next step?

    A. Notify management that there has been a breach.

    B. Stop the audit.

    C. Select additional samples.

    D. Complete the audit report.

44. What U.S. law regulates the protection of medical care–related data?

   A. PIPEDA

   B. HIPAA

   C. GLBA

   D. GDPR

45. The regulation "Security and Privacy Controls for Federal Information Systems and Organizations" is better known as what?

   A. ISO/IEC 27001

   B. ISO/IEC 27002

   C. NIST CSF

   D. NIST SP 800-53

46. Jeffrey is a CISO in an organization that performs financial services for private organizations as well as government agencies and U.S. federal agencies. Which is the best information security controls framework for this organization?

   A. CIS CSC

   B. ISO/IEC 27001

   C. NIST CSF

   D. NIST SP 800-53

47. What is the scope of requirements of PCI DSS?

   A. All systems that store, process, and transmit credit card numbers, as well as all other systems that can communicate with these systems

   B. All systems that store, process, and transmit credit card numbers

   C. All systems that store, process, and transmit unencrypted credit card numbers

   D. All systems in an organization where credit card numbers are stored, processed, and transmitted

48. Which of the following statements is true about controls in the Payment Card Industry Data Security Standard?

   A. Many controls are required, while some are "addressable," or optional, based on risk.

   B. All controls are required, regardless of actual risk.

   C. Controls that are required are determined for each organization by the acquiring bank.

   D. In addition to core controls, each credit card brand has its own unique controls.

49. PCI DSS is an example of what?

   A. An industry regulation that is enforced with fines

   B. A private industry standard that is enforced with contracts

   C. A voluntary standard that, if used, can reduce cyber-insurance premiums

   D. An international law enforced through treaties with member nations

50. Which of the following statements about control frameworks is correct?

   A. Control frameworks are used only in regulated environments.

   B. All control frameworks are essentially the same, with different control groups.

   C. It doesn't matter which control framework is selected, as long as controls are operated effectively.

   D. Different control frameworks are associated with different industries.

1. C	18. C	35. B
2. B	19. A	36. A
3. C	20. B	37. B
4. D	21. D	38. D
5. B	22. B	39. C
6. C	23. A	40. D
7. C	24. D	41. A
8. A	25. C	42. A
9. B	26. D	43. C
10. B	27. A	44. B
11. A	28. B	45. D
12. D	29. C	46. D
13. C	30. A	47. A
14. C	31. C	48. B
15. B	32. A	49. B
16. D	33. C	50. D
17. D	34. D	

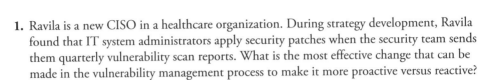

1. Ravila is a new CISO in a healthcare organization. During strategy development, Ravila found that IT system administrators apply security patches when the security team sends them quarterly vulnerability scan reports. What is the most effective change that can be made in the vulnerability management process to make it more proactive versus reactive?

   A. Have IT system administrators run vulnerability scans on their own systems.

   B. No change is needed because this process is already working properly.

   C. Revise the patching process to ensure patches are applied on a defined process schedule based on the risk of the vulnerability. Leverage the quarterly scanning process as a QA.

   D. Run vulnerability scan reports monthly instead of quarterly.

   ☑ **C.** In an effective vulnerability management process, engineers proactively apply security patches and other configuration changes according to a process that may include analysis of new available patches, as well as a regimen of testing to ensure that patches do not introduce new problems. Then vulnerability scans serve as a QA (quality assurance) check to ensure that all systems and devices are configured and patched within established timelines.

   ☒ **A, B,** and **D** are incorrect. **A** is incorrect because this change does not get at the root of the problem of IT system administrators patching only when they are given a scan report. **B** is incorrect because the vulnerability management process as described is not working properly but is reactive instead. **D** is incorrect because patching will still be reactive, although this still may result in security patches being applied earlier. This option would reduce risk but is not the best answer.

2. An organization has outsourced most of its business applications and IT operations to software as a service (SaaS) providers and other service providers. Currently, the organization has no master list of service providers. Instead, IT, legal, procurement, and security have separate lists that are not in alignment. What is the first step that should take place?

   A. Implement a cloud access security broker (CASB) system to discover what other service providers are in use.

   B. Create a master list of service providers from the lists from IT, legal, procurement, and security.

   C. Develop a policy that requires that the security team assess all new service providers.

   D. Develop a policy that requires the legal team to review all contracts with all new service providers.

☑ **B.** The best first step is to create a master list of all known service providers that combines information available from legal (because they manage contracts), IT (because they manage network connections), procurement (because they acquire new vendors and service provider relationships), and security (because they manage or audit firewalls). Many other steps need to follow so that the organization will have a sound third-party management program that ensures that all stakeholders (IT, legal, procurement, security, and possibly others) are involved and can perform their functions as needed.

☒ **A, C,** and **D** are incorrect. **A** is incorrect because this is not the best available answer. However, implementing a CASB or similar capability will provide information about additional service providers that may be used. **C** and **D** are incorrect because neither is the best next step. However, the organization will need to develop policy and a process regarding the use of third-party service providers. The best first step is one of discovery, through the combining of lists of service providers.

3. A global manufacturing organization has decided to develop a SaaS solution in support of one of its products. What security-related resources will need to be acquired in support of this new endeavor?

A. Functional requirements, source code control system, and IDEs

B. Secure coding training, web content scanning tools, and a web application firewall

C. Secure coding training, DAST and SAST tools, and a web application firewall

D. Secure coding training, web application scanning tools, and a web application firewall

☑ **C.** To support security-related needs of the new software as a service (SaaS) endeavor, the organization needs to acquire secure coding training for its developers, dynamic application security testing (DAST) and static application security testing (SAST) tools to discover security defects in its software, and a web application firewall to block layer 7 attacks on its SaaS system. Different organizations will need different combinations of security tools and capabilities, depending upon several factors not addressed in this question.

☒ **A, B,** and **D** are incorrect. **A** is incorrect because these items are not security-related resources. **B** is incorrect because web content scanning tools are used to prevent internal users from the hazards encountered when visiting websites with their browsers, not for protecting web applications. **D** is incorrect because "web application scanning tools" is less specific and using them may be less effective than the use of DAST (dynamic application security testing) and SAST (static application security testing) tools.

4. What is the purpose of developing security awareness content in various forms?

A. To provide unexpected messages that users are less likely to notice

B. To maximize the value of security awareness training content licensing

C. To relieve personnel of boredom from only one form of messaging

D. To address the issue that different people have different learning and cognition styles

☑ **D.** The most effective security awareness training programs include content in various forms (including but not limited to computer-based training, newsletters, e-mail messages, poster, flyers, and promotional items) in recognition of the fact that people have different learning and cognition styles. Workers are more likely to be receptive to messages when they appear in different forms.

☒ **A, B,** and **C** are incorrect. **A** is incorrect because security awareness training is not trying to surprise people or send unexpected messages; it is intended to keep the topic of a secure culture on the minds of workers through a variety of messages. **B** is incorrect because a variety of media types and product licenses have little, if anything, to do with one another. **C** is incorrect because creating messages in a variety of different forms is an attempt to reach people in the most effective way, not to relieve their boredom.

5. The CISO in a venture capital firm wants the firm's acquisition process to include a cybersecurity risk assessment prior to the acquisition of a new company, not after the acquisition, as has been done in the past. What is the best reason for this change?

   A. To discover compliance risks prior to the acquisition

   B. To discover cybersecurity-related risks that may impact the valuation of the company

   C. To get a head start on understanding risks that should be remediated

   D. To understand cybersecurity-related risks prior to connecting networks together

   ☑ **B.** The identification of cybersecurity-related risks prior to the acquisition of a company will, at times, affect the true value of the company being acquired. For instance, if serious vulnerabilities were identified and evidence of a breach was discovered, this would have significant impact on the value of the company.

   ☒ **A, C,** and **D** are incorrect. **A** is incorrect because, although compliance risks would be useful to know, this is not the best answer. **C** is incorrect because the matter of company valuation is more important than risk remediation. **D** is incorrect because venture capital firms do not typically connect their networks to companies they acquire. But even if they do, this is still not the best available answer.

6. What is the purpose of sending security questionnaires to third parties at the start of the due diligence process?

   A. To determine the firewall rules required to connect to a third party

   B. To determine which controls need to be added or changed

   C. To address risks during contract negotiations

   D. To register the third party with regulatory authorities

   ☑ **C.** The purpose of sending a questionnaire to a third-party service provider early in the process is to understand the risks involved that would be related to a business relationship with a third party. Better organizations send questionnaires not just to the selected third party but to other candidate third parties, to help the business make a sound selection that takes cyber risks into account. By sending out questionnaires early, any issues identified can be addressed during contract negotiations.

☒ **A**, **B**, and **D** are incorrect. **A** is incorrect because the determination of firewall rules is a minor matter that can be addressed during the onboarding process. **B** is incorrect because this is not the best answer, even though it may be necessary to make changes to the control environment based upon a third party, the services it provides, and any risks that have been identified through questionnaires and other means. **D** is incorrect because only in narrow circumstances does an organization need to register the use of a third party with regulatory authorities.

7. An organization's CISO has examined statistics and metrics and has determined that the organization's software development organization is introducing a growing number of serious security vulnerabilities. What new control would be most effective at ensuring that production systems are free of these vulnerabilities?

   A. Implement an intrusion prevention system.

   B. Implement a web application firewall.

   C. Perform a security scan during the software build process and require that no critical or high-level vulnerabilities exist in software released to production.

   D. Administer secure code training to all developers once per year.

   ☑ **C.** Control and remediation of security-related software defects is not a simple undertaking. Performing vulnerability scans during a nightly build process will identify any new vulnerabilities. Requiring that software releases contain no critical or high-level vulnerabilities can be a successful control, particularly if it is measured to see how effective it is. This control works only when both of these mechanisms are implemented: scans during nightly builds will inform developers of defects, and the control permitting no release of critical or high-level vulnerabilities is achievable because the nightly scans inform them of vulnerabilities that must be fixed.

   ☒ **A**, **B**, and **D** are incorrect. **A** is incorrect because, although an intrusion prevention system (IPS) may be at least partially effective at protecting applications, the question asks what controls will result in the application being free of serious vulnerabilities. **B** is incorrect because a web application firewall may be effective in protecting applications, but the question asks what controls will result in the application being free of serious vulnerabilities. **D** is incorrect because, although secure code training may help reduce the number of new security-related software defects over time, it will not have an immediate effect on existing vulnerabilities.

8. What is the most effective way of ensuring that personnel are aware of an organization's security policies?

   A. Require personnel to acknowledge compliance to security policies in writing annually.

   B. Require personnel to acknowledge compliance to security policies at the time of hire.

   C. Post information security policies on the organization's intranet.

   D. Distribute hard copies of information security policies to all personnel.

☑ **A.** Requiring annual written acknowledgement of compliance to security policies is the best choice here. Better still is requiring written acknowledgement at the time of hire AND annually thereafter.

☒ **B, C,** and **D** are incorrect. **B** is incorrect because new workers are often overwhelmed with a lot of information at the time of hire, and there is a possibility they will not recall this acknowledgment, particularly when it is not required ever again. **C** is incorrect because posting security policies on an intranet site does not ensure that personnel will be aware of them. **D** is incorrect because there is no assurance that personnel will read or understand security policies; further, the absence of written acknowledgment may mean that workers will not take the policies seriously.

9. What is the best method for determining whether employees understand an organization's information security policy?

   A. Require employees to acknowledge the information security policy in writing.

   B. Incorporate quizzes into security awareness training.

   C. Require employees to read the information security policy.

   D. Distribute copies of the information security policy to employees.

   ☑ **B.** Incorporating quizzes into security awareness training establishes a record of employees' knowledge about information security policy and acceptable use policy, particularly when quiz scores are retained for each employee. Quizzes help to reinforce learning, and they also deter nonrepudiation: an employee who violated policy cannot later claim they did not remember their security awareness training when confronted with records showing they correctly answered questions about policy.

   ☒ **A, C,** and **D** are incorrect. **A** is incorrect because requiring employees to acknowledge information security policy in writing does not mean they read, understood, or retained knowledge about the contents of the policy. **C** is incorrect because requiring employees to read the policy does not ensure they will retain the information. **D** is incorrect because distributing hard copies to employees does not ensure that they will read or retain knowledge about it.

10. An access management process includes an access request procedure, an access review procedure, and an access termination procedure. In the access request procedure, an employee submits an access request; it is approved by the application owner, and it is provisioned by the IT service desk. Which party should periodically review access requests to ensure that records are complete and that accesses were properly provisioned?

    A. IT service desk

    B. Internal audit

    C. Application owner

    D. Employee's manager

☑ **B.** Internal audit is the best party to perform the access review.

☒ **A, C,** and **D** are incorrect. **A** is incorrect because the IT service desk would be reviewing its own work, and this would represent a conflict of interest. **C** is incorrect, although the application owner may want to participate in such a review. **D** is incorrect, because employees' managers could be numerous, and they may not be in a position to review accesses if they are unfamiliar with business processes associated with the system being reviewed.

11. When is the best time for the legal department to review a contract with a third-party service provider?

   A. After a security questionnaire has been completed by the service provider

   B. At the start of the procurement process

   C. At the vendor selection stage

   D. Before a security questionnaire has been sent to the service provider

   ☑ **A.** The best time for the legal department to perform contract review is after a service provider has completed and returned a security questionnaire. Any issues identified in the questionnaire can be mitigated during contract negotiations. For example, if the service provider says that they do not undergo penetration testing, the contract can require the service provider to start undergoing periodic penetration tests.

   ☒ **B, C,** and **D** are incorrect. **B** and **C** are incorrect because there is insufficient information available at these early stages in the process. **D** is incorrect because if the contract is finalized before a security questionnaire is completed and returned by a service provider, it will be too late to address any issues identified in the questionnaire.

12. What aspects of security access reviews would best be reported to senior management?

   A. Number of accounts reviewed in security access reviews

   B. Number of security access reviews completed

   C. Number of security access reviews performed

   D. Number of exceptions identified during security access reviews

   ☑ **D.** The number of exceptions identified during security access reviews is the best operational metric to report to senior management. This metric provides an indication of the quality of the access request and provisioning process. A higher number of exceptions would indicate that personnel are either violating business rules or not paying attention to detail. A low number of exceptions would indicate that employees understand and follow the rules and are paying attention to their work.

   ☒ **A, B,** and **C** are incorrect. **A** is incorrect because the number of accounts reviewed provides little insight into how well the access request and provisioning process is performing and whether controls are effective. **B** and **C** are incorrect because the number of reviews performed and completed also provides little insight into the effectiveness of the access request and provisioning process.

13. In an audit of the user account deprovisioning process for a financial application, three out of ten randomly selected samples indicated that user accounts were not terminated within the 24-hour control limit. How should the audit proceed from this point?

- **A.** Publish audit findings and declare the control as ineffective.
- **B.** Select another sample of ten records and publish audit findings based on the twenty samples.
- **C.** Test all remaining termination requests to see if more were missed.
- **D.** Publish audit findings and declare the control as effective.

☑ **C.** With three out of ten samples failing, this important control is clearly ineffective. Because of the importance of the user account deprovisioning process, it's not enough to publish audit results at this point; instead, all records must be examined so that a more thorough understanding of the control failure can be determined and to deprovision all accounts that were missed.

☒ **A**, **B**, and **D** are incorrect. **A** is incorrect because this is not the best course of action. Although it is true that the control is ineffective, all remaining records should be examined better to understand why the control is in such a poor state of effectiveness. **B** is incorrect because this is not the best course of action. Although pulling another sample will help the auditor better understand what has happened, the gravity of the situation calls for more drastic action—namely the examination of all records. **D** is incorrect because the control is not effective. This option is the worst course of action because a determination that this control is effective is wrong.

14. The board of directors in a manufacturing company has asked for a report from the CISO that describes the state of the organization's cybersecurity program. Which of the following is the best way for the CISO to fulfill this request?

- **A.** Meet with the board at its next scheduled meeting, provide a state of the state for the cybersecurity program, and answer questions by board members.
- **B.** Send the most recent penetration test to the board members.
- **C.** Send the most recent risk assessment to the board members.
- **D.** Send the risk register to the board members.

☑ **C.** The best available option is for the CISO to send the most recent risk assessment. That said, none of the four options is entirely adequate. A better response by the CISO would be to send a report containing some key risk indicators (KRIs), a list of significant security incidents (if any), and short narratives on recent accomplishments and future projects.

☒ **A**, **B**, and **D** are incorrect. **A** is incorrect because the board asked for a report, not simply airtime with the CISO in their meeting. The board wants something to read that explains the state of security in the organization. **B** is incorrect because a penetration test is not appropriate content for a board of directors: it's too detailed and too narrow in focus. **D** is incorrect because the contents of the risk register will not tell the board enough about what is going on. This would be a good second choice, however.

15. One of the objectives in the long-term strategy for an organization's information security program states that a concerted effort at improving software development will be undertaken. Which of the following approaches will be *least* effective at reaching this objective?

A. Enact financial compensation incentives for developers based on reductions in security defects.

B. Implement web application firewalls (WAFs) and intrusion prevention systems (IPSs) to protect applications from attack.

C. Enact a policy stating that new software release packages cannot be released until critical and high-level vulnerabilities are remediated.

D. Provide mandatory secure development training for all software developers.

☑ **B.** While implementing WAFs and IPSs to protect applications from attack will be effective at reducing the probability and impact of layer 7 attacks, this approach is least effective and only serves to cover up and enable what could be sloppy development practices with regard to the reduction of security defects.

☒ **A, C,** and **D** are incorrect. **A** is incorrect because financial incentives, when implemented correctly, can be a powerful means for helping a development organization focus on the reduction of security defects. **C** is incorrect because a policy forbidding the release of software containing critical and high-level security defects can help reduce the number of exploitable defects in production applications. **D** is incorrect because secure development training can help developers better understand how to avoid producing security defects in their code.

16. The human resources arm of a large multinational company is planning to consolidate its HR information systems (HRIS) onto a single platform. How can the information security function align its strategy to this initiative?

A. Contractors and temporary workers can be managed in the new global HRIS.

B. Workers in all countries can acknowledge compliance with the information security policy.

C. Workers in all countries can be enrolled in security awareness training.

D. The identity and access management function can be integrated with the new global HRIS.

☑ **D.** The best alignment opportunity lies in the potential to integrate the new global HRIS to the organization's identity and access management platform. Although this may be a challenge in an organization with many identity systems and many HRISs, the consolidation to single platforms should greatly simplify identity and access management processes and technologies.

☒ **A, B,** and **C** are incorrect. **A** is incorrect because the organization may already be managing contractors and temporary workers in some or all of its HRIS platforms. Many organizations' HR departments resist having anything to do with contractors and temporary workers, but better organizations' HR departments fully embrace their mission to manage information for all workers, regardless of employment status (full time, part time, contractor, consultant, temporary worker, and so on). **B** is incorrect because acknowledgement of compliance to policies, while important, is a minor consideration. **C** is incorrect because the management of security awareness training, while important, is not as important an opportunity as is the alignment of a global HRIS platform with a global identity and access management platform.

17. What is the most effective way to confirm overall compliance with security policy?

   A. Perform penetration tests of key systems and applications, and scan source code if applicable.

   B. Review test scores from security awareness training quizzes.

   C. Circulate questionnaires to process owners and ask them to attach evidence.

   D. Interview process owners and examine business records.

   ☑ **D.** The most effective way to confirm compliance to security policy is to perform audits of policies and controls: interview control owners, examine process documents, and look over business records and other evidence. And because resources are often limited, it's common for an organization to audit the higher-risk controls rather than all controls.

   ☒ **A**, **B**, and **C** are incorrect. **A** is incorrect because penetration tests and code reviews will measure only a small portion of an organization's overall policy—and perhaps not even its most important parts! **B** is incorrect because test scores from security awareness training reveal only the workers' understanding of policy, not whether policies are being carried out. **C** is incorrect because questionnaires and evidence are not an effective means for gathering information about processes. However, for a risk-based approach, it would be appropriate to interview control owners for the highest-risk controls and to use questionnaires and requests for evidence for low-risk controls.

18. What is the purpose of a phishing exercise?

   A. Determine whether phishing messages can bypass phishing controls

   B. Determine whether the links in phishing messages can be confirmed

   C. Determine how many personnel can be tricked by phishing messages

   D. Determine how many actual phishing messages bypass antiphishing defenses

   ☑ **C.** The purpose of a phishing exercise is to determine what proportion of the workforce is potentially susceptible to actual phishing campaigns. Phishing testing consists of the creation of e-mail messages that resemble phishing messages and are released into the workforce. Typically, phishing testing tools track each user's response to test phishing messages and gather statistics on the percentage of the workforce that is successfully tricked by these test phishing messages. In a proper security awareness program, the results of phishing testing help management understand the effectiveness of end-user training on recognizing actual phishing messages and responding appropriately.

   ☒ **A**, **B**, and **D** are incorrect. The purpose of phishing test messages is not to bypass phishing controls, determine whether links are confirmable, or to test antiphishing defenses.

19. A security team has performed a risk assessment of a third-party service provider that hosts the organization's financial accounting system. The risk assessment has identified some critical risks. How should the security team and its leader respond?

   A. Discuss the matter with the service provider to see what mitigations can be implemented.

   B. Enact controls to mitigate the critical risks.

   C. Negotiate a new agreement with the service provider.

   D. Select a different service provider based on the absence of these risks.

   ☑ **A.** When an organization has performed a risk assessment of a third-party service provider, the best course of action is for the organization to engage with the service provider to understand these risks better and to determine what actions (in the form of additions or changes to existing controls or the enactment of new controls) can be taken that will partially or completely mitigate the identified risks.

   ☒ **B, C,** and **D** are incorrect. **B** is incorrect because an organization cannot simply enact new controls in another organization. Only the third-party organization can make changes to its operations, including changes to existing controls and the enactment of new controls. **C** is incorrect because the initiation of contract negotiations during the term of a contract is often not fruitful. However, if a contract is about to expire and be renewed, that may be a good opportunity to bring new language into the agreement between the organization and its third-party service provider. **D** is incorrect because the discovery of new risks is rarely enough cause to compel an organization to change service providers. Terminating a relationship with a service provider is usually an action of last resort.

20. What is the best time to identify security and privacy requirements in a project to identify and evaluate a software service provider?

   A. Just prior to implementation

   B. At the same time that business functional requirements are identified

   C. Post-implementation after the first penetration test

   D. Post-implementation before the first penetration test

   ☑ **B.** The best time to identify security and privacy requirements is at the earliest possible phase in the project—typically when business requirements and other requirements are also identified.

   ☒ **A, C,** and **D** are incorrect. **A** is incorrect because the identification of security requirements just prior to implementation removes the opportunity to select a software service provider based upon its security capabilities (alongside all of its other capabilities). This also removes the opportunity to implement security controls and features in the service, since "just prior to implementation" implies that controls, features, and capabilities have already been determined. **C** and **D** are incorrect because post-implementation is far too late to identify security requirements. When security requirements have not been identified until after implementation, there is a high probability that the service will have been implemented with numerous security weaknesses.

21. What is the primary reason for discontinuing the use of SMS for two-factor authentication?

    A. SMS messages can be easily spoofed.

    B. SIM switching attacks can cause SMS messages to be sent elsewhere.

    C. SMS messages are not encrypted in transit.

    D. One-time passwords sent via SMS do not prove physical possession of a trusted device.

    ☑ **D.** SMS messages are not as secure as they used to be, and several methods are available (cellular carrier websites and services such as Google Voice) for users to obtain SMS messages without having their mobile device (the second factor), with just a user ID and password.

    ☒ **A, B,** and **C** are incorrect. **A** is incorrect because SMS spoofing alone would not pose a threat to two-factor authentication. **B** is incorrect because this is not the best answer, although SIM switching attacks are a threat. **C** is incorrect because encryption of SMS messages does take place at lower layers.

22. An organization recently experienced a security incident in which an employee leaked vital information via an unapproved cloud-based storage provider. The employee stated that she "did not know" that it was against policy to store company data in unapproved cloud-based services. What is the best automatic control to prevent this type of event in the future?

    A. Require employees to acknowledge compliance to security policy annually in writing.

    B. Implement a CASB system.

    C. Implement endpoint-based DLP.

    D. Implement a GPO to block the use of USB mass storage devices.

    ☑ **B.** A cloud access security broker (CASB) system is specifically designed to provide visibility and control into the use of cloud-based services. This is the best available option of those listed.

    ☒ **A, C,** and **D** are incorrect. **A** is incorrect because signing an acknowledgment of policy is not an automatic control, but an administrative control. **C** is incorrect because endpoint data loss prevention (DLP), while potentially effective, is not as effective as a CASB solution, because the CASB solution prevents users from contacting unapproved systems. **D** is incorrect because restriction of USB mass storage does not address the use of cloud-based storage.

23. Which of the following is the best vulnerability management process?

    A. Proactive patching and hardening according to SLAs and security scanning as a QA activity

    B. Security scanning reports initiate patching and hardening according to SLAs

    C. Proactive patching according to SLAs and security scanning as a QA activity

    D. Security scanning reports initiate patching according to SLAs

☑ **A.** The best vulnerability management process is one in which system and device patching and hardening are proactively performed according to established service level agreements (SLAs) and where security scanning (and examination of hardening activities) is a quality assurance (QA) activity to confirm that proactive patching and hardening activities are effective.

☒ **B, C,** and **D** are incorrect. **B** is incorrect because vulnerability scanning should not be the driving force for patching and hardening. **C** is incorrect because vulnerability management should also include proactive system hardening according to established local standards that are based upon accepted industry standards. **D** is incorrect because this method relies on vulnerability scanning that drives patching; hardening, another important aspect of vulnerability management, is not even mentioned in this option.

24. What is the greatest advantage of implementing smaller units of security awareness training quarterly as opposed to all-at-once training annually?

    A. More straightforward recordkeeping for compliance purposes

    B. Less disruption to workers in an organization

    C. Decreased license costs from security awareness training content providers

    D. Keeping the topic of information security current through more frequent training

☑ **D.** The primary purpose for conducting smaller units of security awareness training several times per year, versus a single larger session once per year, is to keep the topic of information current and to keep security awareness on the minds of workers in an organization.

☒ **A, B,** and **C** are incorrect. **A** is incorrect because recordkeeping for security awareness training is already straightforward; maintaining training records for annual or quarterly training events is not burdensome. **B** is incorrect because, although training may be seen as disruptive, security awareness training courses are generally limited to a few hours or a portion of a day. **C** is incorrect because license cost differences between quarterly and annual training should be minimal or insignificant.

25. What is the purpose of periodically assessing risks at a third-party service provider?

    A. Periodic assessment of third parties is required by PCI DSS.

    B. Assessing a third party is wise when the business relationship changes or increases.

    C. Assessing periodically helps with detection of changes in risk that may not have existed at the start of the third-party relationship.

    D. Periodic assessments determine the need to perform penetration tests of specific third-party service providers.

☑ **C.** Periodic assessments of risk in third-party service providers is needed because business conditions in any given third-party service provider can change in ways that influence risk for better or for worse.

☒ **A, B,** and **D** are incorrect. **A** is incorrect because this is too narrow a position; although PCI DSS does require that organizations confirm the ongoing compliance status, this fails to address the phenomenon of changing risk in service provider organizations. **B** is incorrect because risk assessments are *also* needed when a relationship with a third-party service provider changes, but this does not address the need for periodic assessments while the relationship does not change. **D** is incorrect because the outcome of a risk assessment of a third party will not ordinarily determine the need for penetration tests. Rather, the level of inherent risk and the specific role of a third-party service provider will together determine the need for a penetration test.

26. In large organizations, what is the best technique for incorporating cybersecurity-related language into contracts with third-party service providers?

    A. Develop custom legal terms for each service provider based on questionnaires.

    B. Develop custom legal terms for each service provider based on risk.

    C. Develop templates of legal terms for various types of service providers.

    D. Develop templates of legal terms for various types of service providers, and tailor them as needed.

    ☑ **D.** Large organizations with better security programs develop templates of security terms and conditions for various types of situations. Then, for each third party, specific changes are made as needed.

    ☒ **A**, **B**, and **C** are incorrect. **A** and **B** are incorrect because the development of purely custom security terms and conditions is too time consuming. **C** is incorrect because, although the use of a template is a good starting point, each contract will need specific changes based on several factors, including the nature of the business relationship and specific risks that are identified through questionnaires and other means.

27. The security leader in an organization learned about a security breach at a strategic service provider that provides data storage services. What first step should the security leader take regarding the relationship with the service provider?

    A. Examine the agreement to see what the service provider's obligations are.

    B. Terminate the contract if there is a breach exit clause.

    C. Request a copy of the security incident from the service provider.

    D. Perform a penetration test of the service provider's service endpoints.

    ☑ **A.** Before the security leader can take action, he or she needs to first understand what security-breach-related activities the service provider is obligated to perform. Knowing this will help the security leader take the right steps as a part of their organization's response to the breach.

    ☒ **B**, **C**, and **D** are incorrect. **B** is incorrect because a contract termination should be an action of last resort, not the first action to take, even in the event of a breach. Further, it is rarely the security leader's decision to terminate a contract; instead, the security leader may offer his or her opinion regarding such remedies. **C** is incorrect because this may or may not be applicable or available. First, the agreement needs to be examined to see what obligations, if any, are included. **D** is incorrect because a penetration test may not be permitted or appropriate.

28. Which of the following is the best method for testing the following control: "Only authorized persons may approve user access requests"?

    A. Make some dummy access requests and see who approves them.

    B. Interview at least two process SMEs and review business records.

    C. Interview process owners and ask who the approvers are.

    D. Review business records and see who approved access requests.

    ☑ **B.** The best way to test this control is to interview two or more subject matter experts on the access request process and examine business records to see who has reviewed access requests.

    ☒ **A**, **C**, and **D** are incorrect. **A** is incorrect because process owners and operators may be aware that "the auditors are watching" and may behave differently during audit tests than they normally would. **C** is incorrect because this option lacks the examination of business records (which would hopefully show the names of individual process approvers). **D** is incorrect because this option lacks interviews with two or more business process owners.

29. In an organization's information security program, one of the strategy statements reads, "Improve security awareness outreach to company workers." Which activities would best support this objective?

    A. Scan end-user workstations more frequently.

    B. Raise the minimum score required to complete security awareness training successfully.

    C. Publish a quarterly newsletter with security tips and articles.

    D. All of these are correct.

    ☑ **C.** Publishing a quarterly newsletter (in a medium often used in the organization) is the best activity. Security tips and articles will help company workers better understand the nature of cybersecurity risks and actions they can take to reduce risk.

    ☒ **A**, **B**, and **D** are incorrect. **A** is incorrect because scanning end-user workstations will not improve users' awareness of cybersecurity issues. **B** is incorrect because this does not improve outreach, but the level of competency required. **D** is incorrect because not all answers help to meet this objective.

30. A company's IT organization has decided to implement a single sign-on (SSO) portal in the coming year. What are the most important security-related considerations that should be included in advance planning for the SSO portal?

    A. SAML integration with applications

    B. Password quality and password reset

    C. Multifactor authentication

    D. HMAC integration

    ☑ **A.** The point of single sign-on is to make authentication to a large number of applications a matter of clicking a button. Without Security Assertion Markup Language (SAML) or equivalent integration capabilities, it will take considerably more effort to integrate an SSO portal with an organization's business applications.

☒ **B**, **C**, and **D** are incorrect. **B** is incorrect because password quality and password reset, while vital capabilities, are not always controlled by an SSO portal. **C** is incorrect because multifactor authentication, while vital, is not always controlled by an SSO portal. **D** is incorrect because HMAC is a deprecated protocol for authentication.

31. What is the purpose of a security awareness program?

    A. Helps personnel understand proper computer usage

    B. Informs personnel about security policy

    C. Helps personnel develop better judgment when handling company information

    D. Meets compliance requirements for PCI DSS and SOX

    ☑ **C.** The main purpose of security awareness is to help personnel be more aware of cybersecurity-related risks and to help them develop better judgment so that they will make better decisions in a wide variety of situations.

    ☒ **A**, **B**, and **D** are incorrect. **A** is incorrect because security awareness training includes content on proper computer usage, but also on safe computer usage and other topics such as security while traveling and workplace safety. **B** is incorrect because security awareness training goes beyond security policy. **D** is incorrect because compliance is not the only driver for security awareness training.

32. What is meant by the term "move to the left" in the context of information security and systems development?

    A. Introduce security earlier in the development life cycle.

    B. Introduce security later in the development life cycle.

    C. Remediate security flaws more slowly.

    D. Remediate security flaws more quickly.

    ☑ **A.** The term "move to the left" signifies that security is introduced earlier in the systems development life cycle. For instance, if an organization performs vulnerability scans after a new software version is released to production, then performing vulnerability scans on prerelease software before it is released to production would be a "move to the left." In another example, if an organization performs static code scans during the nightly build run, then performing static code scans at code check-in would be a "move to the left."

    ☒ **B**, **C**, and **D** are incorrect. **B** is incorrect because "move to the left" means that security is introduced earlier, not later, in the systems development life cycle. **C** and **D** are incorrect because "move to the left" is not related to the timing of remediation.

33. An organization performs phishing testing on a monthly basis. Over the past year, the average of click-through rates has changed from 42 percent to 14 percent. What conclusion can be drawn from this trend?

    A. End users are more likely to click actual phishing messages.

    B. Phishing messages are more likely to reach end users' inboxes.

C. End users are less likely to click actual phishing messages.

D. Phishing messages are less likely to reach end users' inboxes.

☑ **C.** A reduction in click-through rates in phishing testing means that fewer end users are being tricked by test phishing messages that are sent to them via e-mail. Provided the quality of the test messages was good, this is an indication that end users are less likely to click actual phishing messages that are sent to them.

☒ **A**, **B**, and **D** are incorrect. **A** is incorrect because the trend indicates they are less likely to click actual phishing messages, not more likely. **B** and **D** are incorrect because this metric provides no indication on the likelihood of actual phishing messages to arrive in end-user inboxes.

34. What is the best approach for initial implementation of a DLP system in an organization's e-mail environment?

A. Develop a data classification policy, and implement active controls.

B. Develop a data classification policy, train users, and perform scans of unstructured data stores.

C. Develop a data classification policy, train users, and implement active controls.

D. Develop a data classification policy, train users, and implement passive controls.

☑ **D**. Success in a data loss prevention (DLP) implementation requires that the organization have a well-defined data classification policy, together with handling procedures. User training is a must, as organizations will need to rely at least partly on individual end-user judgment. Implementing DLP tools in passive (monitoring) mode enables the organization to learn more about data movement; once use cases become clear, active (intervention) controls can be slowly implemented.

☒ **A**, **B**, and **C** are incorrect. **A** is incorrect because the implementation of active controls right away is highly likely to disrupt key business process and draw ire from end users and department heads whose business operations are being impacted. **B** is incorrect because static data discovery is not highly related to e-mail use. **C** is incorrect because it is first important to implement passive (monitoring) controls to learn about data flow before implementing active (blocking) controls, so that blocking controls do not disrupt business operations.

35. An organization has experienced numerous instances of unintended data exfiltration via its corporate e-mail system. All of the following approaches for solving this problem are valid *except* which one?

A. Warn users who are sending e-mail to external recipients so they can double-check recipients.

B. Automatically encrypt attachments in outgoing messages to external recipients.

C. Disable e-mail recipient auto-complete.

D. Warn users who are sending e-mail with attachments to external recipients so they can double-check recipients.

☑ **B**. Automatic encryption of attachments in outgoing messages is not likely to help in the situation described, where too much data exfiltration is occurring. Depending on the encryption approach used, the solution will either result in no one being able to read attachments or the wrong recipients being able to read attachments anyway.

☒ **A**, **C**, and **D** are incorrect. **A** and **D** are incorrect because warning users about e-mail going to external parties is a valid step to take, particularly if the problem has been about users selecting the wrong recipients. **C** is incorrect because disabling e-mail recipient auto-complete *can* be an effective remedy if there are numerous cases of data being sent to the wrong recipients.

36. In an organization with an established security culture, some personnel complain about the time required to undergo the annual eight-hour security awareness training, claiming that they are already proficient in the subject matter and that the organization would benefit more from their continuing their work duties. What is the best approach to address this matter?

   A. Permit personnel to skip security awareness training topics if they first pass tests on those topics.

   B. Permit those personnel to skip security awareness training.

   C. Permit personnel to skip security awareness training if they achieved good test scores in previous years.

   D. Require all personnel to undergo training because it is required by policy.

   ☑ **A**. Known as "testing out," the technique of permitting students to take tests on various topics and permitting them to skip instruction if they pass those tests is a common practice.

   ☒ **B**, **C**, and **D** are incorrect. **B** and **C** are incorrect because some of the personnel who were proficient in prior years could fail to stay current and be unaware of new threats and practices. **D** is incorrect because this does not directly address their concern, which is reasonable.

37. An organization undergoes quarterly phishing testing to see how proficient its workforce is in detecting phishing messages. What is the best approach to take for individuals who fail to detect test phishing messages and instead click their contents?

   A. Post their names on a "wall of shame" as a way of ensuring that personnel work harder to detect phishing messages properly.

   B. Require that they undergo reinforcement training.

   C. Remove their access privileges for a period of time.

   D. Require that they write a short essay on the risk of phishing messages.

   ☑ **B**. When workers click a test phishing message, the best practice is to send them back to some reinforcement training in the hopes that their proficiency will improve.

☒ **A, C,** and **D** are incorrect. **A** is incorrect because publicly shaming personnel for a mistake is not a productive tool. **C** is incorrect because this could have operational impact on the business. **D** is incorrect because writing an essay is not a typical sanction in a business, although it is more common in academic settings.

38. An organization is required, via a legal agreement, to perform account activity reviews. Which of the following best defines an account activity review?

A. A review to see how many changes to users' accounts are performed during a time period

B. A review to see how frequently users log in to their accounts

C. A review to see how busy users are when they log in to their accounts

D. A review to see whether users have logged in to their accounts during a specific time period

☑ **D.** An account activity review determines whether each user account is active in a given time period, typically a month or a quarter. After such a review, any user accounts with no logins are candidates for being locked or removed. This helps to reduce risks of unauthorized access to a system by reducing the number of personnel who have access to the system.

☒ **A, B,** and **C** are incorrect. **A** is incorrect because an account activity review is not related to the numbers of changes made to user accounts in a system. **B** is incorrect because a user account review is not so much concerned with the frequency of logins, but rather is concerned with whether an account has gone dormant—the user has not logged in for an extended period of time. **C** is incorrect because an account activity review is not concerned with how busy users are in a system.

39. A particular organization is a financial software as a service (SaaS) provider in the financial services industry. Many of the organization's customers claim that they have a regulatory requirement to conduct audits of the SaaS provider. What remedy is available to the SaaS provider to minimize or eliminate these customer audits?

A. Undertake an annual SOC 2 Type 2 audit.

B. Undertake an annual SOC 2 Type 1 audit.

C. Undertake an annual SOC 1 Type 2 audit of relevant controls.

D. Undertake an annual SOC 1 Type 1 audit of relevant controls.

☑ **C.** An organization providing financial-related services to customers can undertake annual (or semiannual) SOC 1 Type 2 audits. This audit is an effective and cost-saving substitute for customers performing their own audits.

☒ **A, B,** and **D** are incorrect. **A** and **B** are incorrect because a SOC 2 Type 1 or Type 2 audit will not effectively dissuade customers' auditors from wanting to perform their own audits. **D** is incorrect because a SOC 1 Type 1 audit will not provide sufficient comfort to auditors in customer organizations.

40. An organization provides training content to corporate customers via a SaaS platform. Because the organization's SaaS platform includes some sensitive information about its customers, some of the customers want to perform audits of the SaaS organization. What can the SaaS organization do to reduce the number of such audit requests?

A. Undergo an annual penetration test of its SaaS application.

B. Undergo an annual penetration test of its infrastructure.

C. Undergo an annual SOC 2 Type 1 audit.

D. Undergo an annual SOC 2 Type 2 audit.

☑ **D.** The best approach for a nonfinancial SaaS organization to fend off audit requests from its customers is to undergo an annual SOC2 Type 2 audit. In a Type 2 audit, auditors (which are required to be public accounting firms) examine business processes as well as business records and develop detailed reports on every control's effectiveness.

☒ **A**, **B**, and **C** are incorrect. **A** and **B** are incorrect because penetration tests reveal only a narrow facet of risk to customers. **C** is incorrect because a SOC2 Type 1 audit is an examination of the organization's business process documents only and does not show whether those processes are being performed properly and effectively.

41. A CISO is turning her attention to the organization's third-party risk management process, which has risk classification tiers into which each third party is classified. The CISO is concerned with "scope creep" among its third parties. In this context, what does this mean?

A. Third parties that, over time, provide additional services that should elevate them into higher-risk tiers

B. Third parties whose security programs degrade over time

C. Third parties that outsource more and more of their operations to fourth parties

D. Third parties that improve their security programs over time

☑ **A.** It is a good practice to establish a risk tier system for third parties and then to perform risk assessments at varying levels of rigor, based on their classification. "Scope creep" in this context means that a third party is initially classified at a low-risk tier. Then a change in the services that the third party provides to the organization changes, resulting in its being placed into a higher-risk tier. Unfortunately, often a CISO is not made aware of the changes in the business relationship with such a third party, and hence it remains in a lower-risk tier, where risk assessments are less rigorous.

☒ **B**, **C**, and **D** are incorrect. **B** is incorrect because, although the degradation of a third party's security program would be a matter of concern, this is not known as "scope creep." **C** is incorrect because the phenomenon of third parties outsourcing services to fourth parties is not known as "scope creep." **D** is incorrect because the improvement of a third party's security program is not known as "scope creep."

42. When in an audit is it acceptable to use a sample instead of an entire population?

A. When the entire population is too large to test

B. When automation is in place to ensure consistency

C. When logging is in place to measure results

D. When alerting is in place to notify personnel of exceptions

☑ **A.** Sampling is acceptable when the entire population of objects is too large to examine one-by-one. During an audit, if an excessive number of exceptions is found, additional samples can be taken to understand the problem better.

☒ **B, C,** and **D** are incorrect. **B** is incorrect because automation is not a requirement for sampling. **C** is incorrect because the presence of logging is generally not a factor on a sampling decision (even if the audit is about logging). **D** is incorrect because alerting is not related to sampling decisions.

43. An audit of a privileged user account has turned up a high number of exceptions from the sample. What is the appropriate next step?

A. Notify management that there has been a breach.

B. Stop the audit.

C. Select additional samples.

D. Complete the audit report.

☑ **C.** Generally speaking, during an audit in which a large number of exceptions has been identified in a given sampling, it is appropriate to select additional samples to determine the extent of the control's ineffectiveness.

☒ **A, B,** and **D** are incorrect. **A** is incorrect because audit exceptions of privileged user accounts does not automatically signify a breach has occurred. **B** is incorrect because this is no reason to stop the audit. **D** is incorrect because the audit is not complete; more samples should be selected and analyzed.

44. What U.S. law regulates the protection of medical care–related data?

A. PIPEDA

B. HIPAA

C. GLBA

D. GDPR

☑ **B.** HIPAA, the Health Insurance Portability and Accountability Act, comprises a Privacy Rule and a Security Rule. The Privacy Rule limits what healthcare organizations are permitted to do with electronic protected healthcare information (ePHI), while the Security Rule stipulates various required processes and tooling for the protection of ePHI.

☒ **A**, **C**, and **D** are incorrect. **A** is incorrect because PIPEDA is the Canadian Personal Information Protection and Electronic Documents Act that is the federal privacy law for private-sector organizations. It sets out the ground rules for how businesses must handle personal information in the course of commercial activity. **C** is incorrect because GLBA is the Gramm-Leach-Bliley Act, which established requirements for the protection of personal information in the U.S. financial services industry. Generally, organizations subject to GLBA are banks, credit unions, insurance companies, and securities trading firms. **D** is incorrect because GDPR is the European Union General Data Protection Regulation, the law that regulates the protection and use of personally identifiable information for European residents.

45. The regulation "Security and Privacy Controls for Federal Information Systems and Organizations" is better known as what?

    A. ISO/IEC 27001

    B. ISO/IEC 27002

    C. NIST CSF

    D. NIST SP 800-53

    ☑ **D.** NIST SP 800-53, also known as NIST 800-53, is the security controls framework developed by the U.S. National Institute for Standards and Technology and published in its Special Publication number 800 library. NIST 800-53 is required of all branches of the U.S. federal government and has also been widely adopted by other government agencies and private industry in the United States and around the world. NIST 800-53 is available from https://csrc.nist.gov/publications/sp.

    ☒ **A**, **B**, and **C** are incorrect. **A** is incorrect because ISO/IEC 27001 is known as "Information technology – Security techniques – Information security management systems – Requirements." **B** is incorrect because ISO/IEC 27002 is known as "Information technology – Security techniques – Code of practice for information security controls." **C** is incorrect because NIST CSF is known as the U.S. National Institute of Standards and Technology: Cybersecurity Framework.

46. Jeffrey is a CISO in an organization that performs financial services for private organizations as well as government agencies and U.S. federal agencies. Which is the best information security controls framework for this organization?

    A. CIS CSC

    B. ISO/IEC 27001

    C. NIST CSF

    D. NIST SP 800-53

☑ **D.** As a service provider for the U.S. federal government, Jeffrey's organization is required to adopt the NIST SP 800-53 controls framework.

☒ **A, B,** and **C** are incorrect. **A** is incorrect because, although CIS CSC (often referred to as just CIS controls) is a high-quality controls framework, service providers that perform information-related services to the U.S. federal government are required to adopt the NIST SP 800-53 controls framework. **B** is incorrect because, although ISO/IEC 27001 is a high-quality information security controls framework, it is not required for service providers that provide services to agencies of the U.S. federal government. **C** is incorrect because, although NIST CSF (Cybersecurity Framework) is a good methodology for building an information security program, it is not a controls framework.

47. What is the scope of requirements of PCI DSS?

   A. All systems that store, process, and transmit credit card numbers, as well as all other systems that can communicate with these systems

   B. All systems that store, process, and transmit credit card numbers

   C. All systems that store, process, and transmit unencrypted credit card numbers

   D. All systems in an organization where credit card numbers are stored, processed, and transmitted

   ☑ **A.** The systems that are in scope for PCI DSS are all those that store, process, or transmit credit card numbers, as well as all other systems that can communicate with those systems.

   ☒ **B, C,** and **D** are incorrect. **B** is incorrect because the scope of PCI DSS is not limited to just those systems that store, process, or transmit credit card numbers but also all other systems that can communicate with those systems. **C** is incorrect because the scope of PCI DSS includes those systems that store, process, or transmit credit card numbers, even if encrypted. **D** is incorrect because the scope of PCI DSS is not necessarily all systems in an organization where credit card numbers are stored, processed, or transmitted. If the organization has implemented effective network segmentation (that is, if systems that store, process, or transmit credit card numbers are isolated on subnets or VLANs where firewalls or ACLs have severely restricted communications to and from in-scope systems), then the systems not in the subnetworks or VLANs where credit card data resides are not in scope.

48. Which of the following statements is true about controls in the Payment Card Industry Data Security Standard?

   A. Many controls are required, while some are "addressable," or optional, based on risk.

   B. All controls are required, regardless of actual risk.

   C. Controls that are required are determined for each organization by the acquiring bank.

   D. In addition to core controls, each credit card brand has its own unique controls.

☑ **B.** All controls are required for all organizations. There are additional controls required for service providers.

☒ **A**, **C**, and **D** are incorrect. **A** is incorrect because no controls are optional. **C** is incorrect because acquiring banks do not make determinations of applicability of controls. **D** is incorrect because individual card brands do not impose additional controls. Individual card brands do, however, impose specific requirements for compliance reporting.

49. PCI DSS is an example of what?

    A. An industry regulation that is enforced with fines

    B. A private industry standard that is enforced with contracts

    C. A voluntary standard that, if used, can reduce cyber-insurance premiums

    D. An international law enforced through treaties with member nations

☑ **B.** PCI DSS was developed by a consortium of the major credit card brands in the world: Visa, MasterCard, American Express, Discover, and JCB. PCI DSS is enforced through credit card brands' operating rules, as well as by acquiring banks.

☒ **A**, **C**, and **D** are incorrect. **A** is incorrect because PCI DSS is not a law or regulation. **C** is incorrect because PCI DSS is not voluntary for merchants and service providers that store, process, or transmit credit card numbers. Compliance with PCI DSS may influence the cost of cyber-insurance premiums. **D** is incorrect because PCI DSS is not an international law.

50. Which of the following statements about control frameworks is correct?

    A. Control frameworks are used only in regulated environments.

    B. All control frameworks are essentially the same, with different control groups.

    C. It doesn't matter which control framework is selected, as long as controls are operated effectively.

    D. Different control frameworks are associated with different industries.

☑ **D.** Different control frameworks are indeed associated with different industries. For instance, PCI DSS controls are used in organizations that store, process, or transmit credit card information, and NIST 800-53 controls are used in U.S. federal government agencies and organizations that provide information services to those agencies.

☒ **A**, **B**, and **C** are incorrect. **A** is incorrect because control frameworks are used in both regulated and unregulated environments. For example, many larger software as a service (SaaS) organizations use the ISO/IEC 27002 or NIST 800-53 control framework. **B** is incorrect because control frameworks can be said to be similar, but not identical, even when accounting for differences in their structure. **C** is incorrect because different control frameworks do have their differences, which in some cases could be significant.

PART IV

Incident Management

Incident Management Readiness

This domain includes questions from the following topics:

- Similarities and differences between security incident response, business continuity planning, and disaster recovery planning
- Performing a business impact analysis and criticality analysis
- Developing business continuity and disaster recovery plans
- Classifying incidents
- Testing response plans and training personnel

This chapter covers Certified Information Security Manager (CISM) Domain 4, "Incident Management," part A, "Incident Management Readiness." The entire Incident Management domain represents 30 percent of the CISM examination.

Supporting Tasks in the CISM job practice that align with the Incident Management / Incident Management Readiness domain include:

29. Establish and maintain an incident response plan, in alignment with the business continuity plan and disaster recovery plan.

30. Establish and maintain an information security incident classification and categorization process.

31. Develop and implement processes to ensure the timely identification of information security incidents.

32. Establish and maintain processes to investigate and document information security incidents in accordance with legal and regulatory requirements.

33. Establish and maintain incident handling process, including containment, notification, escalation, eradication, and recovery.

34. Organize, train, equip, and assign responsibilities to incident response teams.

35. Establish and maintain incident communication plans and processes for internal and external parties.

36. Evaluate incident management plans through testing and review, including table-top exercises, checklist review, and simulation testing at planned intervals.

Our world is full of surprises, including events that disrupt our plans and activities. In the context of IT and business, several unexpected events can cause significant disruption to business operations, even to the point of threatening the ongoing viability of the organization itself. These events include

- Natural disasters
- Human-made disasters
- Malicious acts
- Cyberattacks
- Changes with unintended consequences

Organizations cannot, for the most part, *specifically* anticipate these events. Any of these events may inflict damage on information systems, office equipment, and work centers, making it necessary for the organization to act quickly to continue business operations using alternative means. In the case of a cyberattack, it may or may not be possible to reverse the effects of the attack, eradicate whatever harm was caused to information systems, and continue operations on those systems. But in some cases, it may be necessary for the organization to continue information processing on other systems until the primary systems can be expunged of their attacker and the damage that has been inflicted.

Incident management readiness begins with up-front analyses of business processes and their dependence upon business assets, including information systems. This analysis includes a big-picture prioritization of business processes and an up-close examination of business processes and information systems. This is followed by the development of contingency plans, response plans, and restoration plans. A natural by-product of all of this effort is improved resilience of business processes and information systems—even if disruptive events never occur—because overall weaknesses in processes and systems are identified, leading to steps to make tactical improvements.

1. Ravila, a new CISO in a healthcare organization, is reviewing incident response records from the past several years. Ravila has determined that minor incidents were managed with too much rigor and complexity, while major incidents weren't dealt with thoroughly enough. What might be the cause of this?

   A. Lack of training for incident responders

   B. Inconsistent levels of response to incidents

   C. Lack of a tiered incident response plan

   D. Improperly tuned SIEM use cases

2. Which of the following is *not* a valid objection for using incident response plan "templates" to serve as an organization's security incident response plan?

   A. The templates will lack the specifics about business processes and technology.

   B. The templates will lack the specific regulations the organization is required to comply with.

   C. The templates will lack the names of specific departments and executives.

   D. The templates will not specifically call on the organization's crisis response plan.

3. The purpose of documenting the steps taken during the response to an actual security incident includes all of the following *except* which one?

   A. Helps the organization understand how to respond more effectively during future incidents

   B. Helps the organization understand whether incident responders followed incident response procedures

   C. Helps the organization understand whether the organization recovered from the incident

   D. Helps the organization understand whether the incident response was compliant with applicable laws

4. Why should incident responders participate in incident response tabletop exercises?

   A. Helps incident responders better understand incident response procedures

   B. Helps incident responders find mistakes in incident response procedures

   C. Helps incident responders understand how long it should take to respond to actual incidents

   D. Helps incident responders memorize incident response procedures so they can respond more quickly

5. Why should incident responders be asked to review incident response procedures?

   A. Helps incident responders memorize incident response procedures so they can respond more quickly

   B. Helps incident responders understand how long it should take to respond to actual incidents

   C. Helps incident responders better understand incident response procedures

   D. Helps incident responders find mistakes in incident response procedures

6. James, the CISO in an organization, has reviewed the organization's incident response plans and disaster recovery plans and has determined that incident response plans do not include any provisions should a security incident occur during a declared disaster of the organization. What is James's most appropriate response?

   A. Declare a security incident.

   B. Request that the next tabletop exercise take place at the emergency operations center.

   C. No response is required because security incident response plans are not required for DR sites.

   D. Request that incident response and disaster recovery teams update the IRPs to include procedures during emergency operations mode.

7. Which step in an incident response plan is associated with tabletop exercises?

   A. Remediation

   B. Detection

   C. Analysis

   D. Planning

8. Of what value is a business impact analysis (BIA) in security incident response planning?

   A. Identifies the business owners associated with information systems and, therefore, the escalation path

   B. Identifies the systems that require forensic examination during an incident

   C. Indirectly identifies the most important information systems that require protection from threats

   D. Directly identifies the location of the most critical data

9. Threat analysts in an organization have identified a potential malware threat in an advisory. Detection in production systems will necessitate configuration changes to antivirus systems on production servers. What approach is best for making these configuration changes?

   A. Make the changes as soon as possible on production servers to stop the threat.

   B. Test the changes on nonproduction servers and measure performance impact.

C. Write a rule in intrusion detection systems to block the threat at the network layer.

D. Update antivirus signature files to permit detection of the threat.

10. Which methods are used to test security incident response plans?

   A. Document review, tabletop simulation, actual incident

   B. Document review, walkthrough, parallel test, cutover test

   C. Document review, walkthrough, tabletop simulation, parallel test, cutover test

   D. Document review, walkthrough, tabletop simulation

11. In the European General Data Protection Regulation, how quickly must an organization report a security breach of PII to government authorities?

   A. 72 hours

   B. 48 hours

   C. 24 hours

   D. 4 hours

12. Ravila, a new CISO in a healthcare organization, is reviewing incident response records from the past several years. Ravila has determined that minor incidents were managed inconsistently from one incident to the next. Staff turnover has not been an issue. What is the most likely cause of this?

   A. Insufficient capacity for storage of forensic evidence

   B. Excessive meddling by executive management

   C. Inattention to detail

   D. Lack of detailed incident response playbooks

13. Who are the best parties to develop an organization's security incident response plan?

   A. Business leaders and the general counsel

   B. Security consultants from an outside firm

   C. Internal security specialists and technology subject matter experts

   D. Regulators and security incident response subject matter experts

14. Which sequence correctly identifies the steps in security incident response?

   A. Detection, analysis, containment, eradication, recovery, closure

   B. Analysis, containment, eradication, recovery, closure

   C. Detection, containment, closure, recovery

   D. Detection, analysis, eradication, closure, recovery

15. Designated incident responders would be asked to attend planned incident tabletop exercises for all reasons *except* which one?

    A. Tabletop exercises serve as training for incident responders.

    B. Tabletop exercises are important for estimating the amount of time required to respond to security incidents.

    C. Tabletop exercises help incident responders become familiar with incident response procedures.

    D. Tabletop exercises help identify errors in incident response procedures.

16. What is the best time frequency for conducting tabletop exercises?

    A. When significant changes are made to the incident response plan

    B. Annually

    C. Annually, or when there are significant changes to the incident response plan

    D. Upon inception of the initial incident response plan

17. Incident responders have been asked to review a newly developed incident response plan. Incident responders' feedback suggests confusion regarding what is expected from them and others in the organization during an actual incident. What is the most likely cause of this?

    A. The incident response plan lacks definitions of roles and responsibilities.

    B. The incident response plan lacks a list of key contacts.

    C. The incident responders have not yet been trained in the use of the plan.

    D. Outsourced forensics services have not yet been defined.

18. A multinational organization that is developing its security incident response plan has created its matrix of severity levels based upon data sensitivity, operational criticality, and data location. Why is this severity level scheme feasible or infeasible?

    A. The scheme is feasible because it identifies basic characteristics of its data sets.

    B. The scheme is feasible because of its simplicity.

    C. The scheme is not feasible because of its complexity.

    D. The scheme is not feasible because it is not mapped to business functions.

19. What is the main purpose for including an escalation process in an incident response plan?

    A. Legal is notified only if regulators are required to be notified.

    B. Executives are notified only if the incident is severe enough to warrant their involvement.

    C. Legal is notified only if affected parties need to be notified.

    D. It provides an additional set of resources to help the incident response team.

20. The entirety of a service provider contract on incident response states, "Customer is to be notified within 48 hours of a suspected breach." Why is this statement sufficient or insufficient?

  A. The statement is insufficient because "suspected breach" is ambiguous.

  B. The statement is insufficient because 48 hours is too long an interval.

  C. The statement is sufficient because 48 hours is considered reasonable.

  D. The statement is sufficient because "suspected breach" is a well-known industry term.

21. An organization has successfully completed training and walkthroughs of its incident response plan. What is the next best step?

  A. Repeat training at regular intervals.

  B. Conduct one or more tabletop exercises.

  C. Wait for an actual incident to prove the effectiveness of training and walkthroughs.

  D. Conduct a penetration test of production systems to measure response.

22. In a business-to-business service provider contract, which language is most reasonable for notification of a security incident?

  A. Notify customer within 1 hour of a breach

  B. Notify customer within 48 hours of a suspected breach

  C. Notify customer immediately after a breach

  D. Notify customer within 48 hours of a breach

23. Under what circumstances would a security incident be accompanied by the triggering of a disaster recovery plan?

  A. When the RPO has been exceeded

  B. When the IRP calls out the DRP

  C. When the security incident renders the system unusable

  D. When a disaster has also occurred

24. A network operations analyst has noticed a sharp increase in inbound traffic at the organization's main edge router, to the extent that legitimate traffic can no longer be processed. What has the organization experienced?

  A. Denial-of-service attack

  B. Zero-day malware outbreak

  C. Distributed denial-of-service attack

  D. Configuration error

25. An attacker has launched a Smurf attack against an organization's web server, rendering it incapacitated. What kind of an attack is this?

   A. SYN flood

   B. Ransomware attack

   C. Denial-of-service attack

   D. Distributed denial-of-service attack

26. Which of the following is the best description of the kill chain?

   A. A teaching tool that helps people understand a cyberattack

   B. A model that depicts a typical attack scenario

   C. A method used by wiper malware

   D. A method used by malware droppers

27. When is the best time to develop an incident response plan?

   A. At the start of the next budget cycle

   B. As soon as possible

   C. When an attack is suspected

   D. When an attack is confirmed

28. When is the best time to declare a security incident?

   A. At the start of the next budget cycle

   B. As soon as possible

   C. When an attack is suspected

   D. When an attack is confirmed

29. Organizations should outsource security incident response for all of the following reasons, except:

   A. Difficulty justifying the hire of qualified incident responders

   B. Difficulty estimating the likelihood or impact of incidents

   C. Difficulty affording the compensation for incident responders

   D. Difficulty justifying the hire of workers with specialized skills

30. What is the best method for a new security leader to examine an organization's security incident response plan?

   A. Hire an external auditor to examine the plan

   B. Interview incident responders and solicit their opinion

   C. Conduct a walkthrough and measure the results

   D. Perform a gap analysis to compare the existing plan with the ideal plan

31. What criteria should be used to select the types of incidents chosen for playbook development?

   A. High-impact incidents least likely to occur

   B. High-impact incidents most likely to occur

   C. Incidents in scope of applicable regulations

   D. Incidents that receive the most publicity

32. An organization is conducting a study to identify its most critical business processes. What is this study commonly known as?

   A. Business impact analysis

   B. Enterprise risk assessment

   C. Vulnerability assessment

   D. Enterprise gap assessment

33. "Accounts payable and accounts receivable functions will be unable to process, impacting the availability of services and supplies and resulting in reduced revenue" is an example of which of the following?

   A. An SLA

   B. A consequence

   C. A statement of criticality

   D. A statement of impact

34. What is the purpose of a criticality analysis?

   A. A study of the vulnerabilities of a system or process

   B. A study of the impact of the incapacitation of a system or process

   C. A statement describing the consequences of the loss of a system or process

   D. A study of the dependencies of a system or process

35. Which of the following is the best definition of maximum tolerable downtime?

   A. The time since disaster onset in which the organization's survival is at risk

   B. The time in which the organization is required to disclose a breach

   C. The time since disaster onset in which the organization must recover

   D. The time in which an organization initiates a disaster recovery plan

36. Which of the following best describes the metric maximum tolerable outage?

   A. The dwell time between the onset and the declaration of a disaster

   B. The theoretical period of time since the onset of a disaster in which the organization's survival is at risk

   C. The longest that an organization can operate in emergency operations mode

   D. The greatest allowable loss of data in a disaster or breach scenario

37. Which of the following is the best description of the greatest amount of acceptable data loss in a disaster scenario?

    A. Recovery time objective

    B. Recovery point objective

    C. Service delivery objective

    D. Maximum tolerable downtime

38. Which position is responsible for determining RPO and RTO recovery targets?

    A. Business continuity planner

    B. Disaster recovery planner

    C. IT architect

    D. Business unit leader

39. Disaster recovery planners and management have agreed that the acceptable throughput of a system in emergency operations mode can be one-half of the capacity of the primary system. This is expressed as:

    A. Recovery capacity objective

    B. Recovery point objective

    C. Service delivery objective

    D. Recovery time objective

40. For a given cost level, a disaster recovery planner has determined that the best achievable RTO for a system is 12 hours, even though management has set the RTO at 4 hours. What is the disaster recovery planner's next step?

    A. Inform management that the desired RTO can be met within budget.

    B. Change the RTO from 12 hours to 4 hours.

    C. Change the RTO from 4 hours to 12 hours.

    D. Inform management that the desired RTO cannot be achieved within budget.

41. The architecture of an alternate processing system to be used in the event of a disaster is best determined by:

    A. Management

    B. BC planners

    C. DR planners

    D. IT architects

42. For disaster recovery purposes, why is book value *not* a preferred method for determining the value of assets?

   A. Information assets have no book value.

   B. Book value may vary based on location if a recovery site is located elsewhere.

   C. Some assets may not be tracked for depreciation.

   D. The cost to replace damaged or destroyed assets could exceed book value.

43. For disaster recovery scenarios, which of the following methods for setting the value of computer equipment is most appropriate?

   A. Recovery cost

   B. Replacement cost

   C. Lost revenue

   D. Book value

44. How are security requirements integrated into disaster recovery plans?

   A. Security requirements and controls are a part of the foundation of DR plans and capabilities.

   B. Management selects the most important security controls and requirements to be a part of DR.

   C. The purpose of DR is different from cybersecurity and the two are not related.

   D. Only those controls required by law are a part of DR plans and capabilities.

45. What is the best approach to the development of an organization's security incident response plan?

   A. Developing separate security incident recordkeeping

   B. Developing a general IR plan and leaving the details to subject matter experts

   C. Developing detailed playbooks and relying on the organization's crisis management plan

   D. Leveraging the organization's crisis management plan

1. C	16. C	31. B
2. B	17. A	32. A
3. C	18. A	33. D
4. A	19. B	34. B
5. D	20. A	35. A
6. D	21. B	36. C
7. D	22. D	37. B
8. C	23. C	38. D
9. B	24. A	39. A
10. D	25. D	40. D
11. A	26. B	41. D
12. D	27. B	42. D
13. C	28. C	43. B
14. A	29. B	44. A
15. B	30. D	45. D

1. Ravila, a new CISO in a healthcare organization, is reviewing incident response records from the past several years. Ravila has determined that minor incidents were managed with too much rigor and complexity, while major incidents weren't dealt with thoroughly enough. What might be the cause of this?

   A. Lack of training for incident responders

   B. Inconsistent levels of response to incidents

   C. Lack of a tiered incident response plan

   D. Improperly tuned SIEM use cases

   ☑ **C.** This organization has an incident response plan that has one path of response for incidents of all severities. The result is this: incidents of high severity are treated too lightly, and incidents of low severity are treated with too much rigor.

   ☒ **A**, **B**, and **D** are incorrect. **A** is incorrect because lack of training would more likely result in response to all incidents being subpar. **B** is incorrect because this is another way of describing the question rather than a description of its cause. **D** is incorrect because security information and event management system (SIEM) use case tuning would not likely cause this phenomenon.

2. Which of the following is *not* a valid objection for using incident response plan "templates" to serve as an organization's security incident response plan?

   A. The templates will lack the specifics about business processes and technology.

   B. The templates will lack the specific regulations the organization is required to comply with.

   C. The templates will lack the names of specific departments and executives.

   D. The templates will not specifically call on the organization's crisis response plan.

   ☑ **B.** This objection, that the templates will lack the names of specific regulations that the organization is obligated to comply with, is the weakest objection to the use of templates and is therefore the correct answer.

   ☒ **A**, **C**, and **D** are incorrect. **A** is incorrect because the lack of specifics about business processes and technologies in use is a valid objection to the use of a template. It is critical that an incident response plan be very specific about existing business processes so that the steps in an incident response plan will properly call out existing processes in the steps to respond to a security incident. Similarly, it is critical that an incident response plan has specific information about the technologies in use, as incident response plan steps will often direct responders to utilize technology in place for troubleshooting, isolation, and mitigation. **C** is incorrect because the lack of specific names of departments and executives is a valid objection to the use of such a template. The names of specific departments are needed, so that incident responders understand which departments to work with during various stages of incident response. The names of executives are also useful, as executives do need to be informed about an incident in progress. **D** is incorrect because the lack of specific references to an organization's crisis response plan is a valid objection to such a template. A security incident response plan certainly needs to call out the organization's crisis response plan, as a highly severe security incident may need to trigger an organization's crisis response plan.

3. The purpose of documenting the steps taken during the response to an actual security incident includes all of the following *except* which one?

   A. Helps the organization understand how to respond more effectively during future incidents

   B. Helps the organization understand whether incident responders followed incident response procedures

   C. Helps the organization understand whether the organization recovered from the incident

   D. Helps the organization understand whether the incident response was compliant with applicable laws

   ☑ **C.** Documenting the steps followed during the response to an actual incident does little to help the organization understand whether it actually recovered from the incident. Key personnel in the organization will know whether recovery was complete and successful and whether response steps were recorded or not.

   ☒ **A**, **B**, and **D** are incorrect. **A** is incorrect because documentation of the steps taken during the response to an actual incident does help the organization understand how to respond more effectively during future incidents. **B** is incorrect because documentation of the steps taken during the response to an actual incident does help the organization understand whether incident responders followed incident response procedures. **D** is incorrect because knowing what steps were taken during an actual incident does help the organization understand whether the incident responders' actions were compliant with applicable laws—for instance, whether evidence was properly collected and protected and whether appropriate parties were notified.

4. Why should incident responders participate in incident response tabletop exercises?

   A. Helps incident responders better understand incident response procedures

   B. Helps incident responders find mistakes in incident response procedures

   C. Helps incident responders understand how long it should take to respond to actual incidents

   D. Helps incident responders memorize incident response procedures so they can respond more quickly

   ☑ **A.** Participation in incident response tabletop exercises helps incident responders become more familiar with incident response procedures. Talking through a simulated incident and thinking about each step in incident response helps responders better understand each step—how to perform it and why it is needed.

☒ **B**, **C**, and **D** are incorrect. **B** is incorrect because the identification of mistakes is not the primary purpose of an incident response tabletop exercise, although it does sometimes occur. **C** is incorrect because knowing the length of time required to respond to an incident is not a primary purpose of tabletop exercises. **D** is incorrect because memorization of response procedures is not an objective of tabletop exercises.

5. Why should incident responders be asked to review incident response procedures?

A. Helps incident responders memorize incident response procedures so they can respond more quickly

B. Helps incident responders understand how long it should take to respond to actual incidents

C. Helps incident responders better understand incident response procedures

D. Helps incident responders find mistakes in incident response procedures

☑ **D.** A primary purpose of incident response plan document review is to identify errors in response plans so that they can be corrected prior to an actual incident occurring.

☒ **A**, **B**, and **C** are incorrect. **A** is incorrect because memorization of response procedures is not an objective of a document review of an incident response plan. **B** is incorrect because gaining an understanding of the length of time required to respond to an incident is not an objective of a review of incident response documents. **C** is incorrect because the primary objective of a document review is not to help incident responders be more familiar with incident response procedures. That said, improved familiarity is a valuable by-product of such a review.

6. James, the CISO in an organization, has reviewed the organization's incident response plans and disaster recovery plans and has determined that incident response plans do not include any provisions should a security incident occur during a declared disaster of the organization. What is James's most appropriate response?

A. Declare a security incident.

B. Request that the next tabletop exercise take place at the emergency operations center.

C. No response is required because security incident response plans are not required for DR sites.

D. Request that incident response and disaster recovery teams update the IRPs to include procedures during emergency operations mode.

☑ **D.** The organization's incident response plan needs to be updated to include procedures, contact information, and other relevant information to assist incident responders to respond to a security incident properly should one occur while the organization is in emergency operations mode.

☒ **A**, **B**, and **C** are incorrect. **A** is incorrect because the declaration of an incident is inappropriate; there is no incident happening here. **B** is incorrect because a tabletop exercise in the context of an emergency operations center, while potentially valuable, will be at least somewhat ineffective because there are no security incident response procedures to be followed should a security incident occur while in emergency operations mode. **C** is incorrect because security incidents certainly must be declared should an incident occur at a disaster recovery site.

7. Which step in an incident response plan is associated with tabletop exercises?

    A. Remediation

    B. Detection

    C. Analysis

    D. Planning

    ☑ **D.** Security incident response tabletop exercises are a part of planning. The actual exercise itself will include most of the steps of an actual incident so that responders will be more familiar with response procedures.

    ☒ **A, B,** and **C** are incorrect. Tabletop exercises are not limited to remediation, detection, or analysis, but are concerned with the entire life cycle of incident response.

8. Of what value is a business impact analysis (BIA) in security incident response planning?

    A. Identifies the business owners associated with information systems and, therefore, the escalation path

    B. Identifies the systems that require forensic examination during an incident

    C. Indirectly identifies the most important information systems that require protection from threats

    D. Directly identifies the location of the most critical data

    ☑ **C.** The BIA is a discovery and analysis activity that identifies the most critical business processes in an organization. The BIA also identifies information systems, service providers, and suppliers that support those business processes. In information security and security incident response, the BIA helps to identify an organization's most important information systems.

    ☒ **A, B,** and **D** are incorrect. **A** is incorrect because the identification of business owners is a secondary benefit from the BIA. **B** is incorrect because the BIA does not determine the need for forensic examination. **D** is incorrect because the location of critical data is a by-product of the BIA, but is not necessarily critical for incident response.

9. Threat analysts in an organization have identified a potential malware threat in an advisory. Detection in production systems will necessitate configuration changes to antivirus systems on production servers. What approach is best for making these configuration changes?

    A. Make the changes as soon as possible on production servers to stop the threat.

    B. Test the changes on nonproduction servers and measure performance impact.

C. Write a rule in intrusion detection systems to block the threat at the network layer.

D. Update antivirus signature files to permit detection of the threat.

☑ **B.** Testing configuration changes in a nonproduction environment is the best first step to ensure that the configuration changes will not adversely affect production systems, both in terms of transaction capacity and correct function.

☒ **A**, **C**, and **D** are incorrect. **A** is incorrect because there may be unintended consequences to the configuration changes that may affect server availability. **C** is incorrect because intrusion detection systems cannot block intrusions. **D** is incorrect because threat analysts have already determined that configuration changes are necessary (perhaps activating real-time file access detection that might be normally turned off).

10. Which methods are used to test security incident response plans?

A. Document review, tabletop simulation, actual incident

B. Document review, walkthrough, parallel test, cutover test

C. Document review, walkthrough, tabletop simulation, parallel test, cutover test

D. Document review, walkthrough, tabletop simulation

☑ **D.** The types of tests that can be performed for security incident response are document review (where one or more individuals review the document on their own), walkthrough (where two or more individuals discuss the steps in the security incident response procedure), and tabletop simulation (where an expert moderator progressively reveals a realistic security incident scenario, and incident responders and others discuss their response activities and the challenges encountered).

☒ **A**, **B**, and **C** are incorrect. **A** is incorrect because an actual incident is not considered a purposeful test of an incident response plan. **B** and **C** are incorrect because a parallel test and cutover test are used in disaster recovery planning.

11. In the European General Data Protection Regulation, how quickly must an organization report a security breach of PII to government authorities?

A. 72 hours

B. 48 hours

C. 24 hours

D. 4 hours

☑ **A.** The European GDPR requires that organizations report breaches of personally identifiable information (PII) to authorities within 72 hours. If the organization takes more than 72 hours to notify authorities, an explanation for the delay must accompany the notification.

☒ **B**, **C**, and **D** are incorrect. All are incorrect because organizations are required to notify authorities of a PII breach within 72 hours, not 48, 24, or 4 hours.

12. Ravila, a new CISO in a healthcare organization, is reviewing incident response records from the past several years. Ravila has determined that minor incidents were managed inconsistently from one incident to the next. Staff turnover has not been an issue. What is the most likely cause of this?

    A. Insufficient capacity for storage of forensic evidence

    B. Excessive meddling by executive management

    C. Inattention to detail

    D. Lack of detailed incident response playbooks

    ☑ **D.** Of the available choices, the most likely cause of inconsistent response to security incidents is the lack of detailed procedural documentation in the organization's security incident response plan. These detailed procedures are commonly known as playbooks.

    ☒ **A**, **B**, and **C** are incorrect. **A** is incorrect because insufficient storage capacity for forensic evidence is not a likely cause of inconsistent responses to incidents. **B** is incorrect because meddling by executives is not a likely cause for an inconsistent response. **C** is incorrect because inattention to detail is not the most likely cause.

13. Who are the best parties to develop an organization's security incident response plan?

    A. Business leaders and the general counsel

    B. Security consultants from an outside firm

    C. Internal security specialists and technology subject matter experts

    D. Regulators and security incident response subject matter experts

    ☑ **C.** The best parties to develop a security incident response plan are internal security specialists and experts in relevant information technology.

    ☒ **A**, **B**, and **D** are incorrect. **A** is incorrect because business leaders and general counsel, though essential personnel to participate in the response to a breach, are not the best parties to develop an organization's security incident response plan. **B** is incorrect because, although outside experts may be qualified to write a general-purpose plan, those consultants won't be familiar with the organization's business processes and uses of information technology. **D** is incorrect because regulators do not develop security incident response plans for organizations they regulate.

14. Which sequence correctly identifies the steps in security incident response?

    A. Detection, analysis, containment, eradication, recovery, closure

    B. Analysis, containment, eradication, recovery, closure

    C. Detection, containment, closure, recovery

    D. Detection, analysis, eradication, closure, recovery

    ☑ **A.** Of the choices available here, the correct sequence of steps in security incident response is detection, analysis, containment, eradication, recovery, and closure.

☒ **B**, **C**, and **D** are incorrect. None of these represents the correct sequence of steps in security incident response.

15. Designated incident responders would be asked to attend planned incident tabletop exercises for all reasons *except* which one?

    A. Tabletop exercises serve as training for incident responders.

    B. Tabletop exercises are important for estimating the amount of time required to respond to security incidents.

    C. Tabletop exercises help incident responders become familiar with incident response procedures.

    D. Tabletop exercises help identify errors in incident response procedures.

    ☑ **B**. Tabletop exercises are generally not a suitable opportunity to determine the length of time to respond to an incident. Rather, incident response tabletop exercises are designed to help incident responders become more familiar with incident response procedures.

    ☒ **A**, **C**, and **D** are incorrect. These are all valid reasons for asking incident responders to attend tabletop exercises.

16. What is the best time frequency for conducting tabletop exercises?

    A. When significant changes are made to the incident response plan

    B. Annually

    C. Annually, or when there are significant changes to the incident response plan

    D. Upon inception of the initial incident response plan

    ☑ **C**. Incident response tabletop exercises should be performed at least annually, as well as when significant changes are made to incident response plans. The hiring of new incident responders would present another opportunity to conduct tabletop exercises.

    ☒ **A**, **B**, and **D** are incorrect. **A** is incorrect because tabletop exercises should be conducted at least annually. If no changes are made to the incident response plan, significant time could elapse between exercises. **B** is incorrect because annual tabletop exercises are insufficient if significant changes are made to the security incident response plan. **D** is incorrect because an incident response plan should be exercised at least annually and when significant changes are made to the plan.

17. Incident responders have been asked to review a newly developed incident response plan. Incident responders' feedback suggests confusion regarding what is expected from them and others in the organization during an actual incident. What is the most likely cause of this?

    A. The incident response plan lacks definitions of roles and responsibilities.

    B. The incident response plan lacks a list of key contacts.

    C. The incident responders have not yet been trained in the use of the plan.

    D. Outsourced forensics services have not yet been defined.

☑ **A.** The incident responders are confused because roles and responsibilities are undefined. This is a critical deficiency in an IRP because there will be confusion when important decisions need to be made, including the declaration of an incident, escalation, and notification of regulators, affected parties, and law enforcement.

☒ **B, C,** and **D** are incorrect. **B** is incorrect because the absence of key contacts is not likely to produce this type of confusion. **C** is incorrect because the lack of training is unlikely to result in incident responders not knowing who is responsible for carrying out specific activities during an incident. **D** is incorrect because the absence of a forensic analysis firm is not likely to produce this apparently wider confusion.

18. A multinational organization that is developing its security incident response plan has created its matrix of severity levels based upon data sensitivity, operational criticality, and data location. Why is this severity level scheme feasible or infeasible?

    A. The scheme is feasible because it identifies basic characteristics of its data sets.

    B. The scheme is feasible because of its simplicity.

    C. The scheme is not feasible because of its complexity.

    D. The scheme is not feasible because it is not mapped to business functions.

    ☑ **A.** This scheme, while a bit complex, appears reasonable because it addresses the primary characteristics of data sets. The sensitivity of data is an indication of whether it is protected by regulation or private obligations; the operational criticality of data associates the data to revenue or organizational reputation; the location of data indicates local regulation or perhaps the identity of a local incident response team. Surely, simpler schemes are more common, but this is a multinational organization, which potentially introduces several operational complications.

    ☒ **B, C,** and **D** are incorrect. **B** is incorrect because this scheme is not as simple as most. **C** is incorrect because this scheme, while somewhat complex, can be workable. **D** is incorrect because there is insufficient information to reach this conclusion.

19. What is the main purpose for including an escalation process in an incident response plan?

    A. Legal is notified only if regulators are required to be notified.

    B. Executives are notified only if the incident is severe enough to warrant their involvement.

    C. Legal is notified only if affected parties need to be notified.

    D. It provides an additional set of resources to help the incident response team.

    ☑ **B.** The primary reason for escalation in an incident response plan is to provide a structured way for specific executives to be notified during a serious incident. A structured incident response plan will include incident severity levels that can be objectively identified; severity levels will have varying frequencies of communicated updates, named resources to assist, and executives to notify. Executives need to be aware of a serious incident because it is more likely to have long-term operational and reputational impacts on the organization.

☒ **A**, **C**, and **D** are incorrect. **A** and **C** are incorrect because notification of regulators, legal staff, and affected parties is but a narrow aspect of the need for escalation. **D** is incorrect because escalation, while it may indeed provide additional resources, is a function of the severity of the incident, not the desire for additional help.

20. The entirety of a service provider contract on incident response states, "Customer is to be notified within 48 hours of a suspected breach." Why is this statement sufficient or insufficient?

   A. The statement is insufficient because "suspected breach" is ambiguous.

   B. The statement is insufficient because 48 hours is too long an interval.

   C. The statement is sufficient because 48 hours is considered reasonable.

   D. The statement is sufficient because "suspected breach" is a well-known industry term.

   ☑ **A**. The term "suspected breach" is ambiguous and should be defined more specifically. Otherwise, it would be too easy for an organization to consider nearly every activity a "suspected breach."

   ☒ **B**, **C**, and **D** are incorrect. **B** is incorrect because 48 hours is a reasonable and standard interval for breach notification. **C** is incorrect because, even though 48 hours is a reasonable and standard interval for breach notification, the term "suspected breach" is ambiguous, so the statement is insufficient. **D** is incorrect because "suspected breach" is not a term that is interpreted consistently.

21. An organization has successfully completed training and walkthroughs of its incident response plan. What is the next best step?

   A. Repeat training at regular intervals.

   B. Conduct one or more tabletop exercises.

   C. Wait for an actual incident to prove the effectiveness of training and walkthroughs.

   D. Conduct a penetration test of production systems to measure response.

   ☑ **B**. After successfully completing the training of incident response personnel and a walkthrough of the incident response plan, the next activity that should take place is a tabletop exercise, which is a facilitated simulation of an actual incident to help the organization better understand whether its incident response plan is effective.

   ☒ **A**, **C**, and **D** are incorrect. **A** is incorrect because repeating training, while it may be useful, is not the next best step. **C** is incorrect because there are other preparatory activities that should take place, particularly tabletop exercises. **D** is incorrect because the main purpose of a penetration test is the identification of vulnerabilities, not a test of an organization's incident response capabilities.

22. In a business-to-business service provider contract, which language is most reasonable for notification of a security incident?

   A. Notify customer within 1 hour of a breach

   B. Notify customer within 48 hours of a suspected breach

C. Notify customer immediately after a breach

D. Notify customer within 48 hours of a breach

☑ **D.** Notification of a customer within 48 hours of a breach is the most reasonable language. The term "breach" will need to be clearly defined elsewhere in the contract.

☒ **A**, **B**, and **C** are incorrect. **A** is incorrect because notification within 1 hour is unreasonably fast for notification. **B** is incorrect because the term "suspected breach" is a potentially wide loophole. **C** is incorrect, as "immediately" is ambiguous and unreasonable.

23. Under what circumstances would a security incident be accompanied by the triggering of a disaster recovery plan?

A. When the RPO has been exceeded

B. When the IRP calls out the DRP

C. When the security incident renders the system unusable

D. When a disaster has also occurred

☑ **C.** A disaster recovery plan may need to be triggered after a security incident if one or more systems are incapacitated for any reason—whether that be damage by the intruder or the need to quiesce a system to permit a forensic analysis to be performed on it.

☒ **A**, **B**, and **D** are incorrect. **A** is incorrect because recovery targets such as the recovery point objective (RPO) are not used as triggers for disaster declaration. **B** is incorrect because the incident response plan (IRP) should reference a disaster recovery plan (DRP) to guide incident responders as they investigate a security incident. **D** is incorrect because it is not necessary for a separate disaster to occur to trigger a disaster recovery plan.

24. A network operations analyst has noticed a sharp increase in inbound traffic at the organization's main edge router, to the extent that legitimate traffic can no longer be processed. What has the organization experienced?

A. Denial-of-service attack

B. Zero-day malware outbreak

C. Distributed denial-of-service attack

D. Configuration error

☑ **A.** The organization has experienced a denial-of-service (DoS) attack, in which illegitimate traffic has rendered a system as incapacitated so that it can no longer perform its function.

☒ **B**, **C**, and **D** are incorrect. **B** is incorrect because the description does not indicate a zero-day malware attack. **C** is incorrect because the description does not indicate a distributed denial-of-service (DDoS) attack. **D** is incorrect because the description does not indicate a configuration error—although, indeed, a configuration error may have made the attack possible.

25. An attacker has launched a Smurf attack against an organization's web server, rendering it incapacitated. What kind of an attack is this?

  A. SYN flood

  B. Ransomware attack

  C. Denial-of-service attack

  D. Distributed denial-of-service attack

  ☑ **D.** A Smurf attack involves sending large numbers of ICMP packets to a target system.

  ☒ **A, B,** and **C** are incorrect. **A** is incorrect because a Smurf attack is not the same as a SYN flood. **B** is incorrect because a Smurf attack is a distributed denial-of-service attack, not a ransomware attack. **C** is incorrect because a Smurf attack is better characterized as a distributed denial-of-service attack rather than a denial-of-service attack.

26. Which of the following is the best description of the kill chain?

  A. A teaching tool that helps people understand a cyberattack

  B. A model that depicts a typical attack scenario

  C. A method used by wiper malware

  D. A method used by malware droppers

  ☑ **B.** In a general sense, a kill chain is a model that depicts a typical attack scenario, consisting of 1) target identification, 2) selection and deployment of forces, 3) attack on target, and 4) accomplishment of attack objective.

  ☒ **A, C,** and **D** are incorrect. **A** is incorrect because a kill chain is not merely a teaching tool, but a realistic model that depicts the stages of a typical attack. **C** and **D** are incorrect because the term "kill chain" does not signify any specific type of malware.

27. When is the best time to develop an incident response plan?

  A. At the start of the next budget cycle

  B. As soon as possible

  C. When an attack is suspected

  D. When an attack is confirmed

  ☑ **B.** An incident response plan should be developed as soon as possible, as it is nearly impossible to know when an attack is likely to occur. It is far better to be prepared than to be unprepared.

  ☒ **A, C,** and **D** are incorrect. **A** is incorrect because waiting for a future event to begin incident response plan development is unwise. **C** and **D** are incorrect because an incident response plan should be developed, tested, and used to train responders prior to an incident.

28. When is the best time to declare a security incident?

   A. At the start of the next budget cycle

   B. As soon as possible

   C. When an attack is suspected

   D. When an attack is confirmed

   ☑ **C.** A security incident should be declared when an attack is suspected, as this generally will trigger the initiation of investigative activities that may lead to confirmation of a breach.

   ☒ **A**, **B**, and **D** are incorrect. **A** and **B** are incorrect because a security incident should be declared as soon as one is known or suspected. **D** is incorrect because incident responders should not wait until the attack is confirmed to declare an incident.

29. Organizations should outsource security incident response for all of the following reasons, except:

   A. Difficulty justifying the hire of qualified incident responders

   B. Difficulty estimating the likelihood or impact of incidents

   C. Difficulty affording the compensation for incident responders

   D. Difficulty justifying the hire of workers with specialized skills

   ☑ **B.** Difficulty in estimating the likelihood or impact of an incident is not related to a decision to outsource security incident response.

   ☒ **A**, **C**, and **D** are incorrect. All are incorrect because they all are valid reasons for outsourcing security incident response.

30. What is the best method for a new security leader to examine an organization's security incident response plan?

   A. Hire an external auditor to examine the plan

   B. Interview incident responders and solicit their opinion

   C. Conduct a walkthrough and measure the results

   D. Perform a gap analysis to compare the existing plan with the ideal plan

   ☑ **D.** Performing a gap analysis is the best available choice. The security leader can compare the characteristics of the existing plan with those of an ideal plan.

   ☒ **A**, **B**, and **C** are incorrect. **A** is incorrect because it should not be necessary to pay an external audit firm to audit a plan. **B** is incorrect because incident responders may or may not be qualified to opine on the effectiveness of an incident response plan. **C** is incorrect because a walkthrough may or may not reveal improvement areas in an existing plan.

31. What criteria should be used to select the types of incidents chosen for playbook development?

   A. High-impact incidents least likely to occur

   B. High-impact incidents most likely to occur

   C. Incidents in scope of applicable regulations

   D. Incidents that receive the most publicity

   ☑ **B.** The best criteria for developing incident response playbooks are those high-impact incidents that are most likely to occur. Examples may include ransomware attacks, business e-mail compromise, and stolen login credentials.

   ☒ **A, C,** and **D** are incorrect. **A** is incorrect because high-impact incidents that are least likely to occur do not warrant the development of an incident response playbook. **C** is incorrect because the scope of regulations is not necessarily a primary driver for incident response playbook development. **D** is incorrect because publicity should not be a primary driver for selecting the types of incidents for playbook development.

32. An organization is conducting a study to identify its most critical business processes. What is this study commonly known as?

   A. Business impact analysis

   B. Enterprise risk assessment

   C. Vulnerability assessment

   D. Enterprise gap assessment

   ☑ **A.** The organization is undergoing a business impact analysis (BIA), used in business continuity planning to identify the most critical business processes.

   ☒ **B, C,** and **D** are incorrect. **B** is incorrect because the purpose of an enterprise risk assessment is to identify the most significant risks. **C** is incorrect because the purpose of a vulnerability assessment is to identify weaknesses in systems, business processes, or procedures. **D** is incorrect because a gap assessment is performed to identify the differences between the existing state of a system or process and a standard.

33. "Accounts payable and accounts receivable functions will be unable to process, impacting the availability of services and supplies and resulting in reduced revenue" is an example of which of the following?

   A. An SLA

   B. A consequence

   C. A statement of criticality

   D. A statement of impact

   ☑ **D.** This is a statement of impact that is a part of a business impact assessment (BIA). A statement of impact describes the consequence of the loss of a critical asset in business terms.

☒ **A**, **B**, and **C** are incorrect. **A** is incorrect because this statement is not a service level agreement (SLA). **B** is incorrect because, although this statement describes a consequence, this is not the best answer. **C** is incorrect because this is not a statement of criticality.

34. What is the purpose of a criticality analysis?

    A. A study of the vulnerabilities of a system or process

    B. A study of the impact of the incapacitation of a system or process

    C. A statement describing the consequences of the loss of a system or process

    D. A study of the dependencies of a system or process

    ☑ **B**. A criticality analysis is a specialized risk assessment, focused on a particular system or process, to understand threats and vulnerabilities in the context of business continuity and disaster recovery planning.

    ☒ **A**, **C**, and **D** are incorrect. **A** is incorrect because a criticality analysis includes, but is not limited to, a study of the vulnerabilities of a system or process. **C** is incorrect because a statement of the consequences of the failure of a process or asset is known as a Statement of Impact. **D** is incorrect because a study of the dependencies of a system or process is a part of a Business Impact Assessment.

35. Which of the following is the best definition of maximum tolerable downtime?

    A. The time since disaster onset in which the organization's survival is at risk

    B. The time in which the organization is required to disclose a breach

    C. The time since disaster onset in which the organization must recover

    D. The time in which an organization initiates a disaster recovery plan

    ☑ **A**. Maximum tolerable downtime (MTD), also known as acceptable interruption window (AIW), is the theoretical period of time since the onset of a disaster in which the organization's survival is at risk.

    ☒ **B**, **C**, and **D** are incorrect. **B** is incorrect because MTD is not related to breach disclosure. **C** is incorrect because MTD is not a measure of recovery. **D** is incorrect because MTD is not a measure of initiation of a disaster recovery plan.

36. Which of the following best describes the metric maximum tolerable outage?

    A. The dwell time between the onset and the declaration of a disaster

    B. The theoretical period of time since the onset of a disaster in which the organization's survival is at risk

    C. The longest that an organization can operate in emergency operations mode

    D. The greatest allowable loss of data in a disaster or breach scenario

☑ **C.** Maximum tolerable outage, or MTO, is the longest period of time that an organization can operate in emergency operations mode, otherwise known as disaster recovery mode. MTO drives the need to reestablish normal production operations within a specific period of time.

☒ **A**, **B**, and **D** are incorrect. **A** is incorrect because MTO is not a measure of dwell time between disaster onset and declaration. **B** is incorrect because this definition is known as maximum tolerable downtime (MTD). **D** is incorrect because the maximum data loss is known as recovery point objective, or RPO.

37. Which of the following is the best description of the greatest amount of acceptable data loss in a disaster scenario?

    A. Recovery time objective

    B. Recovery point objective

    C. Service delivery objective

    D. Maximum tolerable downtime

☑ **B.** The recovery point objective, or RPO, is the maximum data loss from the onset of a disaster.

☒ **A**, **C**, and **D** are incorrect. **A** is incorrect because the recovery time objective (RTO) is a measure of time from the onset of a disaster until the resumption of service. **C** is incorrect because the service delivery objective (SDO) is a measure of the level of quality of an alternate process or system. **D** is incorrect because maximum tolerable downtime (MTD) is the theoretical time from disaster onset that an organization's survival is at risk.

38. Which position is responsible for determining RPO and RTO recovery targets?

    A. Business continuity planner

    B. Disaster recovery planner

    C. IT architect

    D. Business unit leader

☑ **D.** The establishment of recovery targets, including recovery point objective (RPO) and recovery time objective (RTO), is performed by the business unit leader or department head responsible for the operations of key business processes.

☒ **A**, **B**, and **C** are incorrect. **A** is incorrect because business continuity planners do not set RTO and RPO targets. **B** is incorrect because disaster recovery planners do not set RTO and RPO targets. **C** is incorrect because IT architects do not set RTO and RPO targets.

39. Disaster recovery planners and management have agreed that the acceptable throughput of a system in emergency operations mode can be one-half of the capacity of the primary system. This is expressed as:

A. Recovery capacity objective

B. Recovery point objective

C. Service delivery objective

D. Recovery time objective

☑ **A.** The measure of transaction throughput for a recovery system is expressed by the recovery capacity objective (RCapO).

☒ **B, C,** and **D** are incorrect. **B** is incorrect because the recovery point objective (RPO) is a measure of maximum data loss in a disaster scenario. **C** is incorrect because the service delivery objective (SDO) is a measure of quality of service of a recovery system. **D** is incorrect because the recovery time objective (RTO) is a measure of the time from disaster onset until a recovery system has resumed service.

40. For a given cost level, a disaster recovery planner has determined that the best achievable RTO for a system is 12 hours, even though management has set the RTO at 4 hours. What is the disaster recovery planner's next step?

A. Inform management that the desired RTO can be met within budget.

B. Change the RTO from 12 hours to 4 hours.

C. Change the RTO from 4 hours to 12 hours.

D. Inform management that the desired RTO cannot be achieved within budget.

☑ **D.** A DR planner needs to inform management when desired recovery targets cannot be met with the resources provided. Management will need to either change the RTO to a larger figure or provide additional resources so that the RTO can be met.

☒ **A, B,** and **C** are incorrect. **A** is incorrect because the scenario states that the RTO cannot be met. **B** and **C** are incorrect because the DR planner should not be changing recovery targets.

41. The architecture of an alternate processing system to be used in the event of a disaster is best determined by:

A. Management

B. BC planners

C. DR planners

D. IT architects

☑ **D.** When recovery targets, including RPO and RTO, have been established by management, the architecture of an alternate processing system should be developed by IT architects.

☒ **A**, **B**, and **C** are incorrect. **A** is incorrect because management should not be determining the architecture of an alternate processing system, although management does specify recovery targets that will influence that architecture. **B** and **C** are incorrect because BC and DR planners are not the best parties to develop the architecture of an alternate processing system.

42. For disaster recovery purposes, why is book value *not* a preferred method for determining the value of assets?

    A. Information assets have no book value.

    B. Book value may vary based on location if a recovery site is located elsewhere.

    C. Some assets may not be tracked for depreciation.

    D. The cost to replace damaged or destroyed assets could exceed book value.

    ☑ **D.** For disaster recovery purposes, organizations should use replacement or redeployment cost versus book value for asset value. If assets are damaged or destroyed in a disaster, they must be replaced; costs for replacements may be much higher than book value.

    ☒ **A**, **B**, and **C** are incorrect. **A** is incorrect because this question is not specifically about information assets. **B** is incorrect because this is not a true statement. **C** is incorrect because this statement is not relevant.

43. For disaster recovery scenarios, which of the following methods for setting the value of computer equipment is most appropriate?

    A. Recovery cost

    B. Replacement cost

    C. Lost revenue

    D. Book value

    ☑ **B.** Replacement cost may be best suited for disaster recovery scenarios. In a disaster situation, computer equipment may need to be replaced rather than repaired.

    ☒ **A**, **C**, and **D** are incorrect. **A** is incorrect because recovery cost is not usually associated with computer equipment, but instead with information. **C** is incorrect because this is not the best method. If in cases where revenue derived from computer equipment is greater than its replacement value, this would underscore the need for rapid replacement or use of an alternative processing center. **D** is incorrect because it may be difficult to replace lost assets if only book value is available to obtain replacements.

44. How are security requirements integrated into disaster recovery plans?

    A. Security requirements and controls are a part of the foundation of DR plans and capabilities.

    B. Management selects the most important security controls and requirements to be a part of DR.

C. The purpose of DR is different from cybersecurity and the two are not related.

D. Only those controls required by law are a part of DR plans and capabilities.

☑ **A.** All of an organization's security policies, requirements, and controls apply equally to all environments, whether they are normal production environments or disaster recovery environments. At any time, an organization may be compelled to shift its processing from its primary processing facilities to a disaster recovery processing facility, making the DR facility the new (but usually temporary) primary facility. All controls for security and privacy apply to all systems in all locations.

☒ **B, C,** and **D** are incorrect. **B** is incorrect because security requirements and controls cannot be "cherry picked" to be included in DR sites based on management's wishes. Instead, all requirements and controls apply to all information processing facilities, whether they are primary or recovery facilities. **C** is incorrect because security requirements and controls apply to all information processing facilities, whether they are primary or recovery facilities. **D** is incorrect because an organization may have requirements and controls in addition to those required by law that should be applicable to all information processing facilities.

45. What is the best approach to the development of an organization's security incident response plan?

A. Developing separate security incident recordkeeping

B. Developing a general IR plan and leaving the details to subject matter experts

C. Developing detailed playbooks and relying on the organization's crisis management plan

D. Leveraging the organization's crisis management plan

☑ **D.** The best approach for developing any IR plan is to leverage existing processes wherever possible, including the corporate crisis management plan, an IT incident response plan, and emergency communications plans. Leveraging existing processes is more effective than building separate parallel processes.

☒ **A, B,** and **C** are incorrect. **A** is incorrect because existing incident recordkeeping should be leveraged instead of building a separate record. **B** is incorrect because detailed IR playbooks should also be developed so that SMEs understand what steps to take for various incident scenarios. **C** is incorrect because an overall IR plan is needed, even when there are detailed IR playbooks and a crisis management plan.

Incident Management Operations

This domain includes questions from the following topics:

- The steps involved in security incident response
- Incident response tools and techniques
- Attorney-client privilege
- Crisis management and communications
- Post-incident review and reporting

This chapter covers Certified Information Security Manager (CISM) Domain 4, "Incident Management," part B, "Incident Management Operations." The entire Incident Management domain represents 30 percent of the CISM examination.

One Supporting Task in the CISM job practice aligns with the Incident Management / Incident Management Operations domain:

37. Conduct post-incident reviews to facilitate continuous improvement, including root-cause analysis, lessons learned, corrective actions, and reassessment of risk.

Security incidents cannot be prevented—at least not all of them. In this asymmetric cyber war, attackers have innovation, time, and the element of surprise on their side. It is imperative that every organization using technology needs to develop formal security incident response plans, train their personnel, and continually practice with walk-throughs, drills, and simulations.

1. Why would an organization consider developing alerts on its security information and event management system, as opposed to using its existing daily log review procedure?

   A. More accurate and timely awareness of security issues requiring action

   B. Compliance with PCI DSS 3.2 requirement 10.6

   C. Reduce costs associated with time-consuming log review

   D. Free up staff to perform more challenging and interesting tasks

2. While responding to a security incident, the person acting as the incident commander is unable to notify a particular executive in an escalation procedure. What should the incident responder do next?

   A. Notify regulators that the organization is experiencing a cyber incident and requires assistance.

   B. Notify law enforcement that the organization is experiencing a cyber incident and requires assistance.

   C. Order incident responders to suspend their activities until the executive has been contacted.

   D. Notify the next highest executive in the escalation chain.

3. Why would PCI DSS requirements require organizations to put emergency contact information for payment card brands in their incident response plans?

   A. An emergency is a poor time to start looking for emergency contact information for outside organizations.

   B. Card brands must be notified of an incident involving card data as soon as possible.

   C. Requirement 12.10 in PCI DSS requires it.

   D. It reminds organizations to notify the card brands in the event of a breach.

4. The purpose of a post-incident review of a security incident includes all of the following *except* which one?

   A. Determine the root cause of the incident.

   B. Identify improvements in incident response procedures.

   C. Determine the motivation of the attacker.

   D. Identify improvements in cybersecurity defenses.

5. Which term in security incident response represents the final activity that takes place during a response to an incident?

   A. Post-incident review

   B. Remediation

   C. Closure

   D. Containment

6. Which of the following criteria would likely *not* be used to classify a security incident?

    A. Data volume

    B. System location

    C. Data sensitivity

    D. Operational criticality

7. An incident response team is responding to a situation in which an intruder has successfully logged on to a system using stolen nonprivileged credentials. Which steps are most effective at containing this incident?

    A. Lock the compromised user account.

    B. Reset the password of the compromised user account.

    C. Kill all processes associated with the compromised user account.

    D. Block the intruder's originating IP address and lock the compromised user account.

8. In what circumstances should executive management be notified of a security incident?

    A. In no cases, other than monthly and quarterly metrics

    B. In all cases

    C. When its impact is material

    D. When regulators are required to be notified

9. Which of the following individuals should approve the release of notifications regarding cybersecurity incidents to affected parties who are private citizens?

    A. General counsel

    B. Chief marketing officer

    C. Chief information security officer

    D. Security incident response commander

10. What is the purpose of a write blocker in the context of security incident response?

    A. Protects forensic evidence against tampering

    B. Creates forensically identical copies of hard drives

    C. Assures that hard drives can be examined without being altered

    D. Assures that affected systems cannot be altered

11. An employee in an organization is suspected of storing illegal content on the workstation assigned to him. Human resources asked the security manager to log on to the workstation and examine its logs. The security manager has identified evidence in the workstation's logs that supports the allegation. Which statement best describes this investigation?

    A. The investigation was performed properly, and the organization can proceed with disciplinary action.

    B. Because forensic tools were not used to preserve the state of the workstation, the veracity of the evidence identified in the investigation can be called into question.

    C. The investigation should enter a second phase in which forensic tools are used to specifically identify the disallowed behavior.

    D. The investigation cannot continue because the initial examination of the workstation was performed without a signed warrant.

12. Under the state of California's data security and privacy law of 2002 (SB 1386), under what circumstances is an organization *not* required to notify affected parties of a breach of personally identifiable information (PII)?

    A. When the organization cannot identify affected parties

    B. When the PII is encrypted at rest

    C. When the number of compromised records is less than 20,000

    D. When the number of total records is less than 20,000

13. Which of the following is *not* considered a part of a security incident post-incident review?

    A. Motivations of perpetrators

    B. Effectiveness of response procedures

    C. Accuracy of response procedures

    D. Improvements in preventive controls

14. Which of the following is usually *not* included in a cost analysis of a security incident during the post-incident review?

    A. Penalties and legal fees

    B. Notification to external parties

    C. Assistance by external parties

    D. Loss of market share

15. Which of the following describes the best practice for capturing login log data?

    A. Capture all unsuccessful login attempts. Capture user ID, password, IP address, and location.

    B. Capture all successful and unsuccessful login attempts. Capture user ID, password, IP address, and location.

C. Capture all successful and unsuccessful login attempts. Capture user ID, IP address, and location.

D. Capture all unsuccessful login attempts. Capture user ID, IP address, and location.

16. What is the best method for utilizing forensic investigation assistance in organizations too small to hire individuals with forensic investigation skills?

A. Utilize interns from a nearby college or university that teaches cyber-forensic investigations.

B. Request assistance from law enforcement at the city, state/province, or national level.

C. Obtain an incident response retainer from a cybersecurity firm that specializes in security incident response services.

D. Use one of several cloud-based, automated forensic examination services.

17. An organization that obtains a SIEM is hoping to improve which security incident response–related metric?

A. Remediation time

B. Dwell time

C. Postmortem quality

D. Damage assessment

18. An organization has developed DLP solutions on its endpoints and file servers, but an adversary was able to exfiltrate data nonetheless. What solution should the organization next consider to detect unauthorized data exfiltration?

A. Network anomaly detection

B. Advanced antimalware

C. Endpoint firewalls

D. DDoS mitigation

19. At what point in the security incident response process should the general counsel be notified?

A. During quarterly reporting of key risk indicators

B. During the post-incident review

C. When the incident is initially declared

D. When notification of regulators or external parties is likely

20. What should a security incident response plan utilize to ensure effective notifications of internal and external parties?

A. Business continuity plan

B. Crisis response plan

C. Contact list

D. Disaster recovery plan

21. An organization recently suffered a security attack in which the attacker gained a foothold in the organization through the exploit of a weakness in an Internet-facing system. The root-cause analysis in the post-incident review indicated that the cause of the incident was the lack of a particular security patch on the system that was initially attacked. What can the security leader conclude from the root cause?

    A. System engineers need additional training in patch management.

    B. The firewall failed to block the attack.

    C. The vulnerability management process needs to be improved.

    D. The root-cause analysis was not sufficient to identify the real root cause.

22. What compensating control is most appropriate for the absence of encryption of backup media?

    A. Store backup media in locked containers in a keycard-access controlled room.

    B. Back up sensitive data to encrypted zip archives, which are backed up to tape.

    C. Obfuscate the names of files backed up to backup media.

    D. Do not permit backup media to be removed from the processing center.

23. The practice of proactively searching for signs of unauthorized intrusions is known as what?

    A. Geolocation

    B. Password cracking

    C. Threat hunting

    D. Log correlation

24. A SaaS-based e-mail services provider backs up its customer data through the replication of data from one storage system in the main processing center to another storage system in an alternative processing center. This data assurance architecture leaves the organization vulnerable to what type of attack?

    A. LUN spoofing

    B. Supply chain

    C. Smurf

    D. Ransomware

25. An organization's SIEM has generated alerts suggesting a user's workstation is being attacked by ransomware. What steps should be taken in an effort to contain the incident?

    A. Disconnect the user's workstation from the network.

    B. Disconnect the user's workstation from the network and lock the user's account.

    C. Lock the user's account and scan the network for other infected systems.

    D. Pay the ransom and obtain decryption keys to recover lost data.

26. What is the likely role of the chief marketing officer in an information security incident?

    A. Keep records of security incident proceedings.

    B. Update marketing collateral to state that security is important to the organization.

    C. Notify regulators of the incident.

    D. Develop press releases that describe the incident and the organization's response to it.

27. An organization has determined that there are no resources who have experience with malware reverse engineering and analysis. What is the organization's best short-term remedy for this deficiency?

    A. Employ log correlation and analysis on the SIEM.

    B. Obtain tools that perform malware reverse engineering.

    C. Obtain an incident response retainer from a qualified security consulting firm.

    D. Train incident responders in malware analysis.

28. Why should forensic analysis tools *not* be placed on incident responders' daily-use workstations?

    A. Workstations would become too costly and be a theft risk.

    B. Incident responders will not be able to complete daily tasks during incident response.

    C. Daily-use workstations do not have sufficient RAM capacity.

    D. Daily-use activities may influence forensic tools and cast doubt on their integrity.

29. A post-incident-review process addresses all of the following *except* which one?

    A. Root-cause analysis

    B. Selection of future incident response personnel

    C. Potential improvements in preventive and detective controls

    D. Potential improvements in security incident response procedures

30. Which of the following techniques best describes the impact of a security incident on management?

    A. Hard costs and soft costs

    B. Hard costs, soft costs, and qualitative impacts

    C. The total of all outsourced professional services

    D. The total of all hardware replacement for affected systems

31. For what reason(s) would an IT service desk incident ticketing system be inappropriate for the storage of information related to security incidents?

    A. Automatic escalations would be timed incorrectly.

    B. A service desk incident ticketing system is designed for a different purpose.

    C. Sensitive information about an incident would be accessible to too few personnel.

    D. Sensitive information about an incident would be accessible to too many personnel.

32. At what point during security incident response should law enforcement be contacted?

   A. When root-cause analysis during post-incident review identifies that a law has been broken

   B. When directed by the incident response plan and approved by the incident response commander

   C. When directed by the incident response plan and approved by the general counsel

   D. When the incident response commander determines a law has been broken

33. SOC operators and the incident response team have confirmed that an intruder has successfully compromised a web server and is logged in to it. The IR team wants to take steps to contain the incident but doesn't want to disrupt operations unnecessarily. What approach should the IR team take?

   A. Test the proposed changes in a test environment first.

   B. Take containment steps as quickly as possible.

   C. Lock the user account and reboot the server.

   D. Turn on firewall debugging.

34. All of the following are metrics for security incident response, *except* which one?

   A. Dwell time

   B. Lag time

   C. Containment time

   D. Time to notify affected parties

35. An organization recently suffered a significant security incident. The organization was surprised by the incident and believed that this kind of event would not occur. To avoid a similar event in the future, what should the organization do next?

   A. Commission an enterprise-wide risk assessment.

   B. Commission a controls maturity assessment.

   C. Commission an internal and external penetration test.

   D. Commission a controls gap assessment.

36. Security analysts in the SOC have noticed that the organization's firewall is being scanned by a port scanner in a hostile country. Security analysts have notified the security manager. How should the security manager respond to this matter?

   A. Declare a high-severity security event.

   B. Declare a low-severity security event.

   C. Take no action.

   D. Direct the SOC to block the scan's originating IP address.

37. Security analysts in the SOC have noticed a large volume of phishing e-mails that originate from a single "from" address. Security analysts have notified the security manager. How should the security manager respond to the matter?

    A. Declare a high-level security incident.

    B. Block all incoming e-mail from that address at the e-mail server or spam filter.

    C. Issue an advisory to all employees to be on the lookout for suspicious messages and to disregard them.

    D. Block the originating IP address.

38. Why is hardware asset inventory critical for the success of security incident response?

    A. Critical processes such as software asset and software licensing depend upon accurate asset inventory.

    B. Incident responders can better understand what assets may be involved in an incident.

    C. Vulnerability scans need to cover all hardware assets so that all assets are scanned.

    D. Penetration tests need to cover all hardware assets so that all assets are scanned.

39. Of what possible value is system classification in the context of security incident response?

    A. System classification informs incident responders on what information is stored in systems.

    B. System classification helps incident responders better understand the relative importance of systems.

    C. System classification helps incident responders understand dependencies between systems.

    D. System classification informs incident responders of the location of systems.

40. The corporate controller in an organization notified the CISO that an employee recently received an e-mail from the CEO with instructions to wire a large amount of money to an offshore bank account that is part of secret merger negotiations. The corporate controller has determined that this was a fraudulent transaction. How should the CISO respond?

    A. Declare a security incident.

    B. Call the bank.

    C. Notify law enforcement.

    D. Conduct a reverse wire transfer.

41. A SOC analyst is using a system to perform queries to determine whether any specific types of attacks or intrusions have occurred in the organization. What is the SOC analyst doing?

    A. Performing a penetration test

    B. Conducting threat hunting

    C. Performing a vulnerability scan

    D. Conducting threat modeling

42. A SOC analyst is using a tool to identify potential weaknesses in one or more information systems. What is the SOC analyst doing?

    A. Performing a penetration test

    B. Conducting threat hunting

    C. Performing a vulnerability scan

    D. Conducting threat modeling

43. Why is it important to take long-term steps to reduce dwell time?

    A. Forensic imaging will take less time to acquire.

    B. Vulnerability scans will take less time to complete.

    C. Organizations will be aware of security vulnerabilities earlier.

    D. Organizations will be aware of security incidents earlier.

44. A chain of custody should be established for all of the following situations, except:

    A. Computer intrusion by an external adversary

    B. Employee terminated for lack of computer skills

    C. Data theft perpetrated by an insider

    D. Employee terminated for security policy violation

45. How are the crisis management and security incident response functions related?

    A. Security incident response leverages crisis management's escalation model.

    B. Crisis management and security incident response are not related.

    C. Crisis management directs security incident response proceedings.

    D. Crisis management leverages security incident response's escalation model.

1. A	**16.** C	**31.** D
2. D	**17.** B	**32.** C
3. B	**18.** A	**33.** A
4. C	**19.** D	**34.** B
5. A	**20.** B	**35.** A
6. B	**21.** D	**36.** D
7. D	**22.** A	**37.** B
8. D	**23.** C	**38.** B
9. A	**24.** D	**39.** B
10. C	**25.** B	**40.** A
11. B	**26.** D	**41.** B
12. B	**27.** C	**42.** C
13. A	**28.** D	**43.** D
14. D	**29.** B	**44.** B
15. C	**30.** B	**45.** A

1. Why would an organization consider developing alerts on its security information and event management system, as opposed to using its existing daily log review procedure?

   A. More accurate and timely awareness of security issues requiring action

   B. Compliance with PCI DSS 3.2 requirement 10.6

   C. Reduce costs associated with time-consuming log review

   D. Free up staff to perform more challenging and interesting tasks

   ☑ A. The best reason for developing alerts in a security information and event management system (SIEM) is the near-instantaneous alerting of personnel of a security matter requiring investigation and potential remediation. Daily log review is time-consuming and infeasible in all but the smallest organizations due to the high volume of log data that is produced in information systems.

   ☒ B, C, and D are incorrect. B is incorrect because PCI DSS requirement 10.6 does not specifically require that an organization employ a SIEM with alerts, although it is suggested as a more effective approach for daily log review. C is incorrect because cost reduction is not the best reason to generate security alerts. D is incorrect because providing staff with professional challenges is not the best answer to this question.

2. While responding to a security incident, the person acting as the incident commander is unable to notify a particular executive in an escalation procedure. What should the incident responder do next?

   A. Notify regulators that the organization is experiencing a cyber incident and requires assistance.

   B. Notify law enforcement that the organization is experiencing a cyber incident and requires assistance.

   C. Order incident responders to suspend their activities until the executive has been contacted.

   D. Notify the next highest executive in the escalation chain.

   ☑ D. The best choice among those available here is for the incident commander to notify the next highest executive in the escalation chain. This is not an ideal situation, but security incident response does not always proceed as expected.

   ☒ A, B, and C are incorrect. A and B are incorrect because notification of outside authorities is not an appropriate alternative action to the inability to contact an executive. C is incorrect because the suspension of security incident response activities may permit attackers to continue inflicting damage to the organization.

3. Why would PCI DSS requirements require organizations to put emergency contact information for payment card brands in their incident response plans?

   A. An emergency is a poor time to start looking for emergency contact information for outside organizations.

   B. Card brands must be notified of an incident involving card data as soon as possible.

C. Requirement 12.10 in PCI DSS requires it.

D. It reminds organizations to notify the card brands in the event of a breach.

☑ **B.** PCI DSS requirement 12.10 implies that card brands' emergency contact information should be included in organizations' security incident response plans because the card brands should be notified as soon as possible after knowledge of a breach of credit card data.

☒ **A**, **C**, and **D** are incorrect. **A** is incorrect because, although it is true that an emergency is a poor time to start looking around for emergency contact information, this is not the best answer. **C** is incorrect because this answer is circular; there is a reason for the requirement, and answer B offers the reason. **D** is incorrect because the presence of contact information does not serve as a reminder; instead, security incident response procedures should explicitly specify when, and under what conditions, an organization is required to notify one or more of the card brands.

4. The purpose of a post-incident review of a security incident includes all of the following *except* which one?

A. Determine the root cause of the incident.

B. Identify improvements in incident response procedures.

C. Determine the motivation of the attacker.

D. Identify improvements in cybersecurity defenses.

☑ **C.** Determination of the motivation of an attacker is not one of the objectives of a review of the response to a security incident.

☒ **A**, **B**, and **D** are incorrect. **A** is incorrect because the determination of the root cause of a security incident *is* one of the main reasons for conducting a post-incident review. **B** is incorrect because the identification of improvements in incident response procedures *is* one of the reasons for conducting a post-incident review. **D** is incorrect because the identification of improvements in defenses *is* one of the objectives of a post-incident review.

5. Which term in security incident response represents the final activity that takes place during a response to an incident?

A. Post-incident review

B. Remediation

C. Closure

D. Containment

☑ **A.** A post-incident review, sometimes casually called a postmortem, is a review of the entire incident intended to help reviewers understand the incident's cause, the role of preventive and detective capabilities, and the effectiveness of incident responders. The purpose of the after-action review is to identify improvements in defenses and response procedures to reduce the probability and/or impact of a similar future incident and to ensure a more effective response should one occur.

☒ **B**, **C**, and **D** are incorrect. These are all steps that take place after containment, mitigation, and recovery. Typically, the steps in security incident response are planning, detection, initiation, analysis, containment, eradication, recovery, remediation, closure, and post-incident review. Evidence is retained after an incident for an unspecific period of time.

6. Which of the following criteria would likely *not* be used to classify a security incident?

   A. Data volume

   B. System location

   C. Data sensitivity

   D. Operational criticality

   ☑ **B.** The location of a system is the least likely factor to be used to classify a security incident, unless the incident constitutes a breach of privacy of individuals, in which case there may be applicable laws such as GDPR or CCPA. Further, one influence of the location of a system might be the selection of personnel to respond to an incident, but this is not a part of incident classification.

   ☒ **A**, **C**, and **D** are incorrect. **A** is incorrect because the volume of data involved in an incident is likely to influence the incident's classification, particularly if the data is sensitive. **C** is incorrect because the sensitivity of data involved in an incident is highly likely to influence the incident's classification because of the possibility that regulators, law enforcement, or affected parties may need to be notified. **D** is incorrect because the operational criticality of a system is likely to influence the incident's classification.

7. An incident response team is responding to a situation in which an intruder has successfully logged on to a system using stolen nonprivileged credentials. Which steps are most effective at containing this incident?

   A. Lock the compromised user account.

   B. Reset the password of the compromised user account.

   C. Kill all processes associated with the compromised user account.

   D. Block the intruder's originating IP address and lock the compromised user account.

   ☑ **D.** Locking the compromised user account and blocking access from the intruder's originating IP address are the best available steps here. Other steps should also be taken, including killing all processes running under the compromised user account.

   ☒ **A**, **B**, and **C** are incorrect. **A** is incorrect because locking the compromised user account may be ineffective, as the intruder may have compromised other accounts. **B** is incorrect because resetting the password will not stop the attack in progress unless the intruder needs to log in again. **C** is incorrect because killing processes alone will not necessarily prevent the intruder from logging in again. None of these choices are completely effective.

8. In what circumstances should executive management be notified of a security incident?

A. In no cases, other than monthly and quarterly metrics

B. In all cases

C. When its impact is material

D. When regulators are required to be notified

☑ **D.** Executive management should be notified of a cyber incident when it has been determined that regulators must be notified. This is not the only circumstance in which executives should be notified; others include incidents that disrupt business operations as well as large-scale incidents involving the compromise of sensitive information.

☒ **A**, **B**, and **C** are incorrect. **A** is incorrect because executives should be notified of serious incidents. **B** is incorrect because it is not necessary to notify executives of small-scale incidents. **C** is incorrect because it is not as good an answer as D.

9. Which of the following individuals should approve the release of notifications regarding cybersecurity incidents to affected parties who are private citizens?

A. General counsel

B. Chief marketing officer

C. Chief information security officer

D. Security incident response commander

☑ **A.** The general counsel—the top-ranking attorney—should be the person who approves the release of notifications to affected parties. An attorney has expertise in the interpretation of applicable laws, and it is these laws that stipulate notifications to outside parties.

☒ **B**, **C**, and **D** are incorrect. **B** is incorrect because the marketing executive generally does not have expertise in the law to decide when to perform a required notification. The marketing executive may, however, assist in the process of notifying those parties. **C** is incorrect because the CISO is generally not the leading expert in the law to determine if and when notification of outside parties is required. Further, because the CISO is generally responsible for security incident response, the CISO, the general counsel, and others function as an executive team responsible for high-level decisions, which is preferable to a single individual who makes all of the strategic decisions. **D** is incorrect because the incident commander is a lower-level person who is responsible for response logistics, but not for making high-level decisions such as notification of external affected parties.

10. What is the purpose of a write blocker in the context of security incident response?

A. Protects forensic evidence against tampering

B. Creates forensically identical copies of hard drives

C. Assures that hard drives can be examined without being altered

D. Assures that affected systems cannot be altered

☑ **C.** A write blocker is used to connect a hard drive that is the subject of forensic analysis to a computer. The write blocker permits the computer to read from the subject hard drive but does not permit any updates to the hard drive. This serves as an important control in a forensic investigation by preserving the integrity of subject hard drives.

☒ **A, B,** and **D** are incorrect. **A** is incorrect because a write blocker does not protect forensic evidence against tampering. **B** is incorrect because a write blocker is not used to create copies of hard drives; however, a write blocker is a supporting tool that ensures that copies of subject hard drives can be made without affecting the subject hard drives. **D** is incorrect because write blockers are not used to protect systems from being altered.

11. An employee in an organization is suspected of storing illegal content on the workstation assigned to him. Human resources asked the security manager to log on to the workstation and examine its logs. The security manager has identified evidence in the workstation's logs that supports the allegation. Which statement best describes this investigation?

   A. The investigation was performed properly, and the organization can proceed with disciplinary action.

   B. Because forensic tools were not used to preserve the state of the workstation, the veracity of the evidence identified in the investigation can be called into question.

   C. The investigation should enter a second phase in which forensic tools are used to specifically identify the disallowed behavior.

   D. The investigation cannot continue because the initial examination of the workstation was performed without a signed warrant.

   ☑ **B.** Because the security manager logged in to the subject's workstation without first taking steps to preserve a forensic copy of the workstation, the security manager could be accused of planting evidence on the workstation, and this allegation would be difficult to refute. The security manager should have first taken a forensic image of the workstation's hard drive before examining its contents.

   ☒ **A, C,** and **D** are incorrect. **A** is incorrect because the investigation was not performed properly: the security manager could potentially have tampered with the workstation's hard drive and even planted evidence. If the disciplined employee brings a legal challenge to the organization, the challenge would cast doubt on the security manager's actions. **C** is incorrect because the damage has already been done: the security manager's initial examination of the hard drive has tainted the integrity of the hard drive; this cannot be undone. **D** is incorrect because a warrant is not required for an organization to conduct an examination and analyze its own property—in this case, a workstation.

12. Under the state of California's data security and privacy law of 2002 (SB 1386), under what circumstances is an organization *not* required to notify affected parties of a breach of personally identifiable information (PII)?

   A. When the organization cannot identify affected parties

   B. When the PII is encrypted at rest

   C. When the number of compromised records is less than 20,000

   D. When the number of total records is less than 20,000

   ☑ **B.** Under the 2002 state of California's security and privacy law (SB 1386), organizations are not required to notify affected parties of the breach of security if the information was encrypted at rest.

   ☒ **A, C,** and **D** are incorrect. **A** is incorrect because even when an organization is unable to identify all of the specific parties affected by a security breach, the organization is required to publicly announce the breach. **C** is incorrect because there is no lower limit on the number of compromised records. **D** is incorrect because there is no limit on the size of a compromised database.

13. Which of the following is *not* considered a part of a security incident post-incident review?

   A. Motivations of perpetrators

   B. Effectiveness of response procedures

   C. Accuracy of response procedures

   D. Improvements in preventive controls

   ☑ **A.** The motivation of the perpetrators is generally not a part of a security incident post-incident review. Of the available answers, this is the least likely to be a part of a post-incident review.

   ☒ **B, C,** and **D** are incorrect. **B** is incorrect because the effectiveness of response procedures is a key focus area in a post-incident review; it helps ensure that similar incidents in the future can be handled more effectively. **C** is incorrect because the accuracy of response procedures is considered; it helps ensure that organizations will handle similar future incidents more accurately. **D** is incorrect because a review of preventive (also detective and administrative) controls is a key focus of a post-incident review; it helps ensure that opportunities for improvements in relevant controls can help reduce the probability and/or impact of future events.

14. Which of the following is usually *not* included in a cost analysis of a security incident during the post-incident review?

   A. Penalties and legal fees

   B. Notification to external parties

   C. Assistance by external parties

   D. Loss of market share

☑ **D.** Market share is generally *not* included in a cost analysis of a security event, because changes in market share may be more long-term and potentially unknown for several months, quarters, or more. Changes in market share are also more difficult to attribute, as many other forces contribute to these changes.

☒ **A**, **B**, and **C** are incorrect. **A** is incorrect because penalties (from regulators, customers, and others) and legal fees are generally included in the overall cost of a security breach. **B** is incorrect as the cost of notification to affected parties is generally included among the costs of a security breach. **C** is incorrect because professional services fees and other costs from outside parties in support of the investigation, forensics, analysis, and other activities are generally included.

15. Which of the following describes the best practice for capturing login log data?

   A. Capture all unsuccessful login attempts. Capture user ID, password, IP address, and location.

   B. Capture all successful and unsuccessful login attempts. Capture user ID, password, IP address, and location.

   C. Capture all successful and unsuccessful login attempts. Capture user ID, IP address, and location.

   D. Capture all unsuccessful login attempts. Capture user ID, IP address, and location.

   ☑ **C.** The best practice for logging authentication events is the capture all successful and unsuccessful login attempts and to capture the user ID, IP address, and location (if known).

   ☒ **A**, **B**, and **D** are incorrect. **A** is incorrect because successful login attempts should also be captured, and passwords should not be captured. **B** is incorrect because passwords should not be captured. **D** is incorrect because successful logins should also be captured.

16. What is the best method for utilizing forensic investigation assistance in organizations too small to hire individuals with forensic investigation skills?

   A. Utilize interns from a nearby college or university that teaches cyber-forensic investigations.

   B. Request assistance from law enforcement at the city, state/province, or national level.

   C. Obtain an incident response retainer from a cybersecurity firm that specializes in security incident response services.

   D. Use one of several cloud-based, automated forensic examination services.

   ☑ **C.** Most organizations cannot justify hiring a cybersecurity specialist who has computer and network forensic investigations skills and experience. Such organizations should obtain an incident response retainer from a qualified cybersecurity professional services firm that will render assistance if and when a security incident occurs.

☒ **A**, **B**, and **D** are incorrect. **A** is incorrect because interns will generally not have sufficient experience to be able to complete a forensic investigation and create a chain of custody. **B** is incorrect because law enforcement agencies, most of which have insufficient computer forensics resources, are generally not available to perform computer or network forensic analysis unless it is associated with a major crime. **D** is incorrect because there are no cloud-based forensic examination services (at the time of this writing).

17. An organization that obtains a SIEM is hoping to improve which security incident response–related metric?

    A. Remediation time

    B. Dwell time

    C. Postmortem quality

    D. Damage assessment

    ☑ **B**. Dwell time, or the time that elapses from the start of an incident to the realization that the incident has occurred (or is still occurring), can be improved through the use of a security information and event management system (SIEM). Collecting log data from systems in the organization, a SIEM correlates log events and produces alerts when actionable incidents are discovered.

    ☒ **A**, **C**, and **D** are incorrect. **A** is incorrect because a SIEM will have a negligible impact on dwell time. **C** is incorrect because a SIEM will have little or no impact on postmortem quality. **D** is incorrect because a SIEM will have only minor impact on damage assessment.

18. An organization has developed DLP solutions on its endpoints and file servers, but an adversary was able to exfiltrate data nonetheless. What solution should the organization next consider to detect unauthorized data exfiltration?

    A. Network anomaly detection

    B. Advanced antimalware

    C. Endpoint firewalls

    D. DDoS mitigation

    ☑ **A**. Network anomaly detection, including NetFlow technology, is designed to baseline normal network behavior and report anomalous network traffic.

    ☒ **B**, **C**, and **D** are incorrect. **B** is incorrect because advanced antimalware is not designed to detect data exfiltration. **C** is incorrect because endpoint firewalls will not appreciably add to endpoint-based data loss prevention (DLP) in terms of detecting data exfiltration. **D** is incorrect because distributed denial-of-service (DDoS) mitigation will not help with the detection of data exfiltration.

19. At what point in the security incident response process should the general counsel be notified?

A. During quarterly reporting of key risk indicators

B. During the post-incident review

C. When the incident is initially declared

D. When notification of regulators or external parties is likely

☑ **D.** The general counsel, sometimes known as the chief legal officer, should be notified when it is determined that there may be a need to report the incident to regulators or other affected parties. The general counsel is responsible for the interpretation of applicable laws and other legal obligations (such as private contracts between organizations) and for making decisions regarding actions required by those laws and contracts.

☒ **A, B**, and **C** are incorrect. **A** and **B** are incorrect because the general counsel should be notified during serious incidents, not after they have concluded. **C** is incorrect because the general counsel does not need to be informed of minor incidents.

20. What should a security incident response plan utilize to ensure effective notifications of internal and external parties?

A. Business continuity plan

B. Crisis response plan

C. Contact list

D. Disaster recovery plan

☑ **B.** A crisis response plan typically contains contact information for parties to be contacted in various business emergency scenarios, including security incidents and breaches.

☒ **A, C**, and **D** are incorrect. **A** is incorrect because a business continuity plan does not generally contain detailed information regarding the notification of internal and external parties. **C** is incorrect because a contact list does not, by itself, define which parties are contacted, at what times, and in what circumstances. **D** is incorrect because a disaster recovery plan does not generally contain detailed information regarding the notification of other parties.

21. An organization recently suffered a security attack in which the attacker gained a foothold in the organization through the exploit of a weakness in an Internet-facing system. The root-cause analysis in the post-incident review indicated that the cause of the incident was the lack of a particular security patch on the system that was initially attacked. What can the security leader conclude from the root cause?

A. System engineers need additional training in patch management.

B. The firewall failed to block the attack.

C. The vulnerability management process needs to be improved.

D. The root-cause analysis was not sufficient to identify the real root cause.

☑ **D.** The root-cause analysis of this security incident is insufficient. It is not appropriate to conclude that the breach occurred because of the lack of a patch. Proper root-cause analysis would further ask the following: Why was the patch missing? Why wasn't this server a part of the patch management process? Why did the server get implemented without being included in the patch management process? Why did the monthly review of patched systems miss this new server? And why did an underqualified person perform the monthly review? In this example string of questions, root-cause analysis keeps asking why until no further information is available.

☒ **A, B,** and **C** are incorrect. **A** is incorrect because this conclusion cannot be reasonably reached based upon a missing patch. **B** is incorrect because there is not enough information to conclude that a firewall rule failure was the cause of the incident. **C** is incorrect because there is not enough information to say which portion of the vulnerability management process requires improvement.

22. What compensating control is most appropriate for the absence of encryption of backup media?

A. Store backup media in locked containers in a keycard-access controlled room.

B. Back up sensitive data to encrypted zip archives, which are backed up to tape.

C. Obfuscate the names of files backed up to backup media.

D. Do not permit backup media to be removed from the processing center.

☑ **A.** Improving the security of unencrypted backup media is the most feasible compensating control. Many organizations still utilize mainframe and midrange computer systems that do not have the capability of encrypting backup media. But organizations, even when using newer hardware, sometimes do not encrypt backup media for a variety of valid reasons.

☒ **B, C,** and **D** are incorrect. **B** is incorrect because there may be insufficient resources to zip archive very large data sets. **C** is incorrect because obfuscating filenames does little to protect the information contained therein. **D** is incorrect because retaining backup media in the processing center eliminates data assurance in certain disaster scenarios in which systems and media are damaged in the data center—for instance, in case of flood or fire.

23. The practice of proactively searching for signs of unauthorized intrusions is known as what?

A. Geolocation

B. Password cracking

C. Threat hunting

D. Log correlation

☑ **C.** "Threat hunting" is the term used to describe the activity by which analysts use advanced tools to search for signs of possible intrusions into systems. An example case of threat hunting involves the search for a specific operating system file that has a particular checksum, indicating that it has been altered with a specific emerging form of malware.

☒ **A, B,** and **D** are incorrect. **A** is incorrect because geolocation is concerned with the identification of the geographic location of a subject. **B** is incorrect because password cracking is used to derive passwords from a hashed or encrypted password archive. **D** is incorrect because log correlation is an activity performed by a SIEM to identify potential intrusions or other unauthorized activity.

24. A SaaS-based e-mail services provider backs up its customer data through the replication of data from one storage system in the main processing center to another storage system in an alternative processing center. This data assurance architecture leaves the organization vulnerable to what type of attack?

   A. LUN spoofing

   B. Supply chain

   C. Smurf

   D. Ransomware

☑ **D.** An organization that replicates data from one storage system to another is likely to be vulnerable to ransomware: storage systems will likely replicate the destructive encryption from the main storage system to other storage systems. This would result in no source of undamaged files from which to recover.

☒ **A, B,** and **C** are incorrect. **A** is incorrect because LUN spoofing is a fictitious term. **B** is incorrect because a supply chain attack is an attack on a manufacturing company in an attempt to alter or substitute components in a manufactured product (which can include software) for malicious reasons. **C** is incorrect because a Smurf attack is an attack in which large numbers of ICMP packets with the intended target source IP are broadcast to a network using an IP broadcast address.

25. An organization's SIEM has generated alerts suggesting a user's workstation is being attacked by ransomware. What steps should be taken in an effort to contain the incident?

   A. Disconnect the user's workstation from the network.

   B. Disconnect the user's workstation from the network and lock the user's account.

   C. Lock the user's account and scan the network for other infected systems.

   D. Pay the ransom and obtain decryption keys to recover lost data.

☑ **B.** Disconnecting the user's workstation and locking the user's account are the best first steps for containment. If the malware is running on the workstation, disconnecting it should prevent the loss of data on file shares that the user is permitted to access. Locking the user's account will help to slow down instances of malware that may be present on other systems.

⊠ **A**, **C**, and **D** are incorrect. **A** is incorrect because there may be other instances of malware running under the user's account on other systems. **C** is incorrect because although the user's account should be locked right away, scanning for other infected systems is a reasonable step later in the containment phase. **D** is incorrect because paying a ransom does not facilitate data recovery in about half of all ransomware cases.

26. What is the likely role of the chief marketing officer in an information security incident?

   A. Keep records of security incident proceedings.

   B. Update marketing collateral to state that security is important to the organization.

   C. Notify regulators of the incident.

   D. Develop press releases that describe the incident and the organization's response to it.

   ☑ **D.** One activity that the chief marketing officer will perform is the development and distribution of press releases that describe the incident and the steps that the organization is taking to contain it and recover from it. Ideally, generic versions of these press releases are written during incident response plan development.

   ⊠ **A**, **B**, and **C** are incorrect. **A** is incorrect because a marketing person is an unlikely choice to serve as the incident response team's scribe. **B** is incorrect because such collateral updates are not a part of incident response, but activities that take place whenever the organization wishes to update its marketing messaging. **C** is incorrect because it is more likely that senior executives or the general counsel will be notifying regulators.

27. An organization has determined that there are no resources who have experience with malware reverse engineering and analysis. What is the organization's best short-term remedy for this deficiency?

   A. Employ log correlation and analysis on the SIEM.

   B. Obtain tools that perform malware reverse engineering.

   C. Obtain an incident response retainer from a qualified security consulting firm.

   D. Train incident responders in malware analysis.

   ☑ **C.** The best short-term solution is to obtain a retainer from a security incident response firm that has staff and tooling available for this purpose. A viable long-term remedy may include training of in-house staff and acquisition of malware analysis tools.

   ⊠ **A**, **B**, and **D** are incorrect. **A** is incorrect because log correlation and analysis on a SIEM will not contribute to the cause of malware analysis. **B** is incorrect because malware analysis tools are not helpful if personnel are not trained in their use. **D** is incorrect because training is not a viable short-term remedy.

28. Why should forensic analysis tools *not* be placed on incident responders' daily-use workstations?

    A. Workstations would become too costly and be a theft risk.

    B. Incident responders will not be able to complete daily tasks during incident response.

    C. Daily-use workstations do not have sufficient RAM capacity.

    D. Daily-use activities may influence forensic tools and cast doubt on their integrity.

    ☑ **D.** The rule of forensic analysis tools is that they must be run on dedicated, isolated systems that are used for no other purpose. Only this will instill confidence that other activities cannot influence the outcome of forensic investigations.

    ☒ **A**, **B**, and **C** are incorrect. **A** is incorrect because theft risk is not a significant risk; still, it can be mitigated through secure storage of forensic computers. **B** is incorrect because this does not address the need for system isolation. **C** is incorrect because RAM capacity does not address the need for the forensic analysis system to be isolated from other activities.

29. A post-incident-review process addresses all of the following *except* which one?

    A. Root-cause analysis

    B. Selection of future incident response personnel

    C. Potential improvements in preventive and detective controls

    D. Potential improvements in security incident response procedures

    ☑ **B.** The selection of future incident response personnel is not likely to be included in a post-incident review. But on the topic of incident response personnel, issues of their training and knowledge may be discussed if there is a need for improvement.

    ☒ **A**, **C**, and **D** are incorrect. **A** is incorrect because a sound incident response post-incident review will include root-cause analysis to identify the root cause of the incident. **C** is incorrect because a post-incident review will strive to identify improvements in controls to increase awareness of an incident and reduce its impact and probability of occurrence. **D** is incorrect because a post-incident review attempts to find improvement opportunities in the incident review process itself.

30. Which of the following techniques best describes the impact of a security incident on management?

    A. Hard costs and soft costs

    B. Hard costs, soft costs, and qualitative impacts

    C. The total of all outsourced professional services

    D. The total of all hardware replacement for affected systems

    ☑ **B.** Because the costs and impact of a security incident can vary, the best approach is to report on specific hard costs, including professional services, tooling, and equipment, as well as soft costs, including the labor hours by in-house staff, together with qualitative impacts such as market share or reputation damage that are difficult to quantify.

☒ **A**, **C**, and **D** are incorrect. **A** is incorrect because hard costs and soft costs ignore qualitative impacts such as loss of market share and reputational damage. **C** is incorrect because the cost of outsourced services probably does not represent the totality of hard costs, and it does not represent qualitative impact such as reputation. **D** is incorrect because hardware replacement, when it is needed at all, is probably a small portion of the total cost of an incident.

31. For what reason(s) would an IT service desk incident ticketing system be inappropriate for the storage of information related to security incidents?

  A. Automatic escalations would be timed incorrectly.

  B. A service desk incident ticketing system is designed for a different purpose.

  C. Sensitive information about an incident would be accessible to too few personnel.

  D. Sensitive information about an incident would be accessible to too many personnel.

  ☑ **D**. The primary reason why an IT service desk incident ticketing system would not be used for security incidents is the potential for highly sensitive information in the ticketing system being available to all service desk and other IT personnel. A potential compromise is to record all incidents in the service desk ticketing system but store the most sensitive information (such as suspected personnel in an insider event or details about sensitive affected data or sensitive exploit information) elsewhere and reference it in the ticketing system.

  ☒ **A**, **B**, and **C** are incorrect. **A** is incorrect because escalations can often be customized for incidents of various types and severities. **B** is incorrect because an IT service desk incident ticketing system is an appropriate system for tracking security incidents. **C** is incorrect because details about a security incident should not be widely available.

32. At what point during security incident response should law enforcement be contacted?

  A. When root-cause analysis during post-incident review identifies that a law has been broken

  B. When directed by the incident response plan and approved by the incident response commander

  C. When directed by the incident response plan and approved by the general counsel

  D. When the incident response commander determines a law has been broken

  ☑ **C**. Law enforcement should be contacted when the incident response plan suggests such contact and when the general counsel has specifically approved it.

  ☒ **A**, **B**, and **D** are incorrect. **A** is incorrect because a post-incident review is generally far too late to notify law enforcement. **B** and **D** are incorrect because the incident commander is not the appropriate party to approve contact with law enforcement.

33. SOC operators and the incident response team have confirmed that an intruder has successfully compromised a web server and is logged in to it. The IR team wants to take steps to contain the incident but doesn't want to disrupt operations unnecessarily. What approach should the IR team take?

    A. Test the proposed changes in a test environment first.

    B. Take containment steps as quickly as possible.

    C. Lock the user account and reboot the server.

    D. Turn on firewall debugging.

    ☑ **A.** When an incident response team is attempting to remove an intruder from a live system, it is often best first to test any changes in a test environment to understand the actual impact of such removal.

    ☒ **B, C,** and **D** are incorrect. **B** is incorrect because hastily made containment steps may disrupt the operations of the system. **C** is incorrect because rebooting the server may have a significant impact on operations (it is not revealed whether the affected server has no counterparts or is part of a server farm). **D** is incorrect because firewall debugging is not likely to help in incident containment.

34. All of the following are metrics for security incident response, *except* which one?

    A. Dwell time

    B. Lag time

    C. Containment time

    D. Time to notify affected parties

    ☑ **B.** "Lag time" is not a common term in information security metrics and is not likely to be reported.

    ☒ **A, C,** and **D** are incorrect. **A** is incorrect because dwell time, or the time that elapses between the start of an incident and the organization's awareness of the incident, is a common and meaningful metric. **C** is incorrect because containment time is a common and meaningful metric. **D** is incorrect because the time to notify affected parties is a common and meaningful metric.

35. An organization recently suffered a significant security incident. The organization was surprised by the incident and believed that this kind of event would not occur. To avoid a similar event in the future, what should the organization do next?

    A. Commission an enterprise-wide risk assessment.

    B. Commission a controls maturity assessment.

    C. Commission an internal and external penetration test.

    D. Commission a controls gap assessment.

☑ **A.** An enterprise-wide risk assessment is the best option here so that risks of all kinds can be identified and remedies suggested for mitigating them.

☒ **B, C,** and **D** are incorrect. **B** is incorrect because it's possible that there are missing controls; a controls maturity assessment takes too narrow a view here and focuses only on existing controls, when the problem might be controls that are nonexistent. **C** is incorrect because the nature of the incident is unknown and may not be related to technical vulnerabilities that a penetration test would reveal (for example, it may have been phishing or fraud). **D** is incorrect because a controls gap assessment takes too narrow a view here and focuses only on existing controls, when the problem might be controls that are nonexistent.

36. Security analysts in the SOC have noticed that the organization's firewall is being scanned by a port scanner in a hostile country. Security analysts have notified the security manager. How should the security manager respond to this matter?

    A. Declare a high-severity security event.

    B. Declare a low-severity security event.

    C. Take no action.

    D. Direct the SOC to block the scan's originating IP address.

    ☑ **D.** The best course of action is to block the IP address that is the origination of the port scan. However, even this may not be necessary because a port scan is not, by itself, a serious matter. However, it may represent reconnaissance by an intruder that is targeting the organization.

    ☒ **A, B,** and **C** are incorrect. **A** is incorrect because a port scan is not a high-severity security matter. **B** is incorrect because this is not the best answer; however, some organizations might consider a port scan a low-level security incident and respond in some way, such as blocking the IP address. **C** is incorrect because taking no action at all is not the best course of action.

37. Security analysts in the SOC have noticed a large volume of phishing e-mails that originate from a single "from" address. Security analysts have notified the security manager. How should the security manager respond to the matter?

    A. Declare a high-level security incident.

    B. Block all incoming e-mail from that address at the e-mail server or spam filter.

    C. Issue an advisory to all employees to be on the lookout for suspicious messages and to disregard them.

    D. Block the originating IP address.

    ☑ **B.** Of the choices available, the best one is to block any new incoming e-mail messages from the offending e-mail address. A better solution would be the use of a system that would do this automatically, as well as retrieve any offending messages already delivered to some users before the message was recognized as harmful.

☒ **A**, **C**, and **D** are incorrect. **A** is incorrect because this is not the best choice. However, depending on the nature of the threat (which is not revealed in this question), if the phishing is known to carry a malicious payload known to infect user machines successfully in the organization, then perhaps a high-severity incident is the right course of action. **C** is incorrect because this is not the best choice. However, in the absence of antiphishing controls, this may be the organization's best choice. **D** is incorrect because this is not the best choice; the adversary may be able to continue sending e-mails from different servers.

38. Why is hardware asset inventory critical for the success of security incident response?

   A. Critical processes such as software asset and software licensing depend upon accurate asset inventory.

   B. Incident responders can better understand what assets may be involved in an incident.

   C. Vulnerability scans need to cover all hardware assets so that all assets are scanned.

   D. Penetration tests need to cover all hardware assets so that all assets are scanned.

   ☑ **B**. During a security incident, an accurate, complete, and up-to-date asset inventory can help incident responders respond more effectively during a security incident.

   ☒ **A**, **C**, and **D** are incorrect. **A** is incorrect because software inventory, while important for security operations, is not as important as vulnerability management, event management, and malware control. **C** and **D** are incorrect because vulnerability management and penetration tests, while important, are only a portion of critical activities that depend upon effective asset management.

39. Of what possible value is system classification in the context of security incident response?

   A. System classification informs incident responders on what information is stored in systems.

   B. System classification helps incident responders better understand the relative importance of systems.

   C. System classification helps incident responders understand dependencies between systems.

   D. System classification informs incident responders of the location of systems.

   ☑ **B**. System classification helps incident responders better understand the relative importance of various systems. This may play a role in incident escalation or communication.

   ☒ **A**, **C**, and **D** are incorrect. **A** is incorrect because system classification may not indicate anything about information stored on, or processed by, a system. **C** is incorrect because system classification does not generally indicate dependencies. **D** is incorrect because system classification does not generally reveal location information.

40. The corporate controller in an organization notified the CISO that an employee recently received an e-mail from the CEO with instructions to wire a large amount of money to an offshore bank account that is part of secret merger negotiations. The corporate controller has determined that this was a fraudulent transaction. How should the CISO respond?

A. Declare a security incident.

B. Call the bank.

C. Notify law enforcement.

D. Conduct a reverse wire transfer.

☑ **A.** The best course of action is to declare a security incident, so that appropriate incident responders can begin an investigation and notify other parties, such as the legal department.

☒ **B, C,** and **D** are incorrect. **B** is incorrect because a security incident should first be declared. It is likely that the bank will soon be notified as a part of incident response proceedings. **C** is incorrect because a security incident should first be declared. Instructions in the incident response plan will determine who is authorized to approve notifications to outside parties, including law enforcement. **D** is incorrect because there is no such transaction as a reverse wire transfer.

41. A SOC analyst is using a system to perform queries to determine whether any specific types of attacks or intrusions have occurred in the organization. What is the SOC analyst doing?

A. Performing a penetration test

B. Conducting threat hunting

C. Performing a vulnerability scan

D. Conducting threat modeling

☑ **B.** The process of looking for signs of intrusions is known as threat hunting.

☒ **A, C,** and **D** are incorrect. **A** is incorrect because a penetration test is an activity used to identify and confirm exploitable vulnerabilities in one or more systems. **C** is incorrect because a vulnerability scan is an activity used to identify vulnerabilities in one or more systems (and often is the first stage of a penetration test). **D** is incorrect because threat modeling is an activity where various types of threat scenarios are identified to determine whether any are likely to occur.

42. A SOC analyst is using a tool to identify potential weaknesses in one or more information systems. What is the SOC analyst doing?

A. Performing a penetration test

B. Conducting threat hunting

C. Performing a vulnerability scan

D. Conducting threat modeling

☑ **C.** The process of identifying potential weaknesses is known as a vulnerability scan.

☒ **A**, **B**, and **D** are incorrect. **A** is incorrect because a penetration test is an activity used to identify and confirm exploitable vulnerabilities in one or more systems. **B** is incorrect because threat hunting is the process of looking for signs of intrusions. **D** is incorrect because threat modeling is an activity where various types of threat scenarios are identified to determine whether any are likely to occur.

43. Why is it important to take long-term steps to reduce dwell time?

   A. Forensic imaging will take less time to acquire.

   B. Vulnerability scans will take less time to complete.

   C. Organizations will be aware of security vulnerabilities earlier.

   D. Organizations will be aware of security incidents earlier.

   ☑ **D.** Dwell time is the time between the onset of a security incident and the organization's realization of the security incident. Reducing dwell time enables the organization to take containment and eradication steps earlier, often resulting in less damage and disruption.

   ☒ **A**, **B**, and **C** are incorrect. **A** is incorrect because dwell time is not related to forensic imaging. **B** is incorrect because dwell time is not related to vulnerability scans. **C** is incorrect because dwell time is not related to an organization's realization of vulnerabilities, but of security incidents.

44. A chain of custody should be established for all of the following situations, except:

   A. Computer intrusion by an external adversary

   B. Employee terminated for lack of computer skills

   C. Data theft perpetrated by an insider

   D. Employee terminated for security policy violation

   ☑ **B.** A situation where an organization is terminating an employee for lack of computer skills is not likely to require a chain of custody, because a skill or performance gap is not usually associated with a security incident requiring a chain of custody.

   ☒ **A**, **C**, and **D** are incorrect. **A** is incorrect because a computer intrusion by an external adversary may require a chain of custody should law enforcement want to prosecute the intruder. **C** is incorrect because data theft perpetrated by an insider is a scenario likely to require a chain of custody. **D** is incorrect because an employee terminated for security policy violations is a scenario likely to require a chain of custody, should the former employee later sue the employer for wrongful termination.

45. How are the crisis management and security incident response functions related?

    A. Security incident response leverages crisis management's escalation model.

    B. Crisis management and security incident response are not related.

    C. Crisis management directs security incident response proceedings.

    D. Crisis management leverages security incident response's escalation model.

    ☑ **A.** In an organization with crisis management, a security incident response plan will borrow from, or utilize, incident escalation and other features from the crisis management plan, as opposed to developing a similar, yet separate, escalation plan.

    ☒ **B**, **C**, and **D** are incorrect. **B** is incorrect because security incident response and crisis management are related, as both are concerned with the principles and procedures to be followed in a business emergency. **C** is incorrect because crisis management, which is a general business emergency plan, will not include the detail present in a security incident response plan. **D** is incorrect because a crisis management plan will not typically borrow techniques from a security incident response plan.

About the Online Content

This book comes complete with TotalTester Online customizable practice exam software with 150 practice exam questions.

System Requirements

The current and previous major versions of the following desktop browsers are recommended and supported: Chrome, Microsoft Edge, Firefox, and Safari. These browsers update frequently, and sometimes an update may cause compatibility issues with the TotalTester Online or other content hosted on the Training Hub. If you run into a problem using one of these browsers, please try using another until the problem is resolved.

Your Total Seminars Training Hub Account

To get access to the online content, you will need to create an account on the Total Seminars Training Hub. Registration is free, and you will be able to track all your online content using your account. You may also opt in if you wish to receive marketing information from McGraw Hill or Total Seminars, but this is not required for you to gain access to the online content.

Privacy Notice

McGraw Hill values your privacy. Please be sure to read the Privacy Notice available during registration to see how the information you have provided will be used. You may view our Corporate Customer Privacy Policy by visiting the McGraw Hill Privacy Center. Visit the **mheducation.com** site and click **Privacy** at the bottom of the page.

Single User License Terms and Conditions

Online access to the digital content included with this book is governed by the McGraw Hill License Agreement outlined next. By using this digital content you agree to the terms of that license.

Access   To register and activate your Total Seminars Training Hub account, simply follow these easy steps.

1. Go to this URL: **hub.totalsem.com/mheclaim**
2. To register and create a new Training Hub account, enter your e-mail address, name, and password on the **Register** tab. No further personal information (such as credit card number) is required to create an account.

    If you already have a Total Seminars Training Hub account, enter your e-mail address and password on the **Log in** tab.
3. Enter your Product Key: **f92b-zjqg-7bxz**
4. Click to accept the user license terms.
5. For new users, click the **Register and Claim** button to create your account. For existing users, click the **Log in and Claim** button.

    You will be taken to the Training Hub and have access to the content for this book.

Duration of License   Access to your online content through the Total Seminars Training Hub will expire one year from the date the publisher declares the book out of print.

Your purchase of this McGraw Hill product, including its access code, through a retail store is subject to the refund policy of that store.

The Content is a copyrighted work of McGraw Hill, and McGraw Hill reserves all rights in and to the Content. The Work is © 2023 by McGraw Hill.

Restrictions on Transfer   The user is receiving only a limited right to use the Content for the user's own internal and personal use, dependent on purchase and continued ownership of this book. The user may not reproduce, forward, modify, create derivative works based upon, transmit, distribute, disseminate, sell, publish, or sublicense the Content or in any way commingle the Content with other third-party content without McGraw Hill's consent.

Limited Warranty   The McGraw Hill Content is provided on an "as is" basis. Neither McGraw Hill nor its licensors make any guarantees or warranties of any kind, either express or implied, including, but not limited to, implied warranties of merchantability or fitness for a particular purpose or use as to any McGraw Hill Content or the information therein or any warranties as to the accuracy, completeness, correctness, or results to be obtained from, accessing or using the McGraw Hill Content, or any material referenced in such Content or any information entered into licensee's product by users or other persons and/or any material available on or that can be accessed through the licensee's product (including via any hyperlink or otherwise) or as to non-infringement of third-party rights. Any warranties of any kind, whether express or implied, are disclaimed. Any material or data obtained through use of the McGraw Hill Content is at your own discretion and risk and user understands that it will be solely responsible for any resulting damage to its computer system or loss of data.

Neither McGraw Hill nor its licensors shall be liable to any subscriber or to any user or anyone else for any inaccuracy, delay, interruption in service, error or omission, regardless of cause, or for any damage resulting therefrom.

In no event will McGraw Hill or its licensors be liable for any indirect, special or consequential damages, including but not limited to, lost time, lost money, lost profits or good will, whether in contract, tort, strict liability or otherwise, and whether or not such damages are foreseen or unforeseen with respect to any use of the McGraw Hill Content.

TotalTester Online

TotalTester Online provides you with a simulation of the CISM exam. Exams can be taken in Practice Mode or Exam Mode. Practice Mode provides an assistance window with hints, references to the book, explanations of the correct and incorrect answers, and the option to check your answer as you take the test. Exam Mode provides a simulation of the actual exam. The number of questions, the types of questions, and the time allowed are intended to be an accurate representation of the exam environment. The option to customize your quiz allows you to create custom exams from selected domains or chapters, and you can further customize the number of questions and time allowed.

To take a test, follow the instructions provided in the previous section to register and activate your Total Seminars Training Hub account. When you register, you will be taken to the Total Seminars Training Hub. From the Training Hub Home page, select your certification from the Study drop-down menu at the top of the page to drill down to the TotalTester for your book. You can also scroll to it from the list of Your Topics on the Home page, and then click on the TotalTester link to launch the TotalTester. Once you've launched your TotalTester, you can select the option to customize your quiz and begin testing yourself in Practice Mode or Exam Mode. All exams provide an overall grade and a grade broken down by domain.

Technical Support

For questions regarding the TotalTester or operation of the Training Hub, visit **www.totalsem.com** or e-mail **support@totalsem.com**.

For questions regarding book content, visit **www.mheducation.com/customerservice**.